Zamani

A HAUNTED MEMOIR OF TANZANIA

Jane Bryce

LEAF BY LEAF

Published by Leaf by Leaf
an imprint of Cinnamon Press,
Office 49019, PO Box 15113, Birmingham B2 2NJ
www.cinnamonpress.com

Print Edition ISBN 978-1-78864-986-5
Ebook Edition ISBN 978-1-78864-987-2

British Library Cataloguing in Publication Data. A CIP record for this book can be obtained from the British Library.

Cinnamon Press is represented by Inpress.

Designed and typeset in Adobe Caslon Pro by Cinnamon Press. Cover design by Adam Craig © Adam Craig.

All images © Jane Bryce except for the photograph of Miss Goodwyn on page 128, which is by Anne Fletcher.

Every effort has been made to contact rights holders where small quotations have been used from works still in copyright. The author is glad to be contacted through the publisher to update permissions in future editions. The author thanks all those who have granted permissions. Quotations from Karen Blixen's *Out of Africa* (1937), now owned by Penguin, Random House, appear under the US Fair Use determination and with permission from the Gyldendal Group Agency, Copenhagen for the UK edition. Two quotations: one from correspondence between Granville, British Secretary of State and Gladstone, Prime Minister, and one from Chief Mandara, are from *Why Kilimanjaro is in Tanzania* by Heinz Schneppen, National Museums of Tanzania Occasional Paper No.9, quoted by kind permission of his daughter Ruth Schneppen. The quotation from Robert Menzies is licensed from the Commonwealth of Australia under a Creative Commons Attribution 4.0 International Licence. The Commonwealth of Australia does not necessarily endorse the content of this publication. Lines from 'Ballad of the Southern Suburbs'/'Ag Pleez Deddy' by Jeremy Taylor on *Wait a Minim*, 1961 Decca, UK, 1964 used by kind permission of Jeremy Taylor.

For Anne and Jock

And all the people, alive and in the spirit world,
who lent me their stories

Utarajeya kama kitofu chako kime jiwe.
'Where your umbilical cord is buried you, too, will return.'
(Swahili proverb)

Njofu yekyephia royapfo.
'An elephant does not die in a strange land.'
(Chagga proverb)

CONTENTS

PART FOUR: LUSHOTO AND THE USAMBARAS

PART FIVE: MOSHI AND THE MOUNTAIN, 2

Zamani

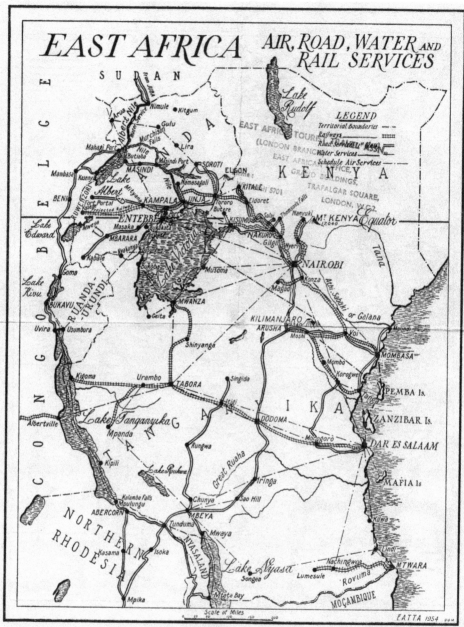

PART 1: HORIZONS

1. Departures and Arrivals

We're flying east, out of darkness into light. Twenty thousand feet below it's still night on the savannah, but here above the clouds it's dawn. The plane banks and levels, and there it is. The mountain, so long a buried memory, materialises in the window, impossibly near. We drift alongside as it floats above rose-tinged clouds, its snowy summit glowing in the early morning sun. Not a memory but as real as rock, as magma from the earth's core. All the years I've been away it's been here, waiting.

Between the mountain and me there's the gulf of years, but I'm the one that's changed. Sitting in this plane, suspended between leaving and arriving, my whole life boils down to this—a woman staring out of a window, looking for confirmation that the past exists. It's dropping behind us now as we drift eastwards, slowly falling out of sight, the way the present endlessly recedes into the past.

The last time I saw Kilimanjaro I was not quite seventeen and flying back to school in England, sick with misery and already longing for home. I had no idea that within six months my parents would be deported and it would be a lifetime before I made my way back here. In Swahili philosophy, Sasa, the present, and Zamani, the past, are inseparable; they swim together in the great sea of time. For twenty years I've lived on an island in the Caribbean, swimming in another sea. Now I'm diving deep into Zamani, but Sasa is the lifeline that will keep me from drowning. As strongly as the past pulls me down, I'm always aware of the ocean's sparkling surface, the present. In coming back to Tanzania, the land of my birth, I hope I'm going forward, open to whatever I may meet, in my luggage a parcel of memories.

I grew up in Moshi, a small town on the plains at the foot of Kilimanjaro. During the day, when it was shrouded in cloud, life went on as if it wasn't there. But in the evening the mountain would emerge shining and afloat on its raft of white. When it was hot and dry and everyone was irritable, sometimes our parents would take me and my sisters to Marangu, a magical place on the mountain, where it was always cool and green and everywhere you went there were streams and waterfalls and the emerald green of banana trees. The turning to Marangu was marked by an ancient baobab on the main road, so vast an entire family couldn't get their arms around it. People said the first baobab had been uprooted by God for daring to complain about something and made to grow upside down with its roots in the air. A tree that size would be at least five hundred years old, my father said. Five hundred years of growing upside down, its branches buried, unable to see. You could live off its bark and the water it contained if you were lost in the savannah. And people were buried in the trunk sometimes, so spirits lived in it. Tree of life and death.

After the tree, the road climbed. The air became clearer and caressed your face, carrying the faintest hint of moisture to revive you after the dust and drought lower down. In Marangu, the two peaks, Kibo and Mawenzi, seemed lower, almost at eye-level. The drama of distance was replaced by the intimacy of connection, so that all the elements were redolent of the mountain—earth dark and rich, air cool and thin, water cold and sparkling like liquid sunlight.

Before the white man came the coastal people had known of the mountain for centuries as a mysterious place, populated by *djinn*. They called it the Land of Djagga, and though they made long perilous journeys there in search of elephant tusks and people to sell in the slave markets of Bagamoyo and Zanzibar, they regarded it with dread. Trudging across the endless plain, a winding caravan of merchants and pack animals, porters and guards would catch a glimpse of something impossibly white rising high on the horizon, and shiver. The wisps of vapour that clung to the peak were the visible sign of spirits.

Though the Chagga had lived there for hundreds of years, for a long time its upper reaches remained a mystery. People believed the mountain was a sacred site, inhabited by supernatural beings that caused death to those who approached. To the Chagga, it wasn't even a single thing, but two peaks embodying distinct personalities. The name Kilimanjaro didn't exist until slave and ivory traders from the coast started to pass that way and the name emerged out of different languages: *kyaro*, a kiChagga word for god, *kilima*, kiSwahili for little mountain. For a long time, white men from different places quarrelled over who owned it; eventually it became an icon, a sign for Africa itself. When Independence finally came to Tanganyika—as it was then—a local man was entrusted with carrying the Uhuru torch to the summit, where its flame was a beacon of freedom to the rest of Africa.

Staring out of the plane window, the mountain already out of sight, I wonder why this homecoming has taken so long. All my adult life I've written and taught about Africa without coming back to Tanzania; when I got a Commonwealth scholarship to study for a PhD, I chose Nigeria and lived there for five years. I've since been in many other countries on the continent, including Kenya—just next door. But I didn't cross the border. Was I afraid of losing all I had so carefully stored in memory? That somehow the past that haunts me, with its peculiar feeling of groundedness in a certain time and space, would have ceased to exist?

In the Caribbean, 'Back to Africa' is a longed-for return to a site of myth, a place of origin beyond the reach of history. For the twenty years I've worked as a lecturer at the University of the West Indies, I've tried through literature and film to connect African descendants with the continent as it is today. I've organised a film festival, brought African directors to show their work and talk to local audiences, and created a dialogue between African and Caribbean filmmakers. For my students, who have never heard African languages or music, experienced its frantic cities or witnessed its contradictions, cinema is a portal to a lived reality. Now, it's brought me here, far from the Black Atlantic, to the Zanzibar International Film Festival, to immerse myself in an Indian Ocean cultural world. To stand in the centuries-old Arab Fort in Stonetown listening to a *taarab* orchestra, eat the spicy food of the Swahili coast, walk with festival goers from all over Africa through narrow winding streets past crumbling palaces. Zanzibar is, for me, the bridge between memory and whatever this country has become in all the years it's carried on without me.

The plane's crossing the water between the city of Dar es Salaam and the islands of Zanzibar, which united with the Tanganyika mainland in 1964 under the new name, Tanzania. Since then, Zanzibar has become a fantasy destination for foreigners in search of the exotic; but I'm not looking for paradise. Beneath the thrum and hustle of today's Tanzania, I'm pursuing a ghostly trail only I can see. That trail leads back to my parents, to their meeting and their fateful posting to Tanganyika in 1949. Before I am even born, the story starts there.

2. Off the shelf

When he emerged from two and a half years as a prisoner of war, Jock Bryce, five foot eleven, weighed 137 pounds (62 kilos). It was May 1945, the War had just ended and he was not yet twenty-four years old. When it started, he was eighteen and marked time getting a war-time degree at Oxford, until he was old enough to join the RAF in 1941. Jock's perfect English enunciation, his public school and Oxford education, belied the fact that he was colonial to the core. His Scottish father, George, was a senior colonial administrator who had been posted successively to Ceylon, New Guinea, Malaya and Nigeria. His mother, Kitty, was Australian. In later years, she lived in a district of Adelaide called Stirling West, while George lived in Stirling, Scotland. Jock had been weaned on separation and distance.

At eighteen, Jock had one ambition—to get airborne and 'do his part killing Germans'. He wrote to Kitty in Adelaide: 'It is harder to receive than to give and I can't have all these people dying for me.' He had to wait till 1942 before his wish was granted and he was posted, still only twenty-one, to RAF Coastal Command in Malta, whose pilots had the job of patrolling the Mediterranean. They not only flew Beaufighter planes but were in control of all the offensive weaponry. This suited Jock, who had scant respect for the idea of a crew and liked to remark sardonically, 'There's only one thing stupider than a bomber pilot and that's a fighter pilot.'

His first mission was flying a Beaufighter over a convoy to protect it from enemy attack. He was disgusted beyond measure when he was shot down on his first flight. Propelled by fury, he fought his way out of the cockpit as the plane sank at speed below the surface of the water. Picked up by an Italian ship, he survived a succession of prison camps, in both Italy and Germany, on Red Cross food parcels, letters from his mother and the companionship of his fellow POWs. One thing that especially sustained him was teaching people to play Bridge—and then beating them. Stakes were high: a single piece of Red Cross chocolate the highest ever. The killer instinct for cards and gambling that grew out of semi-starvation followed him into civilian life. When he was released two and a half years later, he had no idea what he wanted do for a career but knew he wanted to get married, and to whom. He wrote to Kitty that he wanted 'a moll who thinks she has all the answers, who I can bludgeon to her knees'. There not being many women who fitted this description, he looked around meanwhile for a career that would guarantee him maximum freedom and went back to Oxford to read forestry.

Then he met his moll. In May 1949, he sent his mother a telegram: 'Marrying a girl who is older, taller and heavier than I am.' Anne stuck stubbornly to her claim to be five foot ten and three quarters (Jock was five eleven), but in her heels she topped him by an inch. Jock told his mother the part she herself had played in their meeting. While she and George were posted in Kuala Lumpur, Kitty had made friends with a couple called Marguerite and Malcom Macgregor. Their two boys were the first people their own age that Kitty's children, Judy and Jock, met when they came to school in England. Though the elder son—also called Malcolm—was four years older than Jock, they became firm friends. When the War began, Malcolm joined the Navy as a doctor and was posted to a medical station in Tanga, on the Tanganyika coast. The job of looking after wounded troops was greatly eased by the presence of a number of female nursing auxiliaries (VADs), one of whom was Marigold. Marigold was upper-class and beautiful, with an irresistible charm that made you want to warm your hands at its flame. Malcolm was smitten from the moment he met her and they were married in India on his next posting. Conveniently for Jock, when the War ended, they chose to set up home in Warwickshire. He could catch a train in Oxford on a Friday evening, Malcom would meet him in Banbury and they'd be home in time for pre-dinner sherry.

Having become accustomed to viewing their guest room as his, Jock was put out on arriving one weekend by the news that another guest was expected. As he had arrived first, he moved into the spare bedroom before ownership could be contested. The other guest, when she arrived, had the sofa. Anne Millard turned out to be a friend of Marigold's from Tanga, where she'd been posted to the WRNS with the job of decoding enemy communications. Tall she certainly was, but with a gentle grace and a smile that could illuminate a room. She also had a wicked wit to match his own. The family connection and Marigold's friendship were enough to outweigh the fact that she was working for a Labour MP. Since the war she'd been secretary to Eddie Shackleton (son of the famous Antarctic explorer Sir Ernest Shackleton), who had also served with RAF Coastal Command as an intelligence officer. Jock would have been impressed if he hadn't been a High Tory. When he declared that feudalism was the best form of government for Britain, Anne sniffed and said, *droit de seigneur* was all right as long as you were the *seigneur*.

Given her credentials there didn't seem any reason to delay. Jock went up to London and took Anne out to dinner a couple of times just to be sure. Three weeks after their first meeting, Anne was ironing a blouse when the phone rang and a voice like velvet came through the earpiece. When he asked her to marry him, she was so shocked she forgot about the blouse, and when she went back to it, the iron had burnt right through. Of her wartime boyfriends (among them Frank, who gave her a silver bracelet with their names inscribed in a heart; Creepie, who despite his name was very attractive; soulful George; Pete with the jaunty smile) many did not survive. Frank, whom she might have married, was killed early on. Later, many of the naval officers with whom she danced in Tanga were torpedoed at sea. A cardboard folder of typed poems written in her twenties contains as many about death as love. In one she laments:

> Amidst the tragedy of fallen things
> Dreams unfulfilled
> And beating broken wings
> This too must be a part—
> This unhealed hurt
> This numbing of my heart.

Despite this, a lot of her friends got married before the War ended. For people in their twenties who'd survived it, the War was a bond they shared. Besides, Jock was good-looking and made her laugh. He pretended to be cynical and liked to say outrageous things, but she could tell he'd had a hard time. Anne asked Marigold what she thought and her answer was, 'Pure gold.' So she cheerfully sacrificed the blouse.

Jock wrote to Kitty that he had proposed to Anne by offering to 'take her off the shelf'. The War had been over for four years and Anne was twenty-eight. 'I'm glad to say she had the good sense to accept,' he went on. 'I trust you'll approve my choice, because I can't marry anyone you don't like.' In fact, Kitty and Anne recognised each other as allies and were friends the moment they met in September 1949. Afterwards, Kitty wrote Anne a long and personal letter about her struggles with motherhood, her guilt and misgivings about the past. Her honesty cemented a close relationship with Anne: they were each other's champions ever after.

'I feel I must write to tell you of my gratitude that you have agreed to marry my son,' Kitty began. 'I have never felt so instantly drawn to any young thing as when you walked towards me in the restaurant in London, tall and graceful in your elegant New Look suit. As I sat watching you so bravely enduring Jock's dancing, I was surprised by my depth of feeling and hardly dared hope you would really

marry my darling Jock, who has had too much suffering in his short life. Your combined senses of humour seem a gift from Heaven and should make light of any difficulties you encounter. I know from personal experience that marriage is not an easy thing, but the ability to laugh at each other's jokes goes a long way to smoothing rough edges. And Jock has some rough edges, despite my efforts to civilise him.'

It wasn't, she told Anne, entirely his fault. Like all colonial wives in the 1920s, she'd had two choices. Having gone back to Adelaide to have both her children, did she then take them to a harsh tropical environment in Papua New Guinea where there was no suitable housing and rampant malaria, or leave them in Australia and go to join her husband? Kitty's decision, to commit Judy aged three and Jock two to a children's home in Melbourne, was one she continued to struggle with. Until the 1980s, Australia had a large network of such institutions, where many migrant, Aboriginal and white Australian children simply disappeared.

Kitty did what she thought best for her children, regularly spending weeks at sea travelling home to see them. When, on one of these visits, she discovered how miserable Jock was—the extent of deprivation, neglect, abuse and assault in children's homes would only emerge much later, spelled out in a 2004 report titled *Forgotten Australians*—she withdrew them and took them back with her to New Guinea, then to Malaya. When Judy was eight and Jock seven, Kitty reluctantly sent them to boarding schools in Adelaide. She was sick at heart, 'because', she wrote to her own mother, 'I shall be so wretched without them.' When George was posted to Nigeria in 1930, for a few years she continued to spend eight weeks at sea getting to Australia. Eventually she decided she could cut down the distance by moving the children to England, only two weeks away.

So these two young Australians went, aged fourteen and thirteen, to English boarding schools. Kitty bought a cottage in rural Bedfordshire and in the holidays, as young teenagers, Jock and Judy stayed there by themselves and a woman in the village looked after them. Jock was unhappy at school but did well enough to get into Oxford, where, at the age of eighteen, he went to read medicine. But medicine was George's choice, and one thing she would discover about Jock, Kitty warned Anne, was his resentment and anger at his father's preoccupation with work and ignorance of his children's needs. Even after he switched to study English, all he could think of was getting into the forces and joining in the War. He was especially keen on the RAF, because, he told his mother, of 'the possibilities of speed and aerial antics leading straight up into the balmy blue, with, one hopes, a little killing to do when up there.'

Kitty left it to Anne to imagine what it must have meant, after all that training and having finally got to where he most wanted to be—at the controls of a fighter plane—to be shot down and imprisoned in such frightful conditions. For herself, she wouldn't speak of her feelings during the two weeks between the telegram telling them he was lost and the news that he was alive and a prisoner of the Italians. Kitty had frequently thought that his early experiences—emotional deprivation, physical separation and institutional neglect—might have prepared him for what he encountered as a POW and helped him survive. It did not, however, soften him or make him any more amenable, and of this she wanted Anne to be aware. His forestry supervisor at Oxford reported that while he was unquestionably a man of intelligence and ability, he was also cynical and critical, and would show up best when working independently. His judgement that, 'He is likely to be difficult under other conditions,' was one, said Kitty, they would all do well to bear in mind.

'This, my dear Anne,' she concluded, 'is the man you have agreed to marry. I tell you these things not, as I hope, to put you off, but because I trust to your strength of character and that spirit of yours that so appealed to me when we met. If you can overlook the rough edges, I venture to promise that you'll have a husband of sterling worth. But then I am his mother.'

Anne wasn't put off; they were married in October 1949. In the photograph taken as they emerge from the church, they stand shoulder to shoulder, gazing into each other's eyes, and they're laughing. He's dark and dapper in morning suit with a carnation button-hole, she's in a white 1940s wedding dress holding a cascade of roses in her left hand. He's clasping her right hand in his left, and his customary sardonic humour has given way to a teasing hilarity, mirrored in her wide smile beneath her orange-blossom crown. What is he saying to make her smile like that? At this moment they are in perfect equipoise, inhaling a single breath.

Almost immediately afterwards, Jock heard from the Colonial Office that he was to join the Forest Department in Tanganyika, first posting the Rondo Plateau in the Southern Province. They were to leave in November. Anne knew something of Tanganyika, though a southern upcountry posting was going to be different from the northern coastal town where she'd been posted during the War. Jock, from reading the Annual Reports, kept at the Colonial Office, knew that the Southern Province was a territory of some 55,000 square miles—5,000 square miles larger than England but with a population of only a million—so remote it was excluded from the Forest Department until after the War, and since then, 'just permitted to tick over'. Before the War, forestry had been mainly about exploitation and collection of revenue. Now, under the leadership of the visionary Chief Conservator, W.J. Eggeling, it was viewed as protecting natural resources through soil conservation and water control 'for the betterment of the natives.' It was hoped, through Colonial Development and Welfare aid, to introduce sound forest management and Jock was to be one of three forest officers charged with this mission in the Southern Province.

The Rondo Forest had been proclaimed a reserve under German rule in 1912, but no one knew the extent of it. Jock's first job would be to map it on foot. After that, the idea was to allow judicious commercial logging alongside nurseries for reafforestation. According to Eggeling, author of the Annual Reports, 'A forest officer's time should be spent in the forests, not at an official desk.' Jock's sentiments precisely—what could be better? 32,000 acres of forest (an area the size of Manchester) to himself and under orders to get out there where no one could tell him what to do. The Chief Conservator's summation: 'Tanganyika may not be a place fit for kings, but it appears perfectly adequate for foresters to live in,' gave Jock all the encouragement he needed.

Anne, meanwhile, less than a month after her wedding, was preparing to leave behind her friends and family and, once again, live in Tanganyika. On top of an annual salary of £620, they had been given a grant of £30 for equipment. Looking at the camp bed, chair, table and folding canvas bath, the mosquito net, mosquito boots and hurricane lamp, Anne tried to imagine herself in a tent in the bush. For the next three years, they would live with the hiss of the kerosene lantern as their only light source. They had to anticipate what else they would need miles from the nearest grocer or dress shop. Luckily, one of Anne's wedding presents was a Singer sewing machine, and one of Jock's a Phillips wireless they hoped would receive the BBC Overseas Service. Picking out books to take, Jock's tended towards the history of Napoleon's military campaigns, Anne's in the direction of Romantic poetry. It would make for interesting conversation in the long evenings.

There were more personal, feminine, concerns. Needing a companion and advice, Anne thought of her sister Pam, but she was tied down in her Essex village with a toddler and a new-born. So she invited Marigold, who anyway was her closest friend and confidante (and no one had her dress sense) to spend a day in London and help her choose the right clothes for her new life. It was easier for Marigold, who had a nanny, to leave her new-born baby at home. In fact, it was an intense pleasure for them to have the day together in London. It was lovely to sit in a restaurant, just the two of them, and have a really good natter—something that marriage seemed to make so much harder.

'Men,' said Marigold, 'never want to talk about the interesting things, it's all the state of the world and the price of whisky.' Anne agreed.

'What about the price of nail polish and how many bottles to take for three years? And I won't be able to pop into Boots the Chemist for sanitary towels and aspirin either.'

'At least in the War we were all in it together and could borrow each other's.'

'I know. I feel as though I'm going to the ends of the earth with a man I hardly know and no girlfriends to advise me.'

'At least you'll get leave every three years,' Marigold reminded Anne, 'and next time you come you can share the spare room and won't have to sleep on the sofa.'

Cheered by food and talk, they cruised the Oxford Street department stores, but, even though clothes rationing had been lifted in March, it was now late October, the shops were full of winter clothes and lightweight dresses were nowhere to be found. Then Marigold had a brainwave. 'Let's go to Liberty's!' she said, steering Anne towards Regent Street and the half-timbered black and white facade. In the fabric department, they found what they were looking for— exquisite floral-patterned lawn cottons that Anne loved on sight. She selected half a dozen and they spent time in the drapery section, looking at dress patterns. She bought a yard of white linen for contrasting collar and cuffs, bone buttons, a belt— Marigold knew a marvellous dressmaker who could make anything. By the time Anne waved her goodbye at Marylebone Station, it had, they agreed, been a thoroughly satisfactory day.

Anne would wear those cottons every day for three years, until their patterned flowers faded almost away from the onslaught of sunlight and washing.

PART 2: SOJOURN IN THE SOUTH

3. On the Rondo

Anne and Jock sailed from London on November 9th 1949 on the P&O cargo ship SS Matiana, bound for the capital, Dar es Salaam. Arriving in December after a month at sea, they took the 21-seater wartime DC-3 plane to Lindi, then still capital of the Southern Province. Though to Anne's eyes Lindi was nothing like Dar, or even Tanga, it had until very recently been a thriving port, with schools, hospitals, cinema, sports club and a telephone system. Two years before they arrived, the colonial government had decided to promote Mtwara, seventy miles south, as the centre of a major post-war agricultural project, the Groundnut Scheme. As it was now to be the chief trading centre of the region, Lindi's long-established Asian commercial community was induced to move there. By the time they got there, as far as Anne could tell, Lindi had nothing but an old Arab fort and some ramshackle administrative buildings built by the Germans.

They were met by Jock's immediate boss, John Blower, also an Assistant Conservator of Forests, but unlike Jock a bachelor. They took to him immediately. Despite its amenities he hated Lindi. 'I spend most of my time walking in the bush,' he told them. 'In the last year I've spent 198 days on tour and walked 1,300 miles.' When threatened with an office job a few years later, he transferred to the Game Department and became a celebrated game warden in Tanganyika and Uganda, before going to work for Emperor Haile Selassie in Ethiopia. He and Jock hit it off, especially as Jock's job was to deal with the Rondo Plateau, which would free John up to explore the rest of the territory.

They spent the first night in Lindi in an official bungalow, and the next day they went to the office to be briefed. The forestry office was in an underground dungeon with walls four feet thick, beneath the old German headquarters, or *boma*. It had a horrible acrid smell, and Anne was glad Jock didn't have to work there. There were bats roosting in the ceiling, droppings everywhere, and not much else beyond a huge desk next to a barred window. On the wall a tattered map showed the coastline in detail, but the area behind—where they were to live—was labelled vaguely 'Bush' or 'Hills'. John waved at the map. 'Don't take it too literally,' he said. 'It's at least fifty years old and no one's even tried to update it. Last year, it was hailed as a triumph when a jeep made it to the top of the Rondo, because it meant it was actually possible for vehicles to manage the climb. So then they made the road.' Anne managed a smile.

After the briefing, they drove through the town, where the dhow harbour still bustled with life. Then they were allowed to go back to the bungalow and rest, and in the evening, John took them for a drive along the coast, all coconut trees and mangroves. Over a welcome gin and tonic and dinner at his house, John and Jock swapped stories. John had studied forestry in Edinburgh after the War, and delighted Jock with an account of how he released a cageful of rats at a Communist Party meeting. He'd been in Burma during the War and horrified Anne with the story of coming face-to-face with a tiger as he and his men made their way through the jungle in search of Japanese soldiers.

A Bedford truck, assigned by the Forest Department, arrived early the following morning to take them and their luggage to the Rondo. Designed for moving troops and equipment during the War, it was well qualified for the terrain if not passenger comfort. The cab was over the engine with an open metal-floored tray behind, it had a four-wheel drive and weighed three tons. Anne and Jock got into the cab with the driver, who was to show them the way. John had thoughtfully found them a 'houseboy' with rudimentary cooking skills, a man in his forties called Rashidi, who rode in the open back of the truck with their boxes.

It might have been called a road, but to Anne it was sixty-four miles of hell. It was so pitted and bumpy they could only go about fifteen miles an hour, and the journey took over four hours. They arrived at last at a small clearing right on the edge of a ravine that plunged away thousands of feet below. It was spectacular, but Anne was so stiff when she got out, and her eyes so full of red dust, she couldn't appreciate the view. She was longing for a hot bath and a change and a drink, but what she got was cold water, and not a lot of it. They soon found out there was no water up there except what came in a truck every month or so, it had to be boiled because of bilharzia and you had to use as little as possible.

Anne had picked up tummy trouble along the way, and, to her horror, discovered the pit latrine was thirty yards down a forest path. John had warned them that leopard, the most frightening of the big predators, abounded in the forest. It could steal up on its prey in silence and its jaws were deadly. Surrounded as they were on three sides by forest, Anne was queasily aware a leopard could be watching her from the branches of a tree. Women and children were more likely to be victims because they were smaller and easier to dispatch. That first night they made several journeys down that forest path, Anne in front carrying a hurricane lantern in her sweaty hands, trying to still her breath so as to catch the merest rustle in the grass. Jock, walking behind carrying the rifle, tried to focus his eyes outside the small circle of light into which he stepped, trusting it to keep the path clear of snakes. Neither of them fancied diarrhoea as a cause of death.

The house was made of mud blocks, one room deep to allow currents of air to flow through it, with a grass roof populated by creepie-crawlies of every shape and size that swarmed around the flame of the kerosene lanterns. Before dusk, they sat on the verandah sipping minute quantities of whisky from their limited store, but after dark they retreated inside and Rashidi served them dinner cooked on an iron wood-burning stove. His quarters and the kitchen were separate smaller structures at a distance from the house. Though there was a kerosene refrigerator it was hard to keep food fresh, and

their diet would be mainly out of tins. In the wet season they got vegetables from the Benedictine mission fifteen miles away on the plain on the road to Lindi, but when it was dry, nothing grew. A forest messenger brought eggs on foot from thirty miles away and Rashidi laid them tenderly in a basin of water to see if any floated—if they did, they were bad. He guarded them jealously and boiled them for breakfast. It was three weeks before Jock woke up to the fact that the only way they would taste fresh meat was if he shot something. So he went out with the rifle and shot an antelope. Rashidi skinned it expertly and they made themselves popular by giving a lot of it away to the forest guards living nearby. There was no point keeping it to go bad, so for a few days they simply gorged on steak and then went back to tinned sausages and beans.

The few large rooms were cool enough in the dry season at that altitude to warrant a fire at night but there was hardly enough light to read by. Instead, Jock taught Anne how to play Bridge. They hadn't been there long when it became apparent the pitch of the roof was wrong and it had to be rebuilt by local men who lived on the Plateau. The poles and grass, laid in clumps and lashed on, were torn down, releasing a shower of snakes, rats, scorpions, lizards and spiders into the living area. Though they moved from one half of the house to the other until the work was finished, for the nine days it took they had to guard their plates and cups when eating. At night they stripped the bed and remade it before getting in. 'It's a long way from Tipperary,' quipped Jock.

They wasted no time getting on with the job. In a letter to his mother in February 1950, Jock's customary understatement and phlegm barely disguised the dangers they faced: 'Back in good order from the first safari. Anne did a good job of keeping up. We were out for six days and walked about eighty miles, accompanied by a team of porters led by Bernard, one of the better Forest Guards.

It's reassuring to have an experienced Forest Guard because there's a lot of lion and elephant about and we had some exciting moments. It's an interesting thing

to walk in the forest knowing you're observed by large hungry cats which are quite invisible. But the worst thing is hearing elephant and not knowing in which direction they're moving as if they find you in their path they make no detour.'

In these conditions, Jock and his fellow conservators were expected to maintain professional discipline and contribute to scientific knowledge. For Jock, this was a satisfying byproduct of indulging his need for unfettered exploration. The Government had granted a logging concession to Steel Bros of Burma, and he was charged with supervising British interests in the reserve. One of the things he was to look at was how to balance what was taken out with new growth, and which species were most effective. He ran trials with local hardwoods, mahogany and *mvule* (a mighty tree known as *iroko* in West Africa, Latin name *Chlorophora excelsa*). The new forest policy was to enlist local cultivators, who lived in the forest and knew it intimately, to help with reafforestation by planting trees.

Post-war planning was about better administration, beginning with measuring the reserves and increasing the size of the forest estate. They used the Compass and Chain method Jock had been taught at the Forestry School in Oxford: the compass gave you your direction and the chain your distance. The chain was the length of a cricket pitch (twenty-two yards) and consisted of a hundred strong metal links, heavy enough to stay straight when laid on leaves or soft vegetation on the forest floor. He wrote the measurements in a notebook and later, used them to create a map on graph paper.

Alongside that was the identification of botanical species and Jock and his African assistants spent a lot of time on safari collecting specimens. While he was trying out his book-learnt Swahili on the forest guards, he was especially grateful to Bernard, who had grown up with a knowledge of local plants and spoke a little English. As well as leaves, they collected flowers and fruits, for which Bernard knew the local names. They put the specimens—two of each—in rudimentary botanical presses made of crossed strips of plywood nailed into frames, and used layers of newspaper to dry them. With thorny specimens or large fruits it was often difficult to get the newspaper covering—sheets of the *East African Standard*—to stay flat, and it had to be changed frequently to stop things rotting. The frames were stacked and carried back to base on the heads of porters. Through these improvised methods they contributed to science by sending the specimens to the official centres: the Herbarium at headquarters in Morogoro, several hundred miles to the north, and duplicates to the East African Herbarium in Nairobi for naming, as well as Kew Gardens in London and the Imperial Forestry Institute at Oxford.

Anne had other preoccupations. At the end of June 1950, she wrote to Kitty: 'Three letters from you were waiting at the Lindi post office when we were there last week, and were tremendously welcome. It's wonderful to have news from the outside world to remind us it exists. My main reason for braving the road to Lindi was to see a doctor at the hospital, and I have good news. It seems I am to have a baby! I had been feeling a bit off-colour and Jock thought I might have picked up something so I went to be checked. Of course it had crossed my mind, but I hadn't dared to hope I might be pregnant. So here I am, at twenty-nine, expecting for the first time! It should arrive in February, God willing.'

As she quickly outgrew the Liberty print dresses, another trip to Lindi was called for to buy cottons at the Indian *duka* so Anne could make some larger garments. Because of the arduous journey each trip was an occasion, so they took the opportunity to buy as much fruit as they thought they could eat before it went bad. The doctor had told Anne to eat healthily so she saved the bathwater and used it to nurture tomato seedlings she'd bought in Lindi. She waited to see if they would survive.

When Anne told Jock she was pregnant he responded, 'Good, I'll have someone to play cricket with!' It didn't seem to occur to him it might be a girl. He suggested to Anne that she should stay home when he went on safari, but she was having none of it. The dense shade of the forest made it a gloomy place at the best of times and she didn't fancy being left alone. In the morning, she lay in bed and watched the sun rising over the ravine through the expanded metal burglar bars, gradually penetrating the heavy mist in a sinister, silent dawn. The occasional croak from a hornbill, a melancholy plangent sound, only accentuated the silence. During the day the forest was mostly quiet apart from the occasional chattering of monkeys, but towards dusk it whispered and seethed like a great animal coming alive. At night they heard lions roaring terribly close at hand; they had to keep Horatio the terrier (Horry for short) locked up or it would have been like leaving out bait. In fact they had lost two pets almost right away. It was all very well when Jock was there and they could laugh about it, but Anne was adamant she wasn't facing it on her own. She told Jock that until she actually couldn't walk she would continue to go with him on safari, but she did eventually have to brave the loneliness. In November 1950, Jock wrote to his mother: 'I have just returned from safari, for the first time alone. Anne was finally persuaded to stay at home by the fact that she can no longer run out of the path of a charging elephant.'

While Jock was on safari, Anne, eight months pregnant and with only Horry and her tomato seedlings for company, kept herself occupied with the BBC Overseas Service, the Singer she'd brought from home and books. She sewed clothes for the baby and dresses for herself, cut from outdated patterns bought in Lindi. The Swahili she had picked up in Tanga during the War was limited to agreeing with Rashidi what he should cook; though the forest guards also lived on the rim of the Plateau, their wives only spoke the local language, Mwera. When she felt lonely, she listened to the wheeze and crackle from Bush House and pictured the Strand on a rainy day, and meeting a friend for lunch at Lyons. She read a lot of poetry—Tennyson, the Romantics and A.E Housman—and (having published her first poem at nineteen) wrote a few poems herself, a habit she never lost. In one she wrote:

I wish I were in Fleet Street now.
There is always a thrill seeing people rushing
With folders under their arms—
Especially if it is raining,
And inside, the bright lights
And the hammer of typewriters
And the noise of the press turning.

It seemed a long ten days Jock was away, especially when she went out one morning to find Horry's mangled remains right there in the garden. A leopard had come right up to the verandah to snatch him.

Christmas with the Farrers in Mtwara was a welcome relief. It was seventy miles of bumpy, winding coastal road south from Lindi, and the journey on the hard, plastic seat of the Bedford cab was an ordeal to Anne in her unwieldy state. It was worth it for the company and change of scene. Ralph Farrer and Jock had trained together at Oxford, and Ralph had been Jock's best man. He was a gentle, attractive man with a shy smile under his trademark broad-brimmed hat. His wife Ann, who was plump and pretty and laughed a lot, was the first woman Anne had talked to properly since their arrival a whole year earlier. While Jock and Ralph did a lot of comparing of notes on the forestry situation, so did the two women— on their respective pregnancies. They visited the hospital where Anne had her blood pressure checked for the first time. It was a comfort to know everything she was feeling was normal. They played a lot of Bridge and Jock and Ralph played tennis while the two women lolled on the beach and took the occasional dip, though there was too much weed for the swimming to be any good. There were also unlimited supplies of beer and conversation to boost their spirits before taking up their solitary and abstemious existence on the Rondo again.

Mtwara, where the Farrers lived, until recently a fishing village, had been developed in 1947 into an administrative centre and port for the Groundnut Scheme, which was to provide oil for cooking and margarine to a post-war Britain beset by rationing. Along with the new port, a railway had had to be built connecting Mtwara and Nachingwea, a hundred miles inland, so as to import the latest farming equipment to cultivate 150,000 acres of bush. It was one of the most notorious failed colonial experiments. Over Christmas everyone they met was talking about it. As far as Jock was concerned, the Scheme's officials were suffering from collective dementia while the whole miserable affair was the result of the Labour Party's misguided post-war policies, which had poured forty-nine million pounds of tax-payers' money into it.

Almost gleefully, Jock wrote to his mother describing the obstacles in the way of the project. First, they had to bring the tractors by dirt road from Dar, chased by elephant and rhino. Even tractors adapted from Sherman tanks couldn't cope. Baobabs, mighty trees which abounded in that part of the country, impeded progress, but couldn't be cut down because they were used as tombs of important men, for imprisoning miscreants and so on. Their hollow trunks were beloved of bees that savaged the workers. So inhospitable was it to the demobbed recruits of the so-called Groundnut Army that they eventually trained local men to take over the work of ground-clearing. Jock noted that they took to the tractors with enthusiasm, wrecking them in the process. Then the Colonial Office, informed, he supposed, by socialist notions of equality, conceived the idea that the workers should be unionised. No sooner was the union formed than it went on strike in solidarity with dockworkers in Dar. Once they got the first crop planted, the rains washed away all the buildings and brought on a plague of scorpions besides. When the ground dried, it baked so hard they could hardly harvest the nuts.

The government's answer was to send a military man out who marched up and down barking orders no one obeyed, until he got sick and was invalided out. Finally, that January they conceded defeat and cancelled the project, having got precisely two thousand tons of groundnuts for their pains. Now the cleared land was unusable even for subsistence farming. Jock concluded his account by hoping some good might yet come of it—'if the great British public comes to its senses and elects a Conservative government at the first opportunity.' Compared to this, the Forest Department was a model of well-run efficiency.

The next letter, in February, bore news of a different kind: 'Dear Mama, from my telegram you'll know the baby arrived and also that it's a girl: Mary Jane. We couldn't agree which name to give her so ended up giving her both, and so far Jane has won out. Perhaps if she won't play cricket we can teach her to make a third at Bridge.'

I've always loved the drama of my arrival. It was touch and go whether I would arrive on the road or in the hospital at Lindi. When Anne started having pains, Jock put her in the front of the Bedford and they set off down four thousand feet of escarpment to the dirt road that would take them to the coast. Anne was gasping and gripping the truck door whenever they bounced or jolted, which given the state of the road was most of the time. They had sixty-four miles to navigate and on a good day it took four hours. Jock knew if they didn't make it he would be acting as midwife; being at the controls of a Beaufighter when its engines had just been shot out was the only comparable experience he had to draw on. He put his foot down and kept going till they reached a point normally crossed by a small bridge. In the dry season there was nothing there but a furrow that never had anything more than a trickle of water. Now it was the middle of the rainy season, and a torrent of muddy reddish-brown water rushed and gurgled across the road, with no sign of the bridge. He looked at Anne, who was rigid and sweating

profusely, eyes squeezed shut and teeth clenched. 'Hold on old girl,' he said, 'we'll get you there in time.' He swung the steering wheel around and turned the truck back up the road the way they had come on a detour taking them an extra two hours. At last, the simple, one-storey façade of the Lindi hospital, its curved front door beneath a pitched roof held up by verandah posts. Jock brought the truck to a screeching halt and ran to open the door for Anne. She barely made it to the ward before I was born.

Feeling he'd reached his limit and needing back-up, Jock left Anne to navigate the final stage with the help of the nurses. He went in search of John Blower, who luckily was not on safari but in his fusty basement office. John stood up as soon as he entered. It was obvious to both that a drink was in order, so they went back to John's verandah and downed several beers before they felt strong enough to return to the hospital. When they did, they found Anne propped on a narrow iron bed with me in a crib beside her, tearful but none the worse for wear.

'They made me walk up some stairs to the delivery room and I nearly didn't make it,' she told them. 'At one point I collapsed onto a step. I could feel I was sitting on the head.'

'I hope without brain damage being incurred,' said Jock.

Anne, caught between tears and almost hysterical laughter, found herself gasping for breath. When she could speak, she said, 'It was the only one of life's experiences so far that's lived up to expectations.'

They stayed a week in the rest-house in Lindi. Though there was nobody to advise her about caring for a new-born, Anne appreciated being looked after and having people around. The evenings they spent with John Blower, whose gin supplies were welcome. Although Anne and Jock had agreed to hold back the Christening until Kitty could be there, they wanted to ask John to be godfather. This they did over a second pre-dinner gin and tonic. He was silent for a minute.

'What does being godfather involve?' he asked cautiously.

Jock grinned, raising his glass. 'You'll have to swear to abjure the devil and all his works.'

John gave him a sceptical look. 'Must I?' he growled.

The journey back to the Rondo was calmer and slower, and once home, they improvised caring for a baby. They found they had to take all sorts of unforeseen precautions. Indoors, they had to keep the cradle covered at all times because of snakes and scorpions that might drop out of the roof. When Anne wanted to put me outside in the fresh air, Jock said I'd be bait for the leopards and go the way of Horry. He got the local metal-worker to build an iron-barred lion and leopard-proof cage into which they put the cradle. During the day when they put me outside, as an extra precaution they employed Ali, a young boy of fourteen, to sit and watch over me. Observing him from the verandah, Anne wondered how effective he would be as a guard. 'I suppose,' she said, 'the leopard will take Ali first and his screams will alert us in time to rescue the baby.'

They hadn't realised how much would have to be rethought with a baby. Going for a walk in the forest was a different proposition with a pram, and Anne, always nervous of lurking leopard, was perpetually poised to turn and run. She was grateful that her breast milk was plentiful, as there was otherwise no milk at all on the Rondo and African babies were weaned, at three months, straight from the breast onto solid food. With no statistics, no one knew how many babies died, but if they survived the leopard attacks, measles and any number of other minor illnesses could take them. Anne intended to breastfeed for as long as possible.

At last, five months later, in July, came Kitty's long-awaited visit. Reaching the Rondo was a tremendous undertaking, even for a woman accustomed to travelling huge distances. The journey from Adelaide to Dar es Salaam went via Sydney, Singapore, Karachi, Aden and Nairobi and took four days and nights by four different airlines and five planes. As the wife of a colonial government servant Kitty was used to being in a minority, but always with the privilege of being white and British. On the Air India Skymaster she was the only white passenger, and

suspected that in an emergency, she would be jettisoned along with the suitcases. Landing in Aden at 6am, she entered the dining room for breakfast and a Sudanese servant pulled out a chair for her at the head of a table for twenty. The other thirty-five passengers crowded into a far corner of the room and left her to eat in stately solitude.

After Nairobi, the unforgettable sight of Kilimanjaro emerging from early morning mists, and, after the monotony of the plain, Dar es Salaam, a dream city set in a wide sweep of blue water. Then the DC-3 plane to Lindi, where Jock met her with the Bedford. Kitty, who was accustomed to far-flung postings in different corners of the Empire, thought Lindi a sordid little town with the worst European housing she had seen. The Southern Province was known to be the Cinderella state of Tanganyika and had the worst roads. When she arrived at the edge of the great ravine with its abrupt drop of four thousand feet only a hundred yards from the house, she thought it rivalled the Grand Canyon. Even so, she was more impressed by the looming nearness of the forest on the other three sides. Though Anne had tried to warn her, she was unprepared for the sombreness and brooding silence, after the luxuriant beauty of the rainforests of Malaya and the jungles of Ceylon. Kitty greatly admired Anne's courage, for walking three hundred miles with Jock through lion and leopard country, always in danger and sleeping in the bush, and even more for withstanding the isolation when he would be away for a week or two at a time. Taking me for an evening walk she called her 'daily zero hour'.

'I have,' she wrote to her daughter Judy in Adelaide, 'been alone in lonely places, but have never had any ordeal to approach Anne's. Once, we were half a mile from home and pushing the baby in her pram when she looked quickly at me and said, "Did you hear that?" I did indeed—I lived with the sound of elephants trumpeting across the river from us in Ceylon. With one accord we turned for home, pushing the pram as fast as it could go on the rough ground.'

Kitty was shocked to discover on arrival that her new grandchild had no toys. Luckily, she'd brought a teddy bear with button eyes and stuffed with straw, which now lay beside me in the leopard cage. Kitty herself aroused great interest among the few thousand Africans on the Plateau because they had never seen a white person so old. At first they thought she was Jock's Chief Wife; the news that she was his mother caused great hilarity. Perhaps white men, not being quite human, weren't expected to have mothers. They were also impressed by the fact that Kitty had another child, a daughter with five living children. Kitty understood how difficult it was to keep a child alive when she watched Anne trying to feed me with the tomatoes she had so lovingly tended with bathwater. She had cooked and sieved them and I spewed them across the room.

For both Jock and Anne, Kitty's presence was a welcome antidote to their isolation. She religiously observed the colonial ritual of drinks at sundown and was a devotee of Bridge, which at a pinch can be played with three people, so cards enlivened their evenings. Her two-month visit went by too fast for Anne, who appreciated Kitty's experience with children—I was her sixth grandchild. Although she was somewhat grand and had trained Jock as a small boy to sound his vowels 'properly' so as not to sound Australian, she had the same dry humour as her son. Far from doting on him, she liked to apologise ironically to Anne, 'I did my best, but I had *such* poor material.'

The season on the Plateau drew to a close. Having almost completed his first three-year tour of duty, Jock was told he and his fellow assistant conservator in Mtwara, Ralph Farrer, were to go back to the Forestry School in Oxford for a refresher course. He thought he had chosen an outdoor career, but now it seemed that walking, measuring and collecting weren't enough, and he needed further training.

Nor was it only the colonial conservators who were to be trained. The forest rangers' school at Olmotonyi, near Arusha, had also recently reopened to ensure a

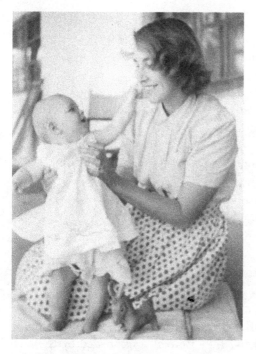

properly trained cadre of African assistants. A rudimentary Silviculture Section, for regeneration and planting of new species, was established at Lushoto, in the Usambara mountains, where Ralph and Ann would go after their time in Mtwara. Meanwhile Eggeling, the Chief Conservator, wanted to put an end to what he saw as the shameful misuse and wastage of timber between felling and use, and make sure when used it was suited to particular purposes. Opportunities for research in this new field of wood utilisation research were wide open and for Eggeling it must be done properly from the start, with adequate staff and funds.

Though Jock didn't yet know which area he felt more drawn to, Silviculture or Utilisation, he didn't fancy being confined to a laboratory and hoped that safari and forays into the bush would continue to be part of his job. Anne, whose life had already been transformed by motherhood, was thrilled at the prospect of a place with electricity, and milk. They both looked forward to a change of diet, and a few of the creature comforts they had learned to live without. When Jock heard that babies were entitled to free orange juice, he rejoiced. 'We can be sure of something to put in our gin, at least!' In July 1952, they set off for Oxford.

So ended my family's first encounter with the *nyika*, the great interior once known as Darkest Africa, or, as Jock called it, 'Darkest'. By the time I returned to retrace our steps, I was just in time to catch the last echoes of an era that had all but faded into silence.

I looked for traces: footprints in the earth, distant voices hanging in the air. And for those among the living who, like me, wanted to recover the past.

4. Safari in the South

When Anne and Jock came to Tanganyika, it was already in a period of transition that would take it, in just over a decade, to Independence. After the demarcation of territories at the Berlin Conference of 1884-5 it had become a German colony; in 1918, after the German defeat in World War One, it had been given to Britain to administer as a mandate of the League of Nations. Three years before their arrival, it had been reclassified a UN Trust Territory.

But all that was recent history. Lindi, which showed little sign of its former glory by the time my parents arrived, was part of a chain of ancient trading settlements strung out along the coast. For centuries before the European scramble for Africa, dhows carrying slaves and other precious goods had come and gone from the East African coast across the Indian Ocean, following the trade winds to Yemen and Oman, Persia, India, Thailand, Burma, Malaysia and Indonesia; and people from those places had followed the trade winds back, and some had settled. It was a place of transplantation. Both the bananas of Kilimanjaro and the coconuts which grow everywhere along the coast, arrived in the fourth century from Indonesia.

There are different versions of how Zanj, the ancient indigenous culture of the first millennium, was replaced by Swahili culture. They range from archaeological dating to legend. The one I like best tells how, in the tenth century, the king of the ancient Persian city of Shiraz had a dream that a giant iron rat was destroying his palace. Deeply disturbed, he equipped seven dhows and set sail from the Persian Gulf with his six sons. Arriving at the eastern shore of Africa, each son built a city at the spot where he landed, from Somalia in the north to Mozambique in the south—though there were no borders, and those countries didn't yet exist—creating, through intermarriage with the locals, the so-called Shirazi empire. This gave birth to the waSwahili—the people of the *sahil*, meaning coastal margin—and their language, kiSwahili. Spoken across a wide swathe of East Africa, it's a living testament to the hybrid history of settlement: Shirazi, Arabic, Portuguese, Hindi, German and English are all to be found in it.

Lindi, my birthplace, is on the coast some hundred miles south of Kilwa, one of the ancient ports allegedly founded by the six Shirazi princes. At its height Kilwa was a major port, its sultan's rule holding sway over hundreds of miles. Gold from the Zimbabwe Plateau travelled to Kilwa through the southern ports of

Sofala and Angoche (in today's Mozambique), and onwards to Asia. Back came ceramics, cotton, silk, beads and glass for distribution throughout the sultanate. Traces of this glorious past linger only in the majestic ruins of Kilwa's Grand Mosque and the fragments of pottery scattered along the coast.

My grandmother called this part of the country the 'Cinderella Province', and it still has little in the way of infrastructure. I had never, since my birth, been back to Lindi, and when I decided to go, it was because it was the nearest town to the Rondo Plateau. I didn't know how easy it would be to get there; all I knew was that the road was bad. When I looked online, what kept coming up was a place a bit further down the coast called Mikindani, and the reason Mikindani came up was the Old Boma, a boutique hotel run by an NGO that also supported local projects. The website showed white-painted walls, cool interiors and a sun-drenched external courtyard with a sparkling swimming pool. I was seduced. If nothing else worked out, at least I might enjoy staying there. But the website also claimed that the Old Boma was set up for trips to the Rondo, with an enticing description of a forest lodge and an overnight stay. I booked a room.

When I landed at the airport at Mtwara, capital of the Southern Province, it was exactly like the one at Moshi in the 1960s—space for one small plane to land at a time and a fire-engine standing by in case you burst into flames. The airport building was not much more than a shed, with a window through which our baggage was passed onto a wooden table. Maendeleo – development – didn't seem to have arrived here.

From the airport, a taxi took me to Mtwara bus park, where I got a *daladala*, one of the small buses ubiquitous in Africa, along the coast to Mikindani. Before the development of Mtwara into a port by the British, Mikindani had been the trade and administrative centre. It suffered the same fate as Lindi, being drained of its merchant class, though for a few years following the ill-fated Groundnut Scheme there was a railway between the two towns. Now there was nothing to see for a long time, then suddenly a cluster of square, earth and thatch Swahili houses and a few larger disintegrating coral stone buildings. Squinting in the midday sun, my eyes were assaulted by a shimmering white castle poised high above the ramshackle village. The Old Boma. Once an Arab palace, then the German administrative headquarters, its size and prominence effortlessly embodied its past status and present luxury. Two little girls ran to carry my bag up the steep hill to the entrance. As we toiled upwards, a small black snake glided across our path.

Dazzled by the brilliance of sunshine on white walls, I was relieved to be swallowed by the welcoming gloom beyond the front door. Inside, the Boma was restored to a level of luxury in keeping with its prominence and well-heeled clientele—government representatives, aid workers on furlough, curious visitors in search of an exotic experience. I sank gratefully into a cushioned sofa and accepted a drink adorned with a hibiscus flower. My room was cool and simply furnished, the walls two feet thick and brushed by bougainvillea. For today's guests, the Boma is what it's always been: an outpost of civilisation in a primitive region, a refuge from the 'horrid country' beyond the door.

Dinner was served at tables around the pool, in an enclosed garden under an inky sky. I shared a table with Cathy, an accountant working for Trade Aid, and Sue, a young volunteer coordinating a project run by the charity EdUKaid. As we visited the charcoal *braai* to select freshly grilled cuts of meat and fish, Cathy and Sue told me about the work the Old Boma was doing. Apart from being a node for tourism, it feeds money into the area by micro-financing small local projects, promoting tree-planting and the teaching of English. A small community of ex-pat volunteers works with locals on different projects. One of the latter, they told me, was Mr Thomas, a retired forester who ran a tree nursery behind the Old Boma. I knew at once Mr Thomas was my man, and asked if I could meet him.

Next day, an alert, spare, sprightly man in his early seventies was at the reception desk. Mr Thomas. I shook his hand and he looked at me in delighted surprise when I said my name.

'The daughter of Bwana Bryce? Of course I knew him. I met him in Moshi when I was at Olmotonyi.'

'The daughter of Bwana Bryce.' These words, like the turn of the lens on an old-fashioned camera, brought my surroundings into tight focus, with me at the centre. I was no longer a slightly lost outsider but right inside the picture. It was the first of many times I would receive from Tanzanians the precious gift of recognition, the acknowledgement of my place in the order of things. For a moment, I couldn't speak. Mr Thomas was telling me how he'd been at Olmotonyi, the training school near Arusha, from 1954-58, running through the list of what he called 'my old foresters'. As he talked, I saw a young Mr Thomas among a group of trainees visiting the Utilisation Section in Moshi, being introduced to Bwana Bryce. 'Of course I knew him.' After Olmotonyi he'd worked on the Rondo from 1958-60, before moving to Mtwara to work with 'Captain' Ralph Farrer—my father's Oxford colleague and friend—a few years after my parents spent

Christmas with him and Ann, his wife. Mr Thomas remembered Captain Ralph with enthusiasm, especially his trademark hat with the big brim.

A first-class honours in forestry whom Chief Marealle of Marangu awarded his certificate in person, Mr Thomas saw himself as a trained man who could promote conservation and help develop the area. He showed me his tree nursery, where he nurtured cedar, ironwood, rosewood, jacaranda and mahogany seedlings, and told me how he was trying to educate the local people about the importance of replanting. He talked to children at Mikindani primary schools and so far had given away over 14,000 seedlings to the community through the tree planting project. Not everyone welcomed his evangelism. When the Vice President attended the local Environment Day exhibition and Mr Thomas took his chance to speak to him about his conservation ideas, he was reprimanded for his forwardness by the Regional Commissioner.

Mr Thomas told me that here, as everywhere else in the country, trees have been regarded as an unending natural resource, and so many have been cut for firewood, charcoal and coral burning that there's now a real danger of deforestation. 'Coral burning?' I asked. Mr Thomas explained that coral, harvested from the reef, is a source of calcium carbonate—lime—used in cement. An image came back to me of women bent double in the water at low tide, harvesting coral with their bare hands. Meanwhile, a canoe can carry twenty years growth of brain coral in a single load. So, said Mr Thomas, the reef was being destroyed all along the coast, along with trees to feed the kilns. It was an ancient practice, hard to eradicate. Many buildings in Mikindani are built of coral, including the Old Boma. Now however, there's a marine reserve and efforts to protect what's left of the reef complement Mr Thomas's efforts to bring back the trees.

I asked Mr Thomas if he would accompany me to the Rondo and he enthusiastically agreed. Although he lived in the same region, he hadn't been back because it's an expensive journey, one he could only make if someone else was paying. But more than that, he had a great deal to say and sensed that I, unlike the Regional Commissioner, was a sympathetic listener. Besides, I was the daughter of one his old foresters, which marked us both as relics of the colonial era of which it's unfashionable and politically incorrect to speak positively or with nostalgia. So together, we embarked on this backwards safari, a secret mission of rediscovery disguised as an eco-trip. Since it appeared the forest lodge and the overnight stay were not an option, we went for the day in the Old Boma Land Rover, escorted by a driver and another man whose role remained unclear.

The first part of the journey was on a reasonably good tarmac road as far as Mnazi Mmoja, where we turned off the Lindi road towards the Rondo. Mnazi Mmoja means 'one coconut tree' and marks the spot where rebels were executed during the infamous repression of the Maji Maji uprising in 1907—one of several violent protests mounted against German rule, resulting in the death thousands.

This flat, featureless countryside is heavily inscribed with history. Trade caravans (looking for slaves and ivory) made their way across it into the interior in the pre-colonial days, as far as Lake Nyasa, several hundred miles to the west. David Livingstone 'discovered' the lake in 1859 by following the river Shire inland from Mikindani to its source, shocked by the human jetsam of the Arab slave trade he encountered along the way. Eventually, in 1871, the journalist Henry Morton Stanley caught up with him when, according to my copy of *Builders of the Empire*: 'Poor Livingstone had not seen a bath or a tent or a civilised man for years, and the effect must have been overwhelming.'

Difficult to imagine now the hardship of those earlier journeys, made in the belief that it was the white man's duty to take charge of those benighted lands for their own good. Tom von Prince, a German officer, drawn by 'the longed-for wonderland, innermost Africa', became station commander at Mikindani in 1890—and thus an inhabitant of the Old Boma. Known to his troops as Bwana Sakkarani, meaning 'a warrior in a state of reckless exaltation', he played a key role in another ruthless German campaign to quell resistance—this time by the Hehe.

A highly organised warrior clan, the Hehe, whose chief was Sultan Mkwawa, lived in the area known as the Southern Highlands. In 1891, the Hehe, under their Sultan's leadership, did that most unpardonable of things—they inflicted a terrible defeat on German forces, during which the German army commander, von Zelewski, who saw Mkwawa as a 'primitive nigger', was skewered by a spear. Station commander Tom von Prince took it as a personal affront: standing on the battlefield, holding Zelewski's skull, he vowed vengeance against Mkwawa. For the next seven years, Mkwawa eluded von Prince, living hand to mouth but protected by his people, until, seeing no way out of his predicament, in July 1898, he killed himself. When a German sergeant-major found his body, he cut off the head and presented it to von Prince, who evidently had a thing about skulls, and sent it as a trophy to the Anthropological Museum in Bremen.

This marked the conclusion of the Hehe chapter for Tom—two years later, he had left the army and was farming in the Usambara mountains, where the local wine is still named Sakkarani after him. It's good—I've tried it. But for the Hehe, Mkwawa wasn't so easily forgotten. After the British had defeated the Germans in World War One and been awarded oversight of the territory, the Hehe sued for the return of their Sultan's skull. Eventually, the Governor, Sir Edward Twining, went in person to Bremen to identify the skull. In 1956, he handed it over to Chief Adam Sapi, Mkwawa's grandson. It was exactly fifty-eight years since Mkwawa's death, but his memory was still fully alive.

My journey, a tiny filament in a web stretched between centuries, spooled out on a road that was nothing like Prince's of a century ago, or even of my mother's some fifty years later. Even so, we had brake damage by the time we turned off the Lindi road at Mnazi Moja and had to stop for makeshift repairs. Shaken to my bones in the Land Rover, I marvelled at the state of the road, one of those red murram trails made by driving a bulldozer through the countryside and thereafter leaving the road to fend for itself. At times we inched along the edges of perilous craters sculpted by successive rainy seasons. It seemed unbearably slow, dusty, and tedious.

I think of my parents and their foot safaris and wonder how they found the stamina to walk those distances. In March 1950, with Bernard as guide and Rashidi as cook, they set out on a round trip of nearly four hundred miles, from the Rondo to Lake Nyasa and back. Beyond a certain point, the only way was to walk. Anne kept a diary of the trip in a small blue notebook she picked up along the way, with the continent of Africa in black silhouette on the front cover and a title, The 'Isiyoshindwa' ('I will not fail') Memo Book.

> We left the lorry at a tiny outpost called Mpapa. To get to the Lake we had first to cross a mountain range, which meant struggling up 6,000 feet and down again the other side. Jock has a rifle with which to see off marauders in the shape of lion, leopard, elephant, poisonous snakes and crocodiles, and to provide meat for the journey.
> The relief of seeing the camp at the end of the day is indescribable. We arrive, footsore and starving, and Rashidi has the tin bath ready, filled with water heated over a wood fire, followed by dinner at a folding camp table, set with a table-cloth and napkins folded into water lilies.

No team of porters for me and Mr Thomas. A devout Christian, his cell phone screensaver was a picture of the Holy Family. As we reached the Rondo, we stopped at St Cyprian's College, an Anglican seminary at a place called Ngala, built about a decade after my parents left the Rondo on the former site of a logging company. While Mr Thomas said a prayer in the chapel, I marvelled at finding such a place, with its stained-glass window depicting the Creation, perched on the edge of the Rondo escarpment overlooking the primaeval forest. Later I discovered it had been built by Bishop Trevor Huddleston, of anti-apartheid fame, soon after his arrival in the diocese of Masasi in 1960. In his view, for the church to show it was moving with the times, its buildings must be the emblem of the future. So he brought an architect from Nairobi to build a chapel that, regardless of its remoteness, would inspire all who saw it.

From the chapel, Mr Thomas led me to the door of a modest bungalow nearby. A man opened the door and escorted us into a sitting room where a hulk of a man sat alone in front of a fat tome, reading. About the resurrection, it turned out. The man was white, elderly and very deaf. Mr Thomas introduced him as the Reverend Richard Norgate. Though I later found out about the Reverend's remarkable life, at this point I had never heard of him. Unsure of why we were there, I began a dialogue by scribbling questions on a piece of paper that he answered in a deep husky voice. He told me he was English, had been on the Rondo for fifty-five years and didn't expect to leave. I calculated quickly and asked, 'Were you here between 1949 and '52? Did you know my father?' In fact, he arrived in 1954. Like Mr Thomas, he remembered Ralph Farrer, my father's close friend and colleague, who lived in Mtwara until 1963.

'What are you doing here?' he asked me.

'I was born in Lindi. My parents were on the Rondo and I want to write about them.'

Something crossed his face. 'I've written my memoirs.' I was filled with excitement.

'Can I read them?' I asked eagerly.

He responded with a firm no.

It was a bitter moment. Here I was, face to face with a living remnant of my parents' past, one from whom I could have learnt so much. In the silence he already inhabited, perhaps through his refusal he was protecting the sanctity of his unseen inner world. And after all, why should I expect everyone I met to be willing to share their secrets with me?

When he died a year later, aged eighty-seven, I discovered from his obituary that he had joined the Navy during the War, winding up in Sydney, from where he dealt with the repatriation of servicemen to Australia. My father, who sailed back to Adelaide in 1946, was one of these. Richard Norgate may never have met my father, but there their lives crossed. He had come to Tanganyika as a mission priest in 1954—the year my parents moved to Moshi—first to the Newala station, then to Masasi. Reverend Norgate was one of a long line of missionaries in this part of Tanganyika. As Jock told Kitty, on the Rondo mission stations surrounded them, god-bothering being one of the ways of civilising the natives. In 1906, German Benedictines set up Ndanda Abbey, which supplied my parents with vegetables; though during World War One these Germans were all repatriated, the Abbey continued to grow and still flourishes today.

A quarter century after Uhuru, something unusual happened: the local clergy and laity of the forty-five parishes of Masasi elected Norgate, a white man, as their bishop. He travelled constantly to these forty-five parishes along the same unmade roads I suffered for a day. Having known and shared his parishioners' hunger (he was often rescued from starvation by the more numerous Roman Catholic community), he also launched an agricultural project to train people in farming, forestry, fish and livestock rearing. When I met him, he had been retired at St Cyprian's for thirteen years; the following year, he was buried in the church he had helped to build as parish priest.

The Europeans who founded these churches left not only buildings and communities constructed on a shared faith, but their memories and the essence of themselves, from Livingstone's heart beneath the mango tree in Ujiji to Norgate's tomb in Mkomaindo. Today, their legacy is alive in the work of Tanzanian priests and believers across the Rondo.

By my belated arrival, I caught the merest glimpse of that long-standing missionary tradition in the south that had sustained and comforted so many weary travellers, my parents included. As my mother's safari notes show, missionaries could be found in the most inhospitable places. No doubt they, too, welcomed the change of company and the chance of conversation. Besides—weren't they all about the same business—bringing European civilisation to Darkest Africa?

After two days, we reached Mbamba Bay on Lake Nyasa. It was a ghastly and unending walk and we staggered on and on, extremely hungry and hot. We arrived at last after nine and a half hours, having left cook and porters far behind. I was obsessed by the thought of a cup of tea, and said wistfully how nice it would be to see a friendly white face which would invite us home. In the distance was a small

steamer loading stores in the harbour, and we walked hopefully towards it. As we got near, two women appeared who turned out to be U.M.C.A. missionaries, a nurse and a teacher. They had come ashore from the steamer and invited us back on board with them. Canon

Cox, Bishop of Nyasaland, was on board, and was extremely nice, insisting that we return later for dinner. Afterwards, we were rowed back across the lake, very calm with a lovely moon, the Southern Cross and Orion both shining out.

At the small town of Ntene, we turned west and finally entered the forest reserve. When my father was here, it was still mainly original or 'closed' forest. For the people of Ntene it was a source of building materials for their houses, fuel, medicinal plants, wild vegetables, fruits, honey and wildlife for hunting. Plantation forestry began in 1952, when my father was involved in introducing pine and teak, along with mvule, a splendid indigenous hardwood tree so strong it

supplied sleepers for the railway. The Rondo became known as the finest mvule forest in East Africa. Today, it's still a source of sustenance for the people of Ntene.

We arrived at a clearing in the forest with a long, low, mud-brick building, one end of which had collapsed into rubble, surrounded by bare earth. The Rondo Plateau Forest Department office. As we got down from the Land Rover, it was hard to tell who was more excited, Mr Thomas or me. We walked along a line of closed doors till we came to an open one and knocked. In the shabby office a single young forestry officer sat scribbling at a desk. He looked up at us with bloodshot eyes. I thought of Eggeling, the Chief Conservator of Forests when my father started work, and his injunction that a forester's proper place was in the forests. This one didn't look pleased to see us. Mr Thomas informed him that he'd worked in this office in 1958, pointing at half a dozen black and white photographs from the 1950s stuck to the wall with tape. In a group of foresters lining up to meet Sir Richard Turnbull, Governor General, Mr Thomas picked out himself.

The young forester looked defensive rather than impressed. When he brought out a map of the forest to show us and I told him my father made the first map survey on foot, his reaction was astonishment and frank disbelief. I asked how many foresters they had to patrol such a big area—54 square miles, 34,744 acres—

and he told me nine, with only one vehicle. There were parts of the forest they couldn't go, he said, because of lions. I didn't tell him my father and his forest guards walked the forest with one gun between them. Nor that, in 1951, Jock Bryce was named among the chief collectors of botanical specimens, with 48 out of a total of 986. Or that that year, five of the six Divisional Officers averaged 7,000 miles of travel each, while the sixth (John Blower, my reluctant godfather) covered 13,000 miles. As we got back in the Land Rover, the silence between me and Mr Thomas contained the understanding of our own irrelevance.

We drove through the forest with Mr Thomas pointing out stands of trees he had planted himself nearly fifty years earlier. At one of them we stopped, and Mr

Thomas got a young man to push him up onto a fallen tree-trunk, in which pose I photographed him pointing to his trees and saying, 'For my old foresters in England'. He also pointed to areas where the trees had been harvested and replanted with pine, displacing the original, or closed, forest. Eventually we came out at the edge of the escarpment falling away thousands of feet below, bush and scrub clinging to its vertical sides. This was the breathtaking view that so impressed my grandmother when she arrived in 1951. We looked for the house my parents lived in, but there was no trace; only the foresters' concrete bungalows. After that, we headed home, a drive of nearly three hours. It was only fifty-five miles to the forest reserve at Rondo, but by driving all day on rough dirt tracks through the forest, we covered a hundred and eighty. By the time I staggered out of the vehicle outside the Old Boma that evening, I was exhausted.

On her foot safari along Lake Nyasa in 1950, my mother recorded:

It was only about 18 miles from Mbamba Bay to Liuli, but it took us two days.

Though I had come a long way and waited a long time for this experience—thousands of miles and half a century—I was left with the rueful recognition that the past was indeed another country. I was grateful to fall into the soft white bed in my thick-walled room in the Old Boma.

> My camp-bed collapsed in the early hours of the morning and I called Jock, who could think of no other reason for being woken than a lion about to enter the tent, so he grabbed his gun. We got the bed up again by torchlight (the porters had the only hurricane lamp, which left us a prey to lions and made me feel very bitter), but Jock nipped his finger in one of the joints and I had to bandage it for him. We were then so thoroughly awake, we sat and smoked a cigarette, hearing the porters sleeping soundly close by. Jock went back to sleep but I lay there imagining every snapping twig and stirring leaf was a lion about to spring through the tent flap. I was very glad to see the dawn.

At dawn I woke and lay in bed, feeling the aches from a day of bouncing along dirt tracks. I had planned to go to Lindi and find the hospital where I was born, but my appetite for safari had waned. I decided to spend the day recovering. Among the books lying on tables in the Old Boma, I found *East Africa and its invaders: from the earliest times to the death of Seyyid Said*, by R. Coupland, published in 1938. I carried it outside to a reclining chair beside the pool and immersed myself in it. The confidently Darwinian tone, the unquestioning belief in white superiority and the rightness of the imperial enterprise, were a reminder of how much things had changed in seventy years. But when my parents arrived here, only a decade after the book was published, such ideas as Mr Coupland's were not in the least outlandish. Away from the coast, what he saw was a wasteland of sand and scrub, backed by a hundred miles of waterless rising ground and a dense jungle of thorn trees and bushes. This 'horrid country', he informed me, known as the Nyika, is

populated by 'black-skinned, fuzzy-haired, thick-lipped Negroes', and everyone who has travelled it on foot 'has put on record how he hated it.' Everyone except my mother.

A lovely evening with a glorious red sunset. We camped right by a little river with water so clean and clear I even washed my hair in it. It was wonderfully cool to dip one's head in such water, so soft you hardly needed soap. We sat outside the tent and ate dinner under the trees.

According to Sir Charles Eliot, author of *The East Africa Protectorate*, published in 1905, and quoted approvingly by Mr Coupland, 'this dense pall of vegetation' coupled with the Slave Trade are what have kept the spirit of the inland African in bondage, preventing him from developing. Sir Charles speculates whether, if European occupation had occurred sooner, East Africa might have emerged from its primitive darkness earlier. Until now, he says, the whole history of the continent has been that of the coast, while 'not many miles back from the settlements and ports and market places a curtain falls, shrouding the vast interior of the continent in impenetrable darkness, "where ignorant armies clash by night".'

We set off from Mbamba Bay, which is the southernmost extent of Tanganyika's bit of the Lake. The rest is in Mozambique and Nyasaland. It was a perfect day, with a bright blue sky and a good breeze. The road twisted round and round the mountain, with a spectacular view of the Lake at every turn. It was thinly wooded on either side and everything was green and luxuriant. We had to climb to 4,000 feet and I had to sit down every hour or so for a drink and a rest. Bernard had sent a messenger to Mpapa telling them to bring the lorry to meet us, but the messenger returned with the news that the lorry had not arrived. As we had no other choice, we continued up the road towards Mpapa, and made camp at dusk.

At dusk in Mikindani, the atmosphere is muted. As I walk away from the Old Boma, people are re-emerging slowly after the day's heat. The rows of Swahili houses are peaceful and orderly, the ground swept clean in front of them. The village sits on a sweep of natural harbour, a curved enclosure of still water. At sunset, it's a golden bowl beneath a scarlet sky. Somewhere in my past, beyond memory, are villages like these, groups of men strolling or praying in the mosque, women sitting at ease outside mud houses and calling out greetings.

An old feeling returns, a childish need to get close to the life inside those houses. I walk freely through the streets, following the path that winds among the houses through the coconut trees, returning greetings and stopping occasionally to look closer. A group of young girls pass me on their way to the pump, buckets on their heads.

Equidistant between two clusters of houses I come on a grove of frangipani trees, white flowers scattered on the ground. As I peer through the gloom, I realise the trees are grave-markers, the old, gnarled ones towards the back marking the older graves, the saplings at the front more recent burials. Elsewhere, chiefs' graves are distinguished by baobabs; here, ordinary people have adopted frangipani as their spirit repository, sharing a patch of ground between different sections of the village. The trees cast long, convoluted shadows, like Makonde spirit carvings, every one a soul.

> When we reached the summit, we met a strange thing: a little cairn of stones that could only have been put there by human hand, one stone laid carefully on top of another. There was no purpose to it that one could see, it gave no shelter and couldn't be seen from any distance. One just came upon it suddenly, at the top of the hill, like a marker whose meaning was lost. It gave me an eerie feeling looking at it, as though the ghosts of everyone who had passed that way were watching us. Bernard, who is an experienced guide, says it's very old. How old, I wonder? Did slave caravans pass this way? Before we walked on, I surreptitiously added my own stone to the cairn.

I turn from the graveyard and, the darkness at my back, retrace my steps towards the sea. Traces of the past are everywhere, in the crumbling two-storey Arab houses, the derelict prison, grand stone ruins among the homely, lived-in houses. At the side of one large deserted house an outside staircase leads to a wide verandah overlooking the harbour, supported by two stone pillars. A gracious house sliding into forgetfulness, it was named for the Aga Khan, a philanthropic king who gave a lot of money to education in Africa. Once a school, now unused, its spacious, empty verandah needs a row of students seated on mats to give it life.

I linger a while on the verandah, half-seeing in the shifting shadows the silhouette of a square-sailed ocean-going dhow slicing the water of the once-great trading port. The harbour fades to black.

5. Transitions: 1952-54

In February 1952, Jock and Anne heard the momentous news of the King's death on the BBC Overseas Service. They were still on the Rondo but change was in the air, both in their corner and the world beyond. In East Africa, the King's subjects, black and white, were stirred by the fact that the newly-married royal couple, Princess Elizabeth and the Duke of Edinburgh, was visiting Kenya. When the BBC broadcast the news of the King's death, they were deep in the bush. At this dramatic moment, it felt as if Kenya, instead of being a remote place in Africa, was right at the centre of world events. Even the Rondo felt a little less cut off.

Soldiers of the King's African Rifles from all three East African countries had fought and died on the British side in both World Wars. Despite the anticolonial feeling gaining ground, to many people 'For King and Country' meant Tanganyika and Kenya as much as England. Jock and Anne shared their patriotic pride. Television had not yet arrived, and all people had seen of royalty up to then was glimpses in British Pathé newsreels or grainy newspaper images. Now, Elizabeth was on African soil, and Africans, Europeans and Indians lined the roadsides to catch a glimpse of her—just as, four years later, I would be one of the schoolchildren waving a flag at the roadside to greet Princess Margaret when she visited Moshi. It was what you did in the 1950s.

While the future queen was in Kenya, Anne and Jock were already anticipating their first 'home leave'. Five months later, in July, they found themselves once again aboard a P&O liner, the SS Uganda, and a few weeks later they were in Oxford. Here Jock was to do the refresher course at the University's Imperial Forestry Institute, along with Assistant Conservators from elsewhere in Africa, the Caribbean and Asia. Despite the poverty and deprivation of the post-war years in Britain, nothing could dent Anne's delight at spending a few months 'at Home'. In the three years they had lived on the Rondo they had become accustomed to making do, so the fact that everyday things—sugar, butter, cheese, margarine, bacon, meat, eggs, tea—were still being rationed didn't really matter. After keeping a baby alive on bathwater-tomatoes, free orange juice from the state looked like bounty. They rented a small house in Lonsdale Road, off the Banbury Road in north Oxford, near enough for Jock to cycle to work.

Two of Jock's colleagues, Ralph Farrer and Dick Willan, were also on the course. While Jock and Anne had been on the Rondo, Ralph and Ann, who lived on the coast in Mtwara, had been their closest friends. In Oxford, they became equally close to Dick. He was thin, his bones so prominent that the planes of his face sliced the air. When he smiled, his thin face was swallowed in the stretching of his lips, the crinkling of his eyes. The year before, on assignment in Moshi, Dick had met Pauline, a very beautiful Irish teacher. They would be married in Moshi in 1954, and remain lifelong friends of Jock and Anne.

Now, in Oxford, Anne and Ann Farrer often met to take their one-year-olds for walks in Port Meadow and the Oxford Parks. After so much solitude it was good to be with friends and share experiences. Even so, it was the 1950s and they, like many women, were not only Home but back 'in the home' after leading their own challenging and interesting lives. While the men were attending lectures and seminars, there were nappies to wash and meals to cook with limited ingredients. By now they were used to cleaning and laundry and cooking being done by someone else, and doing it all with a young child was a full-time job. That December, the smog that descended on London killed thousands of people. Did Anne ever catch herself thinking wistfully of the Rondo, of Rashidi and the African sun and clear air?

If so, there were distractions beyond Oxford. In June the following year they stood in the Mall in the rain to watch the Coronation procession. King George and Queen Elizabeth (now to be known as the Queen Mother) had become patriotic figureheads during the War. The new Queen Elizabeth was only twenty-six years old and with her ascendance it felt as if the War era was well and truly over.

Meanwhile, their old friends, Malcolm and Marigold, lived in the Warwickshire countryside, near enough to Oxford to go and spend weekends. By the time I used to visit them for half-term from Cheltenham, they lived in a large, converted farmhouse deep in the countryside. It was my first encounter with upper class rural life. Marigold was an artist and painted and etched in a studio that shared the ancient barn with her beloved horses. Her spacious, wall-papered kitchen was dominated by an Aga, and I was captivated when Malcolm appeared at the kitchen door with a basket laden with fresh peas and strawberries he'd grown himself. In the hall, uneven floorboards creaked as you approached the little walnut table where a fountain pen lay beside the silk-backed visitors' book. Visiting alone aged fourteen, I was allowed to sign it myself for the first time. Looking back through the pages, I stumbled on evidence of my parents' lives Before Children. With a shock, I realised they had a story that pre-dated us. Jock Bryce's signature appeared several times on its own; then, in 1949, there were both signatures—Jock Bryce and Anne Millard—on the fateful weekend Jock took the spare room and Anne had to sleep on the sofa; in 1952, there were three names in my father's precise angular hand: Jock, Anne and Jane Bryce; four years later, my mother's looser, more rounded script recorded the visit of Jock, Anne, Jane, Mary and Alexandra Bryce, and finally, after her birth in 1961, Sally's name appeared. Our family's history, spelled out in black ink.

When they returned to Tanganyika in August 1953, the new Utilisation Section, where Jock was to be posted, still hadn't opened in Moshi. Meawhile, they were sent instead to Forest Department headquarters in Morogoro, capital of Eastern Province. Though Morogoro District covered eight thousand square miles of mostly bush, Morogoro town itself was the second stop on the Central Line railway, built by the Germans between 1910 and 1914 to connect Dar with the interior. It was in a bowl surrounded by the Uluguru Mountains, rising to six thousand feet and home to a belt of indigenous forest. Here, after several trying months behind a desk, Jock found himself, at last, on safari again.

At Forest Department headquarters Jock worked under the legendary Chief Conservator, W.J. Eggeling. From the moment he took office in 1950, Eggeling's vision for the future went beyond the simple extraction of resources for the benefit of the mother country. As he declared in his first Annual Report: 'Forestry is an important factor… both for the protection of natural resources and the provision of materials vital to the everyday life of the people.' In his view, the primary task for forestry in Tanganyika during the next decade was demarcating forest boundaries, to establish the extent of what was known as 'the forest estate' so as to protect it.

By 1950, the forest estate had already more than doubled, from 4,706 to 8,370 square miles. By 1955, it would be nearly 8% of the entire country: 28,000 square miles. This was accomplished by the collective tramping of Assistant Conservators like Jock, along with their Forest Guards, across thousands of miles of territory, mapping, demarcating and setting forest boundaries. Alongside this they were 'to build up by example and teaching a real understanding among the peoples of the country of the value of forests and forestry to them and their descendants'.

This obscures the impact on the relatively few people who customarily lived or farmed within the newly-declared boundaries, their displacement and loss of land rights, though policing was not the job of the Forest Department but the District Commissioner. But Eggeling was operating in the best tradition of British paternalism, and would have regarded this as a small price for the long-term betterment of 'the everyday life of the people'.

If forestry was above all for the future, for the present there was more than enough to keep Jock busy while he waited for his next posting. As Eggeling said that year in his final Annual Report: 'The Forest Department has become one of the really important departments of the Territory, and... it and Water Development will have an immense bearing on the future prospects of Tanganyika... so Cinderella is to go to the ball at last, and the gown she has been given has the right lines and the new-look.'

Meanwhile, besides looking after me, now two years old, by June the following year Anne would be nursing twins. In the space of ten years, her Tanganyika experience would have included war-service as a naval officer at the coast; living in extreme isolation in a mud-walled thatch-roofed house with her husband while tramping hundreds of miles across the Southern Province; and being the mother of three small girls in circumstances where keeping children alive was a full-time responsibility. Much of this she bore alone since Jock was frequently away from home, but Anne never forgot she was one of the lucky ones. Still there were times, with only me for company, when she looked somewhat wistfully through the heavy album, interleaved with tissue paper, where she had stuck her war-time photos—the parades in uniform, the off-duty picnics and parties and mess dances in Tanga, with Marigold, Lesley, Diana, Creepie, George, Pete... there had been weddings too in Tanga, and babies born since. Babies were to be celebrated even when two arrived unexpectedly at once, six weeks before their due date—as announced by cable to Kitty:

Cable to Mrs K.L Bryce, Stirling West, Adelaide. 9 June 1954.

Early arrival of not one but two babies, both girls. Colleague's comment, 'Good God man, you don't know your own strength!' Jock.

Whether or not attributable to masculine prowess, Anne was quite pleased with herself when the midwife at the small Morogoro Hospital delivered one baby. She was thinking it was all over when the midwife looked at her and said, 'You know, I think there's another one in there!' just before the second baby arrived. Not only was this a complete surprise, they were premature and tiny: at five weeks Mary weighed five and a half pounds and Alexandra, who'd been born first, not quite six. Though Anne was relieved to see that after a week or so they were starting to look quite human, the weight gain came at a cost. There was no neonatal intensive care unit and babies could die of gastroenteritis if they weren't fed on breast milk. Feeding them in rotation was an unending exercise, and for the next nine months she never got more than two hours uninterrupted sleep.

Thanks to a gift from Kitty they could afford a cook, so Anne could put all her energy into feeding the twins. Six weeks after they were born Jock was away on safari and she was confined to the house. When he came home, Jock only realised how exhausted she was when she fell asleep sitting upright on a chair and crashed to the floor. It can't have helped that I, having been sent to stay with friends for two weeks when the twins were born, now started having screaming tantrums nothing could allay. Perhaps this also marked the start of the difficult relationship with Jock that continued until I was about eighteen. Anne reported to Kitty that when she asked me if I loved Daddy, I said, 'No, I'll give him a slug on the lug!' Anne's comment, 'Definitely her father's daughter', was ironic, in view of what was to come.

Anne was hoping Jock would be home in time for his thirty-third birthday in July, but when it came, he was still on safari. As he'd been involved in the negotiations for a forest reserve in the Nguru mountains, another range in Morogoro District, and was the only one who knew how it was to be demarcated, he had no choice but to do it himself. Planning a safari was a complicated business and he wasn't best pleased that, unlike on the Rondo where he had had time to create a safari-organising system and impart essential skills, here he had to make the preparations himself—assembling supplies, packing and sorting into loads, and pitching his own tent. All the effort was made up for by the fact that the people of the Nguru mountains, who rarely saw white visitors, treated him with helpful courtesy. Though remote, they weren't entirely cut off—the local court had a battery-driven wireless that received Swahili broadcasts from Dar es Salaam. Operating it was the prerogative of the chief, and Jock was highly entertained when he told him that, as no one there had previously heard a radio, and as telephones were known to have wires, as chief he was regarded as a more than usually powerful sorcerer for being able to summon up disembodied voices. He confided in Jock that he was held in such awe that he could charge any amount he wanted for the privilege of hearing them. Jock was fairly sure he did so.

Jock's task in Nguru was hard and frustrating. It consisted of climbing alarmingly high steep hills to put beacons on the top, so as to compose a map from a series of triangles that somehow refused to triangulate. He celebrated his birthday by writing to Kitty, describing how he had made camp at 4,500 feet by a very clear and cold stream that bubbled past the front of the tent. The spot—a high valley set among a jumble of peaks—was cool enough at night for Jock to huddle next to his camp-fire inside several of his English jerseys. He didn't, however, enjoy the meals produced by his safari cook, 'who is really the laundry boy with a frying pan'. His birthday dinner consisted of boiled spaghetti and a watery cheese sauce out of a tin, as the bottle of Australian Rosella Tomato Sauce he'd bought to augment his efforts had been left behind by the cook. Accordingly, said Jock, 'I had to confront his cuisine in all its grim reality. Fortunately I had succeeded in acquiring a bottle of beer to alleviate my otherwise teetotal existence.'

This picture of Jock, in his jerseys with his single bottle of beer, making the most of his birthday somewhere in the Nguru mountains, the epitome of loneliness, contrasts with that of Anne, confined to the house with a toddler and two ravenous babies. Although Anne had expected him back in a week, there was a limit to the amount of climbing he could do in a day in pathless country, in head-high elephant grass that brought him up in weals and rashes, and the safari stretched to ten days. He was going back to a house suddenly full of children, so perhaps he secretly relished it.

By the time Jock got home a date had been set for the move to Moshi. Anne contemplated doing the journey in the cab of the Chevrolet truck with a three-year-old and two babies, and wondered about travelling by train instead. Even that would have been an undertaking, so she was filled with gratitude when Fred Hughes, Jock's new boss at the Utilisation Section in Moshi, visited Morogoro and offered to drive her and the babies in his Vanguard saloon.

Late in 1954 they set off in convoy, Jock driving the Chevrolet packed with luggage, Anne and the children with Fred in his relatively comfortable car. She had good reason to be grateful as the tarred road extended barely five miles from Morogoro, after which most of the rest of the journey was on dirt roads, passable in the dry season but a sea of mud in the rains, with bridges washed away; they had been careful to schedule the journey ahead of the short rains, expected at the end of October. But in those days before seat-belts, the rutted roads meant you could be flung against the windscreen or the dashboard, while in the absence of air conditioning, the open windows meant that red dust infiltrated every corner of the car as well as your eyes and hair. It was exhausting, especially if you were trying to breastfeed two babies and keep a three-year-old happy for hour after hour. They did it in two stages with many rest stops, heading first to Lushoto in the Usambara Mountains, a journey of three hundred miles, where they stayed overnight with

Dick Willan (last seen in Oxford and newly married to Pauline), before driving another hundred and forty miles to Moshi. Every mile separated them further

from their early bush-based life. On the Rondo, they had been almost as far south as the Mozambique border; in Morogoro, they had seen the centre of the country. Now they were going to live as far to the north as you could go without spilling into Kenya.

All they knew about Moshi, the town at the foot of Kilimanjaro, was that it was two hundred and twenty miles from the coast and 2,800 feet above sea-level. Neither Jock nor Anne would forget their first glimpse of the highest mountain in Africa, rising out of the plain with its dramatic crown of snow. When in the middle of the nineteenth century German explorers reported they had seen snow on the equator, they were flatly contradicted by the British geographer, William Desborough Cooley, author of *Inner Africa Laid Open*. He had never been to Africa, but was certain that the African mountain had a fiery, not a snowy summit. Nor, with all the explorers and missionaries from different European countries, was it clear who it belonged to, but the Chagga people who lived on the mountain could feel that things were changing. They had lived peacefully enough together in a scattering of settlements on the lower slopes, each with its own chief. The Swahili caravans had not upset the status quo, but now their rulers were competing for supremacy by playing one lot of Europeans against another. But the dice were loaded and they were outplayed.

The British-occupied territory of Kenya lay next to the German-designated country of Tanganyika, with the mountain on the border between them. The German Kaiser knew he wanted it, and in 1884 he told his Chancellor, Bismarck, to convene a great conference in Berlin of all the European countries with colonies in Africa. As the statesmen sat around the map of Africa, pencils poised to draw their boundaries, Kaiser Wilhelm made it known that, as Kilimanjaro was discovered by a German, it must therefore be German. It was a tense moment, but the Kaiser was Queen Victoria's grandson. The British Queen graciously gave the mountain as a birthday present to the Kaiser's young son, with the words, 'William likes everything that is high and big'.

Or did she? There are other versions of this history: Kilimanjaro is a place of stories, and I grew up with some of them. It was many years before I learnt about the hanging of Chief Meli of Moshi, along with eighteen other chiefs, for plotting against German rule. That was in 1900, after which European rule would last another sixty years. On 9 December 1961, the British flag came down and the flame of Uhuru was lit on Mount Kilimanjaro.

But in 1885, all this fuss over a mountain in Africa with fictitious snow was hardly comprehensible to some. In a note to a colleague, William Gladstone, the British Prime Minister, refused a proposal 'to protect the mountain country behind Zanzibar with an unrememberable name.' Which name he meant (Kilimanjaro, the name of the mountain, or Tanganyika, the name of the country) hardly matters. Tanganyika, made up by yoking together the kiSwahili words: *tanga*, a sail and *nyika*, the plain, designates a place where civilisation starts and ends at the coast. All else is 'the dry land behind Tanga'. Seventy years after the Berlin conference, the dry land behind Tanga was where my family came to live.

PART 3: MOSHI AND THE MOUNTAIN, 1

6. Rombo Avenue

For thirty-six years I visited Moshi only in dreams. When I at last went back, I saw with my grown-up eyes a quiet, well-laid out place, wide straight tree-lined streets leading from the bustling town centre to tranquil residential neighbourhoods. I saw the Hindu temple lift its minarets on the main street running directly south-north towards the mountain, the snowy dome of the Greek Orthodox Church give back a reflection of the peak itself. I saw how the roads fanned out from the clock tower at the centre of the roundabout, towards the airport, the industrial district, the town swimming pool, the old European Club, Hellenic Club, Hindu Club,

westwards out of town towards Arusha and eastwards towards the coast. I saw how the town the Germans had designed and built had remained intact, the same streets, the same trees, so that nearly four decades later I could walk with confidence in any direction and know without asking where I was going.

But when we arrived in 1954, I was three years old and for a long time my compass extended no further than the house and garden. The place where memory takes on a joined-up quality is Rombo Avenue. One of a network of quiet residential roads, it was named after a place on the mountain, seat of Horombo, a famous Chagga chief who ruled over the whole of Kilimanjaro in the early years of the 19th century. Jacaranda trees lined the road, their green fronds meeting overhead making a sun-dappled shade on the tarmac. In the dry season they dropped scimitar-shaped seed pods that doubled as swords and rattles. When they flowered, we walked on a soft mauve carpet beneath a canopy of incandescent purple. The volcano, extinct for centuries, had bequeathed the rich red soil beneath our feet, and each house was set in a garden where colonial ladies coaxed roses into bloom, flame trees blazed against bougainvillea hedges and

frangipani branches twisted in intricate patterns, dropping their creamy pink and yellow-tinged flowers on carefully watered grass.

Our house was a modest colonial government bungalow surrounded by a terraced garden and bounded by a hedge. Behind the house was a smaller building designed as a series of self-contained rooms each with their own outside door and one room that served as a communal kitchen. This was the Servants' Quarters, where it was understood grown-ups never went because the Servants lived there and, when there, were Off-Duty and shouldn't be disturbed. But this did not apply to me.

Hamisi, the house-boy, did the cooking and some of the housework, and wasn't a boy but a man. Outside the bathroom was a water tank on a concrete tower with an opening high up where a fire was laid. This was the bombola; every day about five o'clock, Hamisi lit the fire in the bombola so we could have hot water for bathing; twice a week, he lit the bombola in the morning as well so he could wash the clothes he hung to dry in the hot sun. In the early evening, he filled the base of the iron with hot coals and pressed our clothes, which he carried into the house in warm fragrant piles. You were lucky if you found a house-boy or cook who could cook European dishes; if not, you had to train him or supervise the cooking. Hamisi was bright and willing and listened carefully when Anne told him what to do, but still she had to keep it simple. She was caring for three young children and didn't have much energy to spare for niceties, so we lived mainly on shepherd's pie and spaghetti.

Hamisi had a lot of work and stayed mainly in the house, but Ahmed was a young cousin of his who looked after the garden. In time there were flower-beds, flowering shrubs that needed watering in the dry season, and seedlings bought by Anne, which she asked him to look after. Meanwhile, the grass had to be cut often because of snakes, so Ahmed was busy outside, chopping the grass by hand with a flat blade called a panga, or watering, or making bonfires of dry grass and leaves, and I had nothing better to do than follow him around. Hamisi and Ahmed were from the Coast, where the purest Swahili was spoken. Ahmed let me play around him, and spoke Swahili to me so that I soon spoke as much Swahili as English.

One day, Daddy asked me to tell him what I'd learnt that day, and I said, '*Mavi yako ina nuka*'. He spluttered with laughter and called Mummy to listen to me say it again, but wouldn't tell me what it meant.

Apart from Ahmed and Hamisi, there was Martha, our ayah. She came to live with us because Mummy needed someone to help with the babies, and she would carry one on her back while Mummy was feeding the other. She would sing sad slow songs she said were hymns to make them sleep. She looked after me as well, washing and dressing and playing with me when she had time. I loved her from the start for her gentleness and her high-pitched laughter that rang out when we talked or played. She told me stories and explained things to me I wanted to know, like what it meant when you said '*mavi yako ina nuka*'. She giggled and hid her face, but I kept asking, and in the end, she whispered, 'your shit stinks.' She said it was rude so I shouldn't say it to anyone else and she would tell Ahmed not to teach me things like that. She came from the mountain where they spoke Chagga, but had gone to a convent school where she'd learnt some English. Hamisi and Ahmed laughed at her Swahili because it wasn't pure like theirs. In the evenings, she would take me for a walk along the road to the kindergarten school playground, where there were swings and slides. Sometimes we walked back the long way and saw the mountain far away, shining in the setting sun. I looked at it and tried to imagine how you would live there, in all that white, but Martha told me she came from much further down, where there were banana trees instead of snow.

Ahmed worked in the morning before it got too hot, and again in the evening if he was watering. In the garden were dangerous things like centipedes, and even a tarantula. And snakes—one day, Anne found Alexandra face to face with one, each swaying back and forth as if hypnotised by each other. Luckily, Ahmed wasn't afraid of anything and killed snakes with his panga. He cut centipedes in half as well and once he let me use his panga to cut a millipede, even though it wasn't poisonous. He picked up birds, and showed me how to touch them without hurting them, only I didn't like the feathers. We all had to stay inside while he knocked down the hornets' nest that had grown in the space where the roof stuck out beyond the wall. He had a bucket of water waiting and picked up the shattered nest with a spade and pushed it

in so the hornets drowned. One of them stung him first, but he was brave and didn't say anything, he just showed it to Mummy and she took a needle and got the sting out. When he found the tarantula hole he told Daddy, and we all gathered round it while Daddy poured in paraffin. Then he dropped in a match and a flame jumped out but nothing else. A tarantula was a big hairy spider that could kill you with its sting, and Daddy said Ahmed was very useful for protecting us from danger.

Then one day we saw a chameleon, and he ran away. I didn't know what it was, I was just sitting under the frangipani tree when I looked up and saw something strange on a branch. First I thought it was part of the branch because it was the same colour, but then it moved, and I saw something like a big, greenish-brown lizard, with a curly tail and two big eyes with lids that met in the middle when it blinked. Its back was curved and it had four clawed feet it clung on with, and when it moved it lifted one claw and swayed forwards and backwards, ever so slowly, before it took a step. There was an insect on a leaf and it stuck its tongue out—so quick you could have easily missed it—and rolled it back with the insect inside. I scrambled out and called Ahmed, but when he came he only looked once before he ran away. Then I was scared because I had never seen Ahmed scared of anything, and I ran inside to ask Mummy about it. She and Martha came and looked and said it wasn't poisonous, but Martha wouldn't go near it either, so we left it alone. Mummy said it was clever of me to see it because it was camouflaged, which meant its skin could change colour so it would match what it was standing on. I wanted to see it change colour, but when I went back it was gone.

'Why don't you and Ahmed like the chameleon?' I asked Martha.

'Because of what it did to black people,' she replied. 'Long ago, when God made the world, everyone was the same colour, and it was black. Then God made a pool for all the people to wash in, and he called the animals and sent them out as messengers to tell people to come. The cheetah's people arrived first because it was the fastest animal, and they washed all over and became white. The lion's people came second, and there was still plenty of water so they washed and became yellow. The elephant's people came next, and though the water was less, they could still wash well enough to come out brown. The last messenger was the chameleon, and it was so slow its people got there last and there was only a puddle of water left. All they could do was stand in it and bend over and place their palms flat in it, which is why the only part of black people which is white is the palms of their hands and the soles of their feet. And that's why we hate the chameleon, because he cheated us.'

This was the first time I'd heard it was bad to be black, and I felt sorry for Ahmed. But I didn't understand why God didn't just make everybody white in the first place, if that was what he wanted them to be, so I felt sorry for the chameleon too, because God must have made it slow so it wasn't really its fault. I already knew there were many different kinds of people; white people like me and my family and our friends, black people like Martha and Ahmed and Hamisi, and brown people like Mr Mulji in the big shop in town where we went to buy food. White people lived in big houses and black people looked after them, and lived in the Servants' Quarters; or on the Mountain, or at the Coast. Brown people lived in town, in big buildings with names like Mulji's Emporium with a date on the front, and washing hanging over the upstairs balconies. The clothes were different too— black people didn't wear shoes and mostly dressed in old torn clothes, except in the Market where the women wore brightly-coloured kangas, or going to the Mosque, when the men wore long white robes called kanzu and caps on their heads. The brown ladies in the shops in town wore saris and had a red dot in the middle of their foreheads, and they spoke their own language as well as English and Swahili. White people went to the Club to play tennis and golf and snooker and drink beer, and white children swam in the town pool where black children weren't allowed. But even at the Club, not all the white people were the same. Some spoke other languages as well as English, and some went to the Greek Orthodox Church or to the big Catholic Church and not St Margaret's over the road like we did. None of this prepared me for the idea that black was bad. If I hadn't seen Ahmed run away from the chameleon, I wouldn't have known.

The afternoon was a quiet time when the Servants went back to their Quarters for lunch and Mummy had a rest before the twins woke again. I followed Martha. Her room had a wooden shutter she always closed and bolted when she went out, and locked her door with a key. In the afternoon she would unlock the door and the room would be dark and stuffy until she flung open the window-shutter to let in the light, and then you could see her things. She had a bed with a grey blanket with one black stripe, and a wooden box next to it with her Bible and a pretty bead necklace called a rosary she used for praying. Her white church dress hung from a nail on the wall on a wire coat-hanger. In a neat row on the floor were her cooking pots, black on the outside and scrubbed silver inside, with a couple of white enamel bowls and an enamel plate with a blue rim. Everything was clean and tidy, not like our rooms which were full of things. What I liked best was the little picture painted on wood over the bed. In the painting, the Virgin Mary dressed in a blue robe was holding her baby, and they both had a gold halo and were smiling. It was the most beautiful thing I had ever seen.

Next to Martha's room was a kitchen with blackened walls, where she took turns with Hamisi cooking on an open fire surrounded by bricks. Smoke filled the room when she blew on the wood to make it burn, and Martha wafted it away with a fan of newspaper, or she would let me do it. In the corner was the meat-safe, a wooden frame with wire mesh tacked on to keep out flies, its four feet in old condensed milk cans filled with water to stop the ants climbing up. She took a piece of meat from the safe and cut it into chunks along with an onion, before putting them to boil in one of the round black pots. She put a pinch of salt and curry powder to thicken it, and after a while it smelt so good your mouth watered. Then she pushed the meat stew to the back of the fire and put a pot of water on to boil. She took the bag of maizemeal from the shelf and poured it slowly into the bubbling water, turning it with a long wooden stick with a wide flat bit at the end. When all the water was gone and the maizemeal was stiff, she wet the wooden spoon and used it to turn the *posho* onto a plate. We called it *posho*, which Daddy said really meant provisions for a journey. Hamisi used the proper Swahili word, *ugali*.

Martha put a piece of old newspaper on the floor, and placed the two pots on it side by side. The food had a special smell, a mixture of smoke and spices and the starchy scent of the *posho*. We sat on the concrete floor, the steaming mound of *posho* and the small enamel dish of meat and gravy between us, breaking off bits of *posho* and rolling them in our fingers before dipping them in the sauce. Afterwards, I scraped bits of *posho* from under my fingernails and sucked the gravy off my wrist. It was my favourite food.

Sitting there cross-legged, the concrete hard and scratchy beneath my thighs, I asked Martha, 'Martha, can people change their colour?' She looked at me and pinched my leg.

'Why, do you want to be black like me?' she asked, laughing her high-pitched laugh.

I considered this before replying, 'But you said black was bad.'

She was silent and then she said, 'We are all in God's hands.'

We went together to the tap to wash, and I knew it was time to go back to the house where Mummy would be waking up after her rest. It would be a long time before I would understand the mystery of the chameleon.

7. Martha's Dream

Martha was our *ayah*. This word, used in India and Africa in the days of the British Empire, meant maidservant, nursemaid, nanny. To those of us who had one, it meant something more: unshakeable love, loyalty and forbearance. All of which we took for granted. Martha was a house-post, essential to the structure of our lives, but we knew little about her. Where did she come from? How old was she? We knew she was a Catholic and had been to mission school; she had a young

daughter, Ann-Rose; there was no sign of a husband; she was gentle to the point of ineffectiveness; she used to call after the twins 'WaMary', as if they were a tribal group all of their own, and they would run away without answering.

Martha had been with us as long as I could remember, certainly from when we moved to Rombo Avenue when I was five. She was there at Uhuru in 1961, the year Sally, my last sister, was born, when I was ten. She was still there when I was going on thirteen and sprouting breasts. Somewhere along the way she joined the Tanganyika African National Union (TANU), the political party that won power at Uhuru, and started going to night school. The political message must have been powerful because one day she told Anne she was leaving, saying it wasn't right to work for white people. It was shocking not only because we loved her and thought she loved us, but because we didn't think of ourselves as 'white people'—people to be shunned. That must have been around 1965. Was it really only ten years she was with us?

There was an aura of sadness and vulnerability about her. How common could it have been to have to bring up a child on your own? Would the church have condemned her for having a baby out of wedlock? Was that why she had to work for white people? Where were her family? I never asked these questions then; it's only now they occur to me. What was it like for her, living so close to strange men in the servants' quarters? People she didn't know anything about, who she'd never

69

met before they turned up there? People with a different religion, or who drank and sometimes made noise.

And what about us, how did she feel about us? What was it like for her, looking after other people's children, that time before Ann-Rose came to live with her? She and I communicated in Swahili, but how effective was that as a language I'd picked up from the garden-boy? She went to night school to improve her English at one point. She aspired to bettering herself. She must have had dreams, ambitions. Though to me she was a grown-up, I realise now she was young. She must have been in her twenties when she came, in her thirties when she left. She had a whole life after us of which I know nothing.

I remember her carrying my sisters on her back and singing. I see her hands washing me in the bath, squeezing oranges in the kitchen. I used to hang around her and ask questions, and we would talk. I feel that if I could only remember those conversations, I would have the key to something, but all that comes back is an atmosphere, a sense of connection, a sharing of secrets. I know I loved her. Even now, when I think of her, I can feel what she meant to me. But the memory is complicated: need, expectation, affection, admiration, separation, desertion, betrayal. I was a colonial child, she was my *ayah*, my parents' employee. There must always have been a distance between us, even if I was unconscious of it. But she would have known that though she took responsibility for us, played with us, achieved a depth of intimacy with us, we were not her children, and she could be let go at any moment.

Meanwhile, I took it for granted that it was my right to visit Martha in her room, to share her food, ask her questions. I see now that the easy way she had of sharing was a gift she bestowed on me. We talked at intimate moments: brushing teeth, in the bath, getting dressed, or in her hot little room in the soporific afternoons, or at night in the half-lit living room while she baby-sat. We talked in Swahili, a language I didn't speak for many years after leaving the country, though when I hear it, I catch the sense. Swahili is like a secret imprinted in my brain to which I've lost the code. Martha's voice comes to me, muffled by time and distance, and speaking in code. But certain things stand out with startling clarity, moments that have retained a shape as solid as Martha's saucepans, an atmosphere as pungent as the woodsmoke from the bath heater at the back of the house. The time she told me the chameleon story, the time she taught me that there were different ways of viewing the world, and mine wasn't necessarily the right one.

As time went by, I could feel my mother's eyes on me, watching me grow. She watched me with a mixture of anxiety and pride, which made me defensive and shy. I knew she was waiting for me to deliver something, but I didn't know what. It was the early 60s, and in another part of the world, teenagers had been invented. Older children came back from boarding schools in England or Nairobi, wearing jeans and waistless dresses, dancing to an endless chorus of summer holiday, walkin the dog, bachelor boy, it's my party, if I had a hammer, you're the devil in disguise…

The tiny lumps swelling on my chest were uneven in size. When I walked anywhere, my sisters would huddle and giggle behind my back, and I struggled to fill a bra as a way of hiding what was happening. Thoroughly miserable, I complained to Martha, who laughed. 'That's how it is,' she said. 'One grows, then the other one grows, and in the end they're the same.' We were in the bathroom at the time, standing by the mirror side by side. I was naked, gazing disconsolately at my imperfections. She was, as always, wearing her blue uniform, with a starched white cap like a nurse's headdress. Her face in the mirror was on a level with mine, but swamped under the pointed cap, and she was thin in the too-big uniform. I was as tall as she was, and still growing. We used to measure ourselves, back-to-back, waiting for when I would overtake her. I imagine she was saving money out of her wages to send to Ann-Rose, wherever she was. But she was still sharing her food with me.

Other things happened as I grew towards adolescence. I became more rebellious and more difficult to handle. There were frequent storms of tears, choking sobs and going off on my own. My father was bemused by what he called 'emoting', and I decided I hated him, which made my mother unhappy and that gave me satisfaction too. My sisters were a torment, noticing everything and passing comment so I couldn't hide and couldn't pretend. Martha went on being her gentle, forbearing self, and with her I felt I could also be myself, whoever that was. She accepted my tempers and moods as inevitable and never judged, interrogated, or criticised. If she registered any reaction to my turbulence, it was amusement. Except for one indelible moment of dissent.

I don't remember the details of the conflict, but it was probably with my father. It usually was. Between my mother and me there was an unspoken understanding. In his absence, many rules were relaxed. I slept in her bed when he went away, I sat with her at night and read to her, I stood by her dressing table and watched her do her hair and apply her makeup. And she would talk to me, confide things in me that made me feel grown-up and important. At those times, I felt a glimmering of understanding of how it would be to be a woman. When my father returned from safari, I reverted to being a child, sleeping with my sisters and going to bed instead of reading aloud. This arrangement worked for several years, until the breast problem came along, and a demon seemed to take up residence inside me. I found it unbearable, unsupportable, to be relegated like that. I felt I had more right to my mother's attention than he had. I had changed in ways he couldn't see and didn't understand, and he was the one being left behind.

Let's say it happened like this. I wanted to go out, maybe to a film. A friend was going with her mother and invited me. 'You're not watching rubbish like that,' he might have said, with a full stop at the end of his voice. My mother's face would have looked sad and sympathetic, and left alone, she might have talked him into it. 'Come on Jock, it's really not that bad. She's a big girl you know, and Susan's going.' But the demon rose up and snorted through my nostrils, spitting fire and brimstone. 'You never let me do anything I want! All my friends can go out when they want to! I hate you!' and so on. All my father could see was an insolent little girl who wanted her own way. I can't say if he slapped me that time, though he did more than once when driven to it. But almost worse was when he put on a stony expression and his lips became a hard thin line. My heat was no match for his cold, and it was I who was scalded by my own anger.

In a mood like this, I might have flung away into another part of the house, banging the swing door with mosquito netting separating the bedrooms from the living area. I might have stormed and raged for half an hour, my mother trying to comfort me, and quite possibly giving up if the demon really had a grip. Eventually, I'd have calmed down. The house would be quiet, people going about their business regardless of my private drama. Then Martha's knock, her gentle voice, the rustle of that ridiculous starched uniform. 'How are you? Do you feel better? Would you like some water?' Her arms around me and her laugh invite me to rejoin the world of the living. Normally, the demon would have slunk, defeated, back to its lair, and I'd have got up and gone with her to the kitchen and let her pour me a glass of cold water from the Gordon's Gin bottle in the refrigerator. But today, it still lurks, lashing its tail. 'Bring me the water here,' I say, not bothering to add please or look at her. Martha hovers, and tries again. She knows she has to coax me out of the bedroom or I'll sit there festering until I have a headache. Probably my mother has even told her to go and bring me out, and maybe I'm using that against her too. 'Come to the kitchen,' she urges, 'I have work to do and you can help me.' 'Helping' Martha is a privilege I usually leap at, as often I'm forbidden to distract her when she's working. But today I want to inflict as much damage as I can, and turn my face cold like my father's, and say in his voice: 'Bring me the water here.'

Martha is nonplussed, I can tell from her silence. And then I say the thing that has haunted me through the decades since she disappeared, the thing that comes as the last spurt of hellfire from the subsiding fury.

'Do what I say. You have to do what I say, because you're black and I'm white.' There, it's said. No turning back.

Martha doesn't speak, but the air in the room goes cold and clammy. I can feel the sweat on my face and hands, and hear my breath. I still haven't looked at her, and now I don't dare. We stay like that, me feeling her eyes on me but not daring to look, for what feels like eternity. At last I hear her sigh, and rustle. When she speaks, it's so softly I have to strain to catch it.

'Little sister,' she says, and the sadness in her voice lacerates me worse than my father's hardness or my own outrage. 'God made white and black and he made them the same. When you want me, I'm in the kitchen.' I hear the shoosh of her bare feet on the concrete, the click of the door. I am alone, facing myself.

By the time Martha left us, the breast problem was more or less resolved and they were as near the same size as they would ever be. For a long time, we didn't know where she was or what she was doing. Then one day my sisters and I were in town with my mother, and we went for a treat to the KNCU café for Cokes and coffee. A group of women was working at the other end of the long dining room, talking and clattering buckets and brooms. One woman detached herself, and flung herself at my mother exclaiming with joy. With a shock, I recognised Martha. She had changed, was more vibrant than I remembered, her eyes shining, her face filled out. She seemed possessed of a new confidence, as if in shedding her ayah's uniform and passing out into the world she had become someone else. Who she had become was a mystery, and has remained so. I was shy and awkward, but she almost ebullient, asking my mother questions and laughing the high-pitched joyful laugh I remembered from many, many private jokes shared only with me.

That was the last time I saw Martha. After that one reappearance, it was as if she evanesced. I didn't even know her surname, so by the time I went back, decades later, I couldn't ask for her. She left me with the answers to many questions imprinted in my brain, but in a code I can't decipher. I used to think of her as having disappeared from my life, but now I think that it was the other way round—I disappeared from hers. It was me who evanesced, and this existence I'm experiencing is after all only Martha's dream.

8. The Walking Dream

When after thirty-six years I return to Rombo Avenue, it is Martha who dreams me back there. She leads me unerringly up the long shady Hospital Road that makes a T-junction with Rombo Avenue. When I was a child, we walked many times along this road, Martha and I, on the way to kindergarten in the morning, or walking to the playground in the evening. At one end of Hospital Road is St Margaret's Church, where I went on Sundays with my mother, where I was confirmed by the archbishop of East Africa, where Sally, my youngest sister was christened. When my father left government service and joined FAO, the UN's Food and Agriculture Organisation, he was no longer entitled to a house, so we spent a few months in the nearby church bungalow where once a week we had to pack up our beds and hide our things to make way for Sunday School.

Now, as I'm walking past, I see a new, larger church has shouldered the old one aside. Later, I find out that it was built to accommodate the much larger Swahili service congregation—two hundred and fifty people as opposed to the fifty the old church could hold. The simple old rectangular structure stands open, with only the carved golden angels still standing guard over its empty pews. I go in and sit on the altar cushions, breathing in the air of disuse and neglect. An engraved plaque hangs on a rusty nail by the door, unpolished and hard to read. I walk over and peer at it, making out the words. It tells me that the church's oak cross was a gift from St Margaret's, King's Lynn, to St Margaret's, Moshi, in 1955. I didn't know this when I lived in Moshi, but the King's Lynn church, founded by Losinga, first Bishop of Norwich, was one of the oldest in England. The oak from which our cross was made came from the twelfth century bell-chamber. When the cross was reinstalled in the new church the plaque was left behind and with it its history.

I return to the road and walk up it towards Rombo Avenue. It's still lined with jacarandas, most probably planted by the Germans when they controlled Tanganyika before the First World War. The trees were old even when we lived there, their branches meeting in a canopy overhead, the sunlight filtering in shifting patterns onto the tarmac. The house, which is on the corner, used to be surrounded by a hedge with yellow bell-shaped flowers we would wear on our fingertips like witches' talons. At one corner was a small gap, guarded by a guava tree with silver bark, that allowed you to cut across the garden. Between the road and the hedge was a furrow that ran with water in the rains so we would have to jump across.

As I come closer, I see that now the house is surrounded by an ugly concrete wall, so high all I can see is the roof (the same grey tiles). All along the wall is jagged glass, and round the front, a thick metal gate. I try climbing the bank to peer over, but I can't see anything. The house is on the defensive, no longer open to the road, but separate and standoffish. I take a deep breath and ring the bell on the gate.

A young woman, maybe a housegirl, beckons me inside. She leads me to the verandah and asks me to wait. It's the same verandah, the one where the guinea pig cage used to be, where my parents sat with guests in the evenings drinking gin or beer, where I whiled away time with friends as I got older. Only a second, and the door opens, and I'm invited inside.

I have to summon all the will power I possess to cross that threshold. If memory is one of the defining attributes of human beings, what happens when you lose it? I enter the room holding the past in my hands. A man—a Tanzanian—sits in front of a large television, eating. He looks at me calmly, as if a white stranger stepping through the door on a Sunday afternoon were the most ordinary thing in the world, and tells me 'karibu': welcome. He invites me to sit. We exchange pleasant greetings for a few minutes, but he doesn't ask me what I want. So I tell him I used to live in this house. Oh, he responds enthusiastically, then you must have lunch with me. You see, you've met me eating, please join me.

This must be Martha's dream because only she could put that remembered food in front of me at this moment. Thanks to her, I'm eating *ugali* and stew in my parents' old living room with the new owner of my childhood home. His name is Victor, and he bought the house a year or two previously. He likes the house, it has a lot of space, he says. He looks at home, sitting there, comfortable, content. We talk about the old days, and it turns out his father, like mine, was a forester, but in Arusha, not Moshi. Victor himself is the chief engineer of roads for the Kilimanjaro Region.

Three little girls come into the room, two daughters and a friend. They remind me of me and my sisters, when we too were three little girls. They show me their school books, and it turns out the youngest goes to my old kindergarten, two streets away. I ask to see their room, and they lead me through the house—the 'bang-bang' door that separated the bedrooms from the rest of the house has gone, but everything else is the same. They take me into my parents' old bedroom, where there are now four little beds. They lead me through the house, through our old kitchen to the garden. When it was my mother's garden it had big old trees, and terraces with shrubs and carefully watered grass and lovingly nurtured rose beds. Now the trees have gone, and instead there's a *shamba* growing maize and bananas.

When I tell Victor I'm sorry about the trees he tells me he found the garden like this, but he wants to remake it, to enclose the house in green again.

It's late in the afternoon by the time I drag myself away. All this time, no one makes me feel I'm intruding, or that they have better things to do. Victor seems happy for me to stay all day and pours me wine, but something animates me so I can no longer sit still, and after one glass I say goodbye. As I walk away, a great burden lifts, and I realise Martha has dreamed me a healing. She brought me back to my old home to meet its new inhabitants and they let me in and showed me their family life. They showed me that the past I dreaded losing is intact, animating the present.

In a daze, I reach the end of the road, and as I emerge from another canopy of trees, I see the mountain. The two peaks, snow-capped Kibo, and rocky Mawenzi, sit shining in the evening sunlight. Neither dream nor memory, they've been here all the time, solid and real. Waiting.

9. A Contested Kingdom

The best time of day in Moshi was early evening, when the trees threw long shadows and everything stilled. It was a moment of drawn breath between the working day and night. Before I was old enough to venture out on my own Martha and I used to go for a walk in the late afternoon, turning homewards at twilight. We'd walk in a big square, crossing the furrow through the gap at the end of the garden, down Hospital Road as far as the church, past the kindergarten and its playground (where we might go in so I could play on the swings) and onto Kilimanjaro Road. Walking up it as far as the Police Training School, the plangent sound of a bugle rose on the twilight air, lamenting the dying of the light. As if in answer to its summons, the mountain would appear. As we turned back into Rombo Avenue, we were tiny ant-like beings against a huge blue and silver backdrop. Next to the elegant white curve of Kibo, rocky Mawenzi stuck out like a sore thumb. It was as if Cinderella in her snowy ballgown had an ugly sister permanently at her side.

Martha told me that her people, the Chagga, had a story that explained why Mawenzi had a jagged crown. The two peaks really were sisters and their names were Mawensi and Kipoo. Their favourite dish was *shiro*, made of bananas mixed with beans. It was Martha's favourite too. Kipoo was an expert at cooking *shiro*. One day, Mawensi was careless and let her fire go out, so she went to her sister.

'*Hodi?*' she sang out as she knocked on Kipoo's door.

'*Karibu,*' replied Kipoo. 'You've met me eating, why don't you join me?'

Mawensi was happy to join her. Kipoo's food was so good that when Mawensi went home, carrying a smouldering log for her fire, she couldn't think about anything else. How could she make *shiro* that tasted like Kipoo's? Her own was dry and lacked that smoky flavour that made it so delicious. Then she came up with an idea. She put out her own fire on purpose and knocked on Kipoo's door a second time.

'*Hodi?*' she called, feeling her tummy rumble at the thought of her sister's cooking. Kipoo didn't like being disturbed a second time, but she was too polite to say so.

'*Karibu,*' she replied. 'You find me eating, why don't you join me?'

So Mawensi ate her sister's food again and went home feeling satisfied, carrying embers in a fragment of pottery.

Then Mawensi came a third time to ask for fire.

'*Hodi?*' she called, expecting her sister to ask her in as before. Instead, Kipoo met her at the door with her largest wooden cooking spoon in her hand, and beat her sister on the head.

And that, said Martha, is why Mawensi to this day is crowned in jagged fragments.

On the mountain, we had a favourite picnic spot by the river in Marangu, a flat, green space of riverbank, where our parents threw down the rug and spread out the tea things as we struggled into our swimsuits. The river came straight from the mountain, from a glacier which dissolved as it descended, so cold it burnt your skin when you stepped in. You stood on a rock, dipped in a toe and recoiled shrieking, but you couldn't resist, you must be in that water and you slid off the rock and let the current take you, bumping against rocks and  laughing with high-pitched hysteria at the shock. Sebastian, the black Labrador, leapt in too, and when he clambered out onto a rock, he shook off a great spray of freezing droplets. Our parents, glad of a few moments of peace, lay on the bank and breathed the air, inhaling its freshness.

One day, when I was about eleven, after the sandwiches and digestive biscuits, I wandered from the family where they lay on the river bank. I found myself alone. In the intense quiet of the afternoon, colours thrust themselves at me. A cloud of bright butterflies hovered like brilliant dust-motes above a carpet of purple flowers. In the distance, the scarlet bells of a flame tree seared the air. Flat brown rocks in the river like the glossy backs of hippos, half-submerged in the black and silver water. And all around green, green. Almost without knowing what I was doing, I picked my way from rock to rock, winding slowly upstream. After a while, I became aware of a continuous rushing, growing louder and louder. I went forward as if hypnotised, blind and deaf to everything but the colours and sound of the river, until I was at the foot of a sheet of white water, flinging itself over the edge of a black rock-face. It was so tall it seemed to pour from a hole in the sky, and I sat down hard with shock on the rock beneath me. I stayed still, barely breathing. The water raced forward and hurled itself over the edge, dashing itself into a million sparkling shards on the rocks below, then flinging high, high in the air. My skin was covered in tiny glittering drops. The waterfall was framed by white trumpet lilies, and the black of the rock, the white water, the lilies, called to mind a Colobus monkey with its long black hair with a flash of white, glimpsed leaping through trees.

I sat a long time on the rock in the river gazing at the waterfall, mesmerised by its animal roar. When I came to, the sun had slipped behind the cliff and I turned back in a panic, slipping on wet stones as I rushed to reach the picnic spot. I passed an old man standing stock still on the riverbank, seeing only a blur of tattered shorts, nondescript, discoloured shirt, battered tin bucket at his feet.

I arrived, panting, almost in tears, where they stood in a group waiting for me. I thought I was in trouble, but all my father said was, 'You're very lucky this is Chagga country. An old farmer passed by and said he'd seen you at the waterfall.'

Many years later, when I returned to Marangu from the Caribbean, I retraced my path to the waterfall and stood on the same flat stones, listening to the roar and rush of water, seeing the ghosts of my parents sitting on the bank, my sisters in the water. It was then I learnt the Chagga people call the waterfall Ndoro, meaning Colobus.

Sometimes, instead of the river, we used to go to Marangu Hotel to swim in its pool of icy water and drink tea or a cold beer on its lawn, surrounded by birds and brilliant flowers, overseen by the peaks at sunset. On every occasion I've been back, returning to Marangu Hotel has been a kind of homecoming. Countless times I've sat in its dining-room listening to people boast of conquering 'The Big Seven', the great summits of the world of which Kilimanjaro is one. Often they arrive one day, start climbing the next and five days later, they're gone. They don't have time to stop and look at Marangu itself, to notice they're in a paradise of green growth and falling water. To spend a day exploring the narrow earth tracks through the banana farms, crossing tiny sparkling streams and passing little houses where a pebble-lined path leads to a neatly swept yard bounded by a hedge. To hear, enclosed in the penumbral green, the ungainly flapping and raucous croak of hornbills, the tiny, delicate fluttering of a pair of swallows beneath a waterfall. To pause at a crossroad where a girl called Mercy invites you home to meet her grandmother. In a house made of mud, wood and rusty iron sheets built around a central courtyard, you greet the grandmother as she cooks bananas over an open fire. The family live close to their animals, three cows in a shed, a few goats and chickens scuttering in dried banana leaves. Mercy shows you her schoolbooks and talks about her plans, once she passes her school leaving exams. You say goodbye and walk on, and, approaching dusk, you come upon two men sitting outside a shack drinking banana beer. They introduce themselves as Gaudeus and Good Luck, and when they invite you, you taste the beer, fermented, frothy, pungent. As darkness gathers, missing your way, a young boy guides you home. His name is Bless Me.

Before the colonisers came, Marangu was one of several kingdoms on Kilimanjaro; Moshi was another—not the Moshi I grew up in, which was a late invention, but a loose collection of villages and farms on the lower slope of the mountain, known today as Old Moshi. In the middle of the nineteenth century, the ruler of Marangu was Chief Marealle, whose descendants still live there today. When Mandara, a young man of nineteen, became king of Moshi, he and Marealle were at different times rivals and allies. Because Mandara was the first among the chieftains to understand the allure of the mountain to the white explorers, he would become the most notorious. He managed for a while to convince the foreigners he was the only king on the mountain.

Though Mandara was young, thanks to the caravan route from the coast he had a hundred years of trading history to draw on. His people were accustomed to Swahili traders in their long robes, and men from many parts of Africa and India, conscripted into the caravans as porters. Then one day, when Mandara was seven years old, a new kind of traveller had arrived, stranger than any they had seen. All the people who had come to the mountain up to that time had been alike in one respect: their skins were black, or brown, or any shade in between, and they were all bound by a common undertaking, the transport of goods. These caravans had also introduced the mountain people to a new religion, Islam, and some of them went so far as to convert. Conversion brought benefits, because the unconverted were *infidel*, and automatically inferior to the people of the Book.

This new arrival was a puzzle: neither black, nor brown, nor a worshipper of Allah, though he too came with a Book. He was a strange, pale creature, transparent so you could see his insides and vulnerable to all sorts of physical ailments, with a beard so long that when seated on a donkey, it trailed behind him. The year was 1848 and the name of the pale emissary was Johann Krapf, a German missionary and explorer, the first white man to see Kilimanjaro. When he later claimed to have seen snow on the Equator, nobody at home believed him.

Mandara grew up with the caravans and with knowledge of the pale intruder became expert at juggling his desires and aspirations. Because he controlled access to the mountain, attempts to climb it had to go through him. He had no problem with the white man's obsession with climbing, as long as he observed protocols and understood the status quo. Mandara was accustomed to the ebb and flow of demand and supply, to the idea of himself as having the power to give or withhold. As he took over more and more of the mountain kingdoms, he became known by the name of Makindara.

By the time Sir Harry Johnston arrived in 1884, Mandara, now forty-three, had survived various attempts on his position and was at the height of his powers. He was now known as Rindi—'the cloud that covers all'—and greatly feared. In *The Kilima-Njaro Expedition: A Record of Scientific Exploration in Eastern Equatorial Africa*, Sir Harry provides a vivid picture of Mandara, including his extravagantly pierced ears so that his lobes hung low like a Masai warrior's, and the fact that, though he was blind in one eye, 'the other was bright as an eagle's and lay glittering under an eagle's brow.' On first meeting Mandara, Sir Harry, on a mission to acquire data about the mountain for the British Association for the Advancement of Science and the Royal Geographical Society, saw him as 'one of the most remarkable Africans I have ever met... My vagrant habits have sometimes led to my being presented to personages that the world holds distinguished, but in no case did I ever anticipate an introduction to a temporal or spiritual magnate with more anxiety than my first interview with the Sultan of Moshi.' As time went by, Mandara found manifold ways to both court and thwart him, constantly demanding presents and refusing to allow him to collect specimens if money or gifts were not delivered.

Mandara was adept at exacting gifts from his foreign visitors, surrounding himself with exotic decorations. Above his bed hung a watercolour of a German city at dawn. On a small table nearby stood an elaborately carved clock with little tin soldiers on top that marched round and round to a Prussian tune. A rack of meerschaum pipes hung on the wall, and four beer tankards with the arms of the German states lined up underneath them. But the centrepiece of the room was a magnificent sewing machine, black and beautifully oiled, its brass plates gleaming as if on display in a German showroom.

At this time the British Government, unenthusiastic about starting a settlement in such fierce territory, had no official presence around the mountain. Though the Sultan of Zanzibar was their vassal, no one knew how far his influence extended inland and whether it covered Kilimanjaro. Mandara took advantage of the uncertainty to sign treaties with both Britain and Germany, the two competing powers. He changed the flag on his *boma* according to which delegation he was receiving and who was prepared to pay the highest price. When they left, he would bring down the flag and let his wives quarrel over who would use it as a *kanga*. Meanwhile, he freely disregarded all treaties. As he reasonably pointed out, 'The Sultan of Zanzibar wants my country, the Germans want my country, you (the British) want my country. Whoever wants my country must pay for it.'

For the colonisers, mountains, like islands, were useful as bases and bargaining chips. In 1886 the German adventurer Carl Peters brought about a treaty by which the mountain was at last ceded to Germany. Though the British now gave up their claims to Kilimanjaro, German influence on the mountain was still tenuous. Needing a front man, the Germans turned to Mandara as their best bet, promising to elevate him above the other chiefs.

Coastal people are accustomed to looking out to sea, to the idea that a change of wind may bring the unexpected. Mountain people naturally turn towards the mountain, and even when they turn away, it calls to them. In this respect, Mandara was no different from his subjects. His realm was the mountain, his vision only extended to its horizon. Within these confines what he desired was power, and to defeat his rival, Sina of Kibosho, another mountain chieftain. Sina had resisted German attempts to fly their flag on his territory, as well as Mandara's pretensions to predominance. It was natural, then, for the Germans to ally with Mandara to defeat Sina. All it took was six German officers and five hundred *askari*—native soldiers from here and there in the pay of the Germans—along with Mandara's warriors from Moshi and Chief Marealle's from Marangu.

But now the Germans showed the true nature of their respect for their Chagga allies. Instead of installing Mandara as supreme chief, they took over Sina's well-fortified *boma* as well as Marealle's at Marangu, which they made their base. By now it was 1891, and at this point in the drama, Mandara, the snarling lion, died. After him, the great tide of colonial incursion could no longer be held back. Everything changed.

Within two years, the Chagga chiefs, who saw which way the wind was blowing, had capitulated. Carl Peters, now Imperial High Commissioner for the Kilimanjaro Region, had, through violence and cruelty, at last accomplished his aim to enforce peace, earning him the nickname *Mikono wa Damu*—hands of blood. Next, because of his support for the Germans, they elevated Marealle of Marangu to a position of virtual paramountcy. In 1951, the year of my birth, his grandson, Thomas Lenana Mlang'a Marealle II, would be elected the actual Paramount Chief by popular vote, providing a focus for a collective Chagga identity in opposition both to colonial rule and the perceived corruption of lesser chiefs. In 1953, when my parents joined the crowds in the Mall to watch the Coronation procession, Chief Thomas, in his ceremonial leopard skin cloak, and his wife Elifuraha—a politician in her own right—in a Colobus stole, were among the guests at Westminster Abbey.

Though he addressed the UN in 1957 in support of Independence alongside President Nyerere, his brief ascendancy was not to last. After Uhuru, hereditary chieftainship would be seen as unbefitting a socialist nation. After a career as an international diplomat, Thomas died in February 2007 at the age of ninety-two. In a country where the average life expectancy was fifty-five, this was remarkable in itself.

Wandering through the *shambas* on the mountainside later that year, I came on a piece of open ground where a huge billboard had been erected extolling his achievements. He was 'our guiding star which instilled confidence in us'. I saw how in Marangu the name Marealle retained its power, a talisman of Chagga pride in a post-tribal era.

10. Marangu and the Mountain Guides

The first time I return to Marangu, I catch a *daladala* from Moshi bus station. Filling the bus means that everyone has to have someone sitting on top of them. I guess I'm lucky as a large man is only sitting half on top of me, my nose practically in his armpit. I can't see anything and have to guess when I've arrived from the stir of people leaving the bus. When I fall out, I see that I'm at the gates of the hotel and stagger up the drive to the Lanys' old farmhouse, now the reception. My room, in a bungalow set in the middle of a lawn and surrounded by trees, is simple, but so welcoming I want to fling myself on the bed at once. Instead, I head for the tables dotted about on the grass. I'm looking for the owners, the Brice-Bennetts, not knowing how important they'll be, knowing only that we were all here as children. I've spotted a group who aren't talking about climbing, and look relaxed—as if they own the place. I introduce myself, and Desmond, Fionnuala, Seamus and Jackie Brice-Bennett welcome me like an old friend. None of us exactly synchronised in age so we hadn't been friends growing up, but we remember each others' families and they make me sit and have a drink with them. It's five o'clock in the afternoon, and there are several large bottles of Kilimanjaro beer on the table. Anyone who isn't drinking beer is drinking double whiskies. I ask for a gin and tonic, and when the waitress asks 'double or single', Desmond tells her, 'Double of course—she was born here.'

As a treat before going back to boarding school in England, when I was fifteen or so my parents brought me for dinner in the hotel dining room, with its white-washed walls and red cement floor. It was five years after Uhuru but little had changed—then or since. In the old colonial style, uniformed waiters gravely served one course after another on white china plates. Basketwork shades cast a dim light over the faded green tablecloths and heavy wooden sideboard, the dingy curtains and faded prints of Kilimanjaro, so all conversation was somehow hushed to a murmur. Peggy Brice-Bennett, who ran the hotel, sat down and chatted with my parents, along with Seamus, her eight-year old son.

Marangu Hotel started as a guest house in the early twentieth century, when the country was German East Africa. A missionary called Martin Lany and his family came from Czechoslovakia to Marangu, bought land from Chief Marealle and set up a coffee farm. By 1932 they had added the guest house and were organising expeditions up the mountain.

In 1951, Frank Brice-Bennett, who had lived in Tanganyika before the War, drove for six weeks from Nigeria so he could show Peggy, his wife, Marangu. Peggy, who was Republican Irish and brought her children up on rebel songs and myths, loved Marangu because it reminded her of west Cork. Though Frank continued to work in Nigeria, Peggy and the children returned to live in Marangu in 1952, and for the next fifty years Peggy helped Erika, Martin Lany's daughter, run the hotel. Peggy's children, Desmond, Fionnuala and Seamus, grew up in Marangu. My parents knew their parents; as a teenager I knew the older children as occasional exotic visitors to the Moshi social scene.

After her husband died young, Peggy battled valiantly to bring her children up alone. She was an ardent Catholic, friend to many priests and a benefactor of the church at Marangu. Seamus, who was born in Moshi, was thirteen the first time he went to England. It was 1969 and Tanzania had been independent for eight years. It was two years since the president had made his famous Arusha Declaration, which affected people's lives for years: owning property was capitalist; being white or brown and owning property was an affront to socialist Tanzania. Many people fled because the government was appropriating land and property owned by anyone who wasn't considered indigenous. Peggy never knew when she might lose the hotel, the only security she had, where she had lived and worked and brought up four children, losing one in the process. After living from day to day for two years, Peggy took Seamus to England for a break and collapsed in the taxi on arrival. She was in hospital with nervous exhaustion for two weeks.

Miraculously, Peggy kept the hotel and ran it till she died, organising porters and provisions and seeing climbers off up the mountain. The children, who all went to school in Tanzania, grew up and set off to explore the world. When Peggy grew old and started to find running the hotel too much of a burden on her own, they found their way back. Their story—of migration, settlement, dispersal, return—is a Tanzanian one. From the moment our first human ancestor stepped out of Olduvai Gorge more than three million years ago, the people of this region have been on the move. Go far enough back and everyone's a settler: home is where you settle. The Chagga themselves are a conglomerate of immigrants from the surrounding regions who over time established themselves as a farming society, moulding themselves into the mountain, tending their gardens of banana trees mixed with coffee and avocados, diverting streams into furrows to water their crops.

In the course of many double shots with Peggy's children, I hear their stories. For thirty years, says Desmond, he'd been a criminal lawyer in Alaska. He describes the time he spent among the Inuit, trekking through the wilds, steering his sleigh by the sun, building an igloo, fishing through the ice. When he came back, already in his fifties, he married Irene, a Chagga woman, and started a family.

Fionnuala, mother of five sons, now divorced, stayed in Africa, living in Swaziland and Zimbabwe. Seamus, the youngest, describes how he thought, when he was a policeman on the beat in Notting Hill in London, that coming from Africa he would be able to talk to West Indians, and was shocked to discover they saw him as a white man. Like me, Jackie, his wife, grew up in Moshi and attended Lushoto School; like Desmond and Irene, she and Seamus are bringing up their children in Marangu.

It sounded idyllic, this story of reconnection, reunion and return to roots, but it wasn't an easy transition from being widely scattered individuals to running a family business. Marangu was a flawed paradise. They told me how at one time, the hospital had no equipment because it was cleared out by two workers, who by law were retained on half-pay until a case was brought. But one of them had a brother in the police, so the hospital, where a Swedish volunteer doctor and four nurses worked for free, had to keep paying the culprits. Meanwhile, even though some workers at the hotel had been there all their working lives, Desmond said they had to work hard to keep pilfering 'down to a low roar'. Tourism, the face by which Tanzania is mainly known to the world, is its biggest earner of foreign exchange and attracts such an array of government taxes it's sometimes hard to make a profit. It wasn't, then, the sweet haze of nostalgia that sustained them but the reality of earning a living in a difficult environment.

The mountain was their livelihood and the Brice-Bennetts helped fifteen hundred climbers a year make the ascent. My father tried but fell prey to mountain sickness and couldn't make the summit. My mother did, though. She climbed in 1966, aged forty-five, a year after her mastectomy, in clothes borrowed from Terence, a friend who was exactly her height, who wore a monocle and lived with his mother. Both my parents would have experienced Erika Lany's famous briefing to mountain climbers starting out from Marangu Hotel. After Erika's death, Peggy's sons, Seamus and Desmond, took over the briefing, and one day I sat in and listened. I could feel my mother sitting there beside me, listening intently. Seamus, who has been described as looking like a 'mild-mannered accountant' or a 'soft banker', is a spell-binding storyteller. He spins a yarn about the mountain that wraps itself around us, so that together we ascend through each stage of the climb. Seamus's secrets are simple.

'The first thing you need to know is that the mountain runs on tea. You have to stay hydrated and you have to take it slowly. Walk so that you never have to breathe heavily. Old people and children get to the top following this advice; fit people who run a half-marathon every weekend often fail to reach the summit because they can't make themselves go slowly. The reason is altitude sickness. The first hut, named Mandara after the chief, is at 2,700 metres; from there to the second hut at Horombo, on Day 2, you climb a thousand metres in less than twelve kilometres. At Horombo most people suffer headache, nausea, loss of appetite, diarrhoea—the early signs of mountain sickness. If you're one of the 2% who get oedema you must descend immediately. How do you know you've got it? Well, if you become irrational and can't walk in a straight line, you might be drunk but it's more likely you've got cerebral oedema. Pulmonary oedema, on the other hand, may be symptom-free apart from complete exhaustion. If after a rest your breathing is still shallow and fast, the guides will recognise it and send you back down on the spot. If not, you could be dead by seven o'clock next morning.

'In case this is enough to put you off, the solution is simple: drink four litres of fluid a day. Always drink four cups of tea at every rest stop and stop drinking by about 8pm, as even then you'll pee two or three times a night and stumbling about the mountainside in the pitch dark and freezing cold is no fun.'

I'm with my mother as, on Day 3, she ascends a thousand metres from Horombo to Kibo Hut. As we approach Kibo it gets significantly steeper and everyone feels tired and depressed. We go to bed early but anxiety and a fast pulse make it hard to sleep; Seamus tells us to concentrate on a relaxing image. I think about the waterfall, its mesmeric flow, and I'm fast asleep when the guides wake us for tea at 11pm. Seamus warns that when we set off at midnight the temperature will be zero and drop to ten or twenty-five below before dawn. We should wear four or five layers on top, three layers below, two pairs of socks, good gloves, a balaclava. By 8am, as it gets warmer, we'll start taking it all off.

We get up in the dark that final morning and follow Seamus up the last torturous slope. Sleepless and cold, we plod on for four or five hours in the darkness, until we can go no further and despair.

'At this point,' says Seamus, 'you stop for four minutes and eat a piece of chocolate, walk for half an hour and stop again. By Kibo peak it's not uncommon for people to be down to five steps at a time. Eventually you'll arrive at Gillman's Point on the edge of the crater.'

Then the bad news.

'It can take another two hours to get to the summit, Uhuru peak, which is at an altitude of 5,895m. If you can still walk, you should have a go. If you make it, you'll be close to the Southern ice-field which is a hundred metres thick and wonderful to see.'

We struggle on, one foot after another, sliding on the scree, toe to heel, blood pumping so close to the surface we think it will break through our skin. When our lungs threaten to burst, our knees to buckle under the weight of our labouring, useless bodies that seem designed only to hold us back, to make us *not* get there, the story in our heads is the only thing left. If we don't make it, we will forever have missed standing on the lip of the volcano, high above the clouds, looking at infinity. We'll never be more than one of the toilers on the mountain flanks, while others stand, triumphant, at the peak.

Suddenly, somehow, we're there, at the climax of the story, at the highest point in Africa.

I've seen the euphoria on the faces of climbers as they return to the hotel, as they sit in a wide circle in the garden with the guides, singing to celebrate their victory. For my mother, it was a point of honour that she made it when my father didn't. But for me it remains a story. The highest I've been on the mountain is just above the first hut, Mandara.
It was an easy day-trip from Moshi when I was growing up, and one of our favourite things to do. The Forest Department Land Rover covered the bit as far as the road went, then we walked up through the rainforest, following the narrow path, to the first hut. It was just a simple wooden building with a sign saying Bismarck: 2,700m.

We would picnic in the strange moonscape of the sub-Alpine belt, with its tumbled rocks and enormous spiky protea flowers or 'alpine sugarbush', native to just this stretch of Kilimanjaro (other varieties are native only to the South African Cape). There were also red-hot pokers and giant lobelia, like elongated inverted pineapples, and even taller groundsel with stout stems twenty feet high ending in a cluster of yellow flowers called a rosette; further up, near the peak, the only thing that grew was *helichrysum*, a kind of lichen, slow-growing and old— possibly one of the oldest living things on earth. When my mother climbed everyone who reached the summit was crowned with a garland of its tiny, papery white stars, that we knew as everlasting flowers. Since then, they've become too rare to pick, but in the photo of my mother on her triumphant return from the summit, filthy and exhausted, she's wearing her little crown of everlasting flowers. For years I kept it, wrapped in tissue paper in a flat cardboard box, until it dropped to dust.

My mother, like every other person who attempts it, could not have climbed Kilimanjaro without the help of the mountain guides. They are local men, dressed in layers of old sweaters, shabby trousers and rubber plimsolls, a far cry from professional mountain gear. Through the Brice-Bennetts I met two of these guides, who between them had been with the hotel for a century.

We know about foreign travellers from classical times onwards, and the many attempts to climb the mountain. It took a man of Alpine skills, the German geographer Hans Meyer, to reach the summit. This he did in 1889, during the time of the great chiefs Marealle and Mandara, cutting steps in the ice as he went. Meyer, like all those who have followed, was accompanied at least part of the way by a Chagga guide. His guide's name was Johanni Lauwo, then very young, who from keeping bees and hunting for honey knew all the paths through the rainforest. Though Seamus told me that Johanni was only ten years old, and would not have had the skills or even the clothing to ascend to the Alpine region near the summit, his name is recorded along with Meyer's as the first to climb the mountain. Johanni did later train other young men in the skills needed to take climbers safely to the summit—how to go slowly to avoid mountain sickness, the importance of speaking enough English to communicate with climbers (until recently most of those who could afford the trek were European), how to cook appropriate food at the rest stops, how to encourage someone who is close to giving up. He guided climbers for the next seventy years, and reputedly lived to the age of a hundred and fifteen.

The two guides I talked to had been trained as young men by Johanni. Emmanueli Petro Minja, born in 1930, started climbing when he was seventeen and was still climbing when I met him, aged seventy-seven. He was a tall, well-built, dignified man with an expressive, intelligent face, who responded courteously but gave little away. He had a reputation for great calmness and psychological insight. He told me he knew after two days if a guide would be any good, and that with tourists, 'You give them what they want. Never argue, it's all over in five days.' Although he didn't say so, I could imagine how over-confident tourists, having paid the considerable costs of a climb, might regard the guide as their servant.

The other was Fataeli Hezekiah Mangowi, seventy-two, who did his first climb with Emmanueli as leader in 1956. Unlike Emmanueli's dignified reserve, Fataeli painted a more intimate picture of helping climbers, both women and men, to relieve themselves when caught in a freezing storm. When I asked Fataeli what he did if climbers with mountain sickness insisted on going on, he said, 'I point out the direction and tell them to go ahead, but I'm not going with them.' I don't suppose there's any further argument.

Emmanueli and Fataeli were from the same village, Mamba Kokirire. They each had one wife and eight children, both were farmers in the Chagga tradition, both also had another trade, Fataeli as a mason, Emmanueli as a pit-sawyer, cutting trees into planks. The similarity in their stories says something about the close-knit mountain culture, and the way climbing, more than a job, is a test of manhood, a source of pride. They told me how, as children, they walked miles to go to mission schools run by the Lutherans who were a prominent presence in German-controlled Tanganyika.

'Now there are more schools, better roads and more health care. But children were better behaved and more respectful then,' said Emmanueli. 'Now you can buy beer and cigarettes. I had my first taste of beer when I was twenty, when I was already married with a child.'

Although they loved climbing, they didn't see the mountain in sentimental terms. Climbing was a profession, but also a sacred task entrusted to the men of the mountain. The route to becoming a guide, then as now, was to start as a porter, then graduate to assistant guide for two or three years, and eventually, to go for training and become a guide. As chief guide for Marangu Hotel, Fataeli was part of a tradition going back more than eighty years, and had been responsible for organising and training forty or so guides. But even Fataeli was once tempted to try something easier.

According to Seamus, some years before, Fataeli had a love affair with a foreign woman who'd bought him a truck. For five years, he forsook climbing and went into business, but ran into problems when the woman wanted to marry him. He'd neglected to mention he was already married with a family, and when she found out she wanted the truck back. Fataeli went to ground and she eventually gave up and left the area. Perhaps out of relief, Fataeli went on the razzle and turned the truck over, wrecking it. When he came back to the hotel and asked to be allowed to climb again, Erika Lany looked at his body, softened by driving and beer, and patted his paunch. 'Do you think you can still make it?' she asked.

Getting to the summit, though not a difficult feat of mountaineering, takes stamina and determination, and most people wouldn't make it without the encouragement of the guide. Emmanueli showed me a comment book where successive climbers had written their impressions. On 14 September 1963, Stewart Udall, US Secretary of the Interior and an early ecologist, had written: 'I have great respect for all the Chagga guides—their endurance, their willingness to sacrifice their own welfare for that of others is outstanding.' Emmanueli once carried an unconscious climber on his back for six hours from the peak down to the hut where he could be rescued. To another grateful climber he was 'the most courteous, efficient and cheerful guide I have ever observed'.

Leafing through his book, I came on an entry by A.M. Goode, of Adelaide, S. Australia, written on 26 February 1968. This was my father's sister, Alison Mary, known as Judy, who was visiting my parents in the fateful year when they were deported from Tanzania. My father made sure my aunt, who at forty-nine was already a grandmother, shared Emmanueli with only one other climber, while the rest of the party had another guide. In her entry she describes how, just short of the peak, she begged Emmanueli to bring the logbook to her so she could sign as proof that she'd made it. He refused and coaxed her to complete the climb to the summit. Once there, she was so exhausted that they sat for a long time chatting, and when he told her he had six children, she trumped him with seven. Three of his sons became guides, and one a lieutenant colonel in the Tanzanian army. One of hers was, for a while, an expedition guide in the Himalayas before setting up a maintenance business scaling high-rise buildings in Australia. They had a lot in common.

'What are you most proud of?' I asked Emmanueli. He described two occasions when he was given a special responsibility. One was taking ex-US President Jimmy Carter and some of his family up the mountain. The other was at Independence, when the Uhuru torch was carried from place to place lighting torches all over the country. President Nyerere himself came to Marangu with the Uhuru torch. As he handed it to Emmanueli to take it to the summit, he told him, 'If the torch breaks, freedom will break.'

'The torch was very heavy,' Emmanueli confessed to me, 'it gave me pain in my back, but I prayed to God and was able to carry the torch to the summit and down again.' He paused. 'Then I cried, for the only time in my life.'

Besides guiding, he and Fataeli had given years of service to their community as village leaders. In Tanzania's democratic system this is an unpaid elected post of considerable responsibility, presiding over compulsory mass meetings and dealing with disputes, and answerable to central government. Reflecting Tanzania's socialist origins, it's a microcosm of the proper working of the state. When I asked Emmanueli what it took to become village leader, he responded that you had to be 'humble, a gentleman who can reconcile people'. These qualities, valued by the community, also endeared these men to countless mountain climbers for more than fifty years.

Meeting Emmanueli and Fataeli brought home to me the more occluded meaning of the mountain—as a site of stability and permanence. Kilimanjaro is recognised across the world as an iconic sign of Africa. For many people that means the challenge of the wild, the pitting of human strength against nature. It's the soaring peak, rather than the mundane foothills. As it was for Ernest Hemingway, it's still a site of the exotic, a 'destination' to be travelled to from far away. But for the mountain people, in all their variety, its black soil is the bedrock of identity. You can, like Emmanueli and Fataeli, scale the summit for sixty years but ultimately you retire to your *shamba* and the black soil receives you back.

Emmanueli retired at eighty and died a few years later. He was buried in his *shamba* under the banana trees. Everywhere you go on the mountain you see shining white headstones nestled close to family homes, where hens cluck and goats forage for leaves. Each one is a domestic shrine uniting the living and the departed, Sasa and Zamani, in a single space.

11. Myself as a Puff of Dust: a Ghost Story

When I at last returned to Moshi, it was as a shade from a barely remembered past. I was alone, but as I haunted the old familiar places, I felt the presences of all the people I had known. Meanwhile, the girl of seventeen who had last walked these same paths had undergone a transformation, making her unrecognisable. In this limbo state I hovered, watching the life of the town.

The old landmarks were still in place. Julius Nyerere Road, known as Double Road because, although it's only a mile or so long, it has two lanes, runs directly north-south, like the arrow of a compass pointing at the mountain. It's a sort of runway or catwalk for the mountain that most of the time remains shrouded in

cloud. When, from time to time, it emerges in its unstudied grandeur, the ordinary little town is touched by a drama it barely understands; like the moment a diva walks out onto a bare stage and sings. At one end of Double Road is a carefully maintained roundabout with, at its centre, the squat, art deco clock tower and its white, four-way clock-face bearing the red Coca-Cola logo—presumably the epitome of global modernity in the 1940s, when it was erected by Mulji, an important Moshi businessman; at the other end is a roundabout carved out of the red dirt, messy with signs. In this way, the two extremes of Moshi society are brought into contact: the polite, middle-class, colonial and commercial end, and the noisy, haphazard, working-class African end.

Along the pavements many women and a few men are busy with sewing machines, tailoring and dressmaking. You can get something made 'express' in twenty-four hours, if you're ready to pay. Eating houses rub shoulders with shops displaying multi-coloured *kangas*. Outside the mosque a stall of coloured bottles offers traditional remedies for every ailment, from impotence and infertility to stomach ache and sleeplessness. Its hand-painted signboard promises in kiSwahili, 'By the power of God and the inspiration of medicines the sick will recover,' signed in big curly letters M.R. Mdoe Nguzo.

Away from the bustle of the town centre, in the middle of another roundabout is the statue of an *askari*, gun at the ready: a monument to two world wars. From here, wide, tree-lined roads, laid out by German and British town planners, lead to the residential part of town. The Moshi Club with its golf-course and tennis courts. The police training school with its bugle calls and marching feet. The old Greek Orthodox Church, now inhabited by Baptists. The old hospital, where we went for injections to keep the tropical diseases at bay. St Margaret's Church, where we went on Sundays. The kindergarten where I chanted the alphabet, the primary school where I wore my purple and white check dress. The landmarks are familiar, but life has progressed. The primary school, built for sixty white children, now has two hundred black ones. The children kicking a ball

around the rocks on the dusty playing field, the boy selling ices from a cart at the side of the road, the woman turning corn on a brazier, the man in a suit and hat having his shoes polished, see only a shade, a puff of dust, as I pass.

Although I'm a ghost, I'm not alone. I see him now, the old madman who used to haunt the town-centre pavements, dressed in rags that had once been military uniform: an old *askari*. On his chest, bits of iron that could be medals, on his head a battered helmet, on his bare feet, rags tied to resemble boots. As he marches from place to place, he totes a piece of wood over his shoulder for a gun. Every so often, answering some unheard command, he stops, stamps and smartly presents arms, saluting with his free hand. 'He came back crazy from the War,' whispers my mother. Sometimes, as I turn a corner, I catch a glimpse of someone who seems to be following me. I try stopping and turning, but when I do there's no one there. When I turn back and continue, I hear his footfall follow me, his breath a few yards behind. I fancy I can smell his sweat.

One day, looking for a short cut, I follow a dusty track from the town centre and find myself in the cemetery, surrounded by graves as far as the eye can see. The first section is orderly and well maintained, surrounded by a fence and laid out with graves from World War One. I count five neat rows of nineteen headstones, standing to attention just as their occupants would have done in life. These headstones tell a story of men, Muslim and Christian, conscripted to the cause from many points of origin. As I walk down the rows their names call out to me, as if answering a morning roll call: Eronimus Omari, Mumbo Cheria, Felesiano Piason... They served with the King's African Rifles, the East African Engineers, the Army Service Corps or the East African Military Labour Service. I imagine many joined up in 'British' Kenya to march on 'German' Tanganyika, and ended up here, far from home and family. Rajabu Ferrussi and his companions most likely died defending the railway at Voi or Tanga against the legendary German general, von Lettow-Vorbeck, and were 'transferred' here after the Armistice, broken bodies scraped out of shallow graves, transported hundreds of miles in army vehicles. Of fifty thousand soldiers and porters from Britain, India and East, South and West Africa, who died in the World War One East African campaign, Bisiweki Dickson was one who was brought here to rest under a stone inscribed with his name. He and the rest struggled across terrain unmarked by roads, plagued by tsetse fly, thirsty and hot and far from home. Most have no graves, but here in the cemetery the white headstones look like sails mounted on invisible boats sailing in formation towards eternity. Compared to them I am unanchored, drifting like smoke on a windless day.

Away from the war graves, the cemetery loses its military precision. It occupies a space between two roads, with no defining boundaries, no clear entrance or exit. There's no building to give it focus, no layout, no orderly rows or paths between the graves. The dead have built their own community, extending the space they occupy one mound after another, in an organic fellowship of baked earth, wooden crosses and dust. The newer graves are nearer the road, their freshly-painted crosses festooned with tinsel and brightly-coloured plastic flowers. Many of the dates of birth approximate to mine—fifty is a good age for dying. Standing awake and upright in this place where everyone else is sleeping, the scent of scorched dust in my nose, the hum of a million infinitesimal insects in my ears, I'm acutely and foolishly aware of being alive.

I pick my way further in, and gradually the makeshift crosses with tinsel and pink plastic roses give way to carved headstones. The people buried here had the means of proclaiming themselves for posterity, beyond the recording of a name and date in black paint on a wooden cross that would crumble to dust in a few years. Some of them were famous even. The town has seen a stream of explorers since the outside world discovered that there was such a thing as a snow-covered mountain practically on the Equator. From then on, it became a target for geologists, botanists and climbers, despite William Desborough Cooley's denial, in the 1860s, of 'the fantastic assertion that permanent snow lies at 12,500 feet and lower on Kilimanjaro'. Among those who continually proved him wrong was the man whose mortal remains now lie at my feet. I read the epitaph he must have written for himself in anticipation of his death, which happened when his plane crashed between the coast where he lived and the mountain he loved.

> *To the memory of Clement Gillman*
> *28th Nov. 1882—5th Oct. 1946*
> *Who led a common-sense and therefore happy life*
> *Because he stubbornly refused to be bamboozled*
> *By his female relations*
> *By his scientific friends and by the rulers*
> *Spiritual and secular of the society*
> *Into which without his consent he was born.*

Gillman's recipe for happiness was par for the course for an early twentieth century adventurer in Africa. It certainly worked for him, as he ascended to the summit of Kilimanjaro for the first time in 1921. What's interesting is that he was still here, working as a geographer, twenty-five years later, at an age when he should have been cultivating a garden in the Home Counties. He had arrived in 1905 as a surveyor for a German railway company, and stayed when the British took over. Although he wrote a book about the Tanganyika railways, his real memorial is Gillman Point, on the edge of the Kilimanjaro crater. He climbed often, sharing a bottle of champagne with his wife when they got to the summit. With the thin air and the alcohol in their blood they must have floated back down the mountain, but what style, what disdain for scientific warnings about lack of oxygen! I can just hear his female relatives tut-tutting over the contents of his backpack: what, no clean socks but a bottle of Bollinger? Really Clement, don't you think... but Clement was gone, up the mountain, down the railway track, wherever he couldn't hear feminine, scientific, pious or political muttering.

Clement wasn't alone in his choice of resting place. A little further on I stop and read:

> *In Loving and Grateful Remembrance Before God*
> *of Albert Arthur Mangwall Isherwood, CMG, OBE.*
> *Born in Cumberland 1889.*
> *Died at Moshi 1957.*
> *A Colonial Civil Servant*
> *Who Served Tanganyika from 1917-1954.*
> *'For with thee is the well of life*
> *And in thy light shall we see light.'*

I was six when Albert Arthur died, and living here, in Moshi. For a moment, our lives crossed. Where was he as I walked to school in my white and mauve checked dress and grey felt hat? Did he drive by and see me, child of the new generation of colonial servants who flowed in after the War? What made him stay after he had retired, rather than return home to Cumberland? Did he find here the well of life and stay where he could drink? Does his ghost wander with me along the avenues of jacarandas, watching the light fade on that snowy summit that isn't supposed to exist?

Not everyone chose to stay. In another spot, I find the small grave of a child. I remember Jamie, a little boy with white blond hair riding his bike around the neighbourhood. One day he was knocked off it by a truck and killed. His mother, the bank manager's red-haired young wife, was a friend of my mother's. She didn't choose to leave part of herself in the ground, but here he is. These are the colonials, intruders who outstayed their welcome, refusing to go home when their time was up. They take up a corner of the graveyard, surrounded by the people they intruded on, whose graves proliferate, pushing closer and closer to the road. They don't know it, these remnants in their fellowship of dust, but what I feel for them is envy. They found a way to stay, while I was forced to leave.

My mother, who died the year after we left Tanzania, is buried in an English churchyard. My father, who lived for another nineteen years, died in Scotland. There's nothing of my family in this dust, no permanent memorial to our presence. Instead, I'm searching for the grave of Peggy Brice-Bennett, but I can't seem to find it. It should be near the road, it should have flowers and tinsel, and also, because of who she was, a headstone. It turns out the family took down the plaque from Peggy's headstone because people are stealing them.

Seamus tells me the story of Peggy's funeral one day as we're driving down from Marangu. The child of a storytelling Republican Irish mother who grew up among storytellers on the slopes of Kilimanjaro, when Seamus tells a story you don't just listen, you become a part of it.

Peggy was close to a Catholic priest, Father Peter, whom she irreverently called Father Pieta, an Irishman she had nursed when he was sick and who felt he owed her his life. When she was dying, Fr Pieta was called from Lushoto, but couldn't get there till the next day. Although Fr Louis, a Chagga priest who lived in Marangu, gave Peggy the last rites twice, she was still alive when Fr Pieta arrived, and he sat and held her hand for hours until she died. They asked him to officiate at the funeral, but Fr Pieta said he didn't trust himself, so Fr Louis did it. The Catholic Church at Marangu is built on land donated by Peggy and named St Margaret's after her baptismal name. The funeral of such an important elder as Mama Brice-Bennett was a momentous occasion and the church was packed. Afterwards, says Seamus, the procession of cars he led down the mountain road stretched several miles, joined by more cars on the outskirts of town in a long queue to the cemetery.

Peggy wanted to be buried in the same grave as her youngest child, little Sean, who died of eating malaria tablets when he was two years old. So the day before, Seamus's cousin John Bennett hacked through the concrete slabs with a pickaxe. A day or two later, when he had overcome his grief, Fr Pieta called the family together at the graveside for a small ceremony of his own. Borrowing lines from Senegalese poet, Birago Diop, this is what he told them:

> *Those who are dead are never gone…*
> *They are in the fire that is dying,*
> *They are in the grasses that weep,*
> *They are in the whimpering rocks,*
> *They are in the forest, they are in the house,*
> *The dead are not dead.*

Fr Pieta was an Irish Catholic priest, but what he expressed here was the essence of animist belief. In this part of the world, ancestral spirits cohabit with the living. Something of the living being clings to the things that were hers, the air she breathed, the clothes she wore, the walls that sheltered her. The living being is body animated by spirit, which is perceptible as breath, or as shadow, which can be seen but not grasped. The shade of a dead person can take the form of an animal, a dream or a cloud of dust or smoke. It can take up residence in a river, a tree or a stone, and especially on a mountain. Fr Pieta, who owed his life to Peggy, knew that a woman who had lived all her life on the mountain would remain there. He told her children this to comfort them.

Standing in the blazing sun, I feel faint. I sit and put my arms around my knees and rest my head on them. Bunched up on the ground, I'm invisible. I think, what if I die here, in a huddled heap? No one can see me from the road, they won't find my body till someone else comes looking for old graves. The insects will devour me bit by bit, and my bones will fall into dust, and they won't even know who I was. In fact, the insects are devouring me already.

I get up and walk shakily through the graves towards the road. As I leave the cemetery something makes me look back. In the distance, a dark figure stands to attention, one hand raised as if in salute. I blink and look again. The sun is lower now, and shadows spread across the graveyard. I see nothing. I leave.

12. 'They are in the forest, they are in the house.' ('Spirits' by Birago Diop)

A few days later I meet Abdueli Mshiu. He isn't a ghost, but he's in touch with the spirit world through his wife, who is very sick. We meet at the Forest Department, Utilisation Section office, which we used to call 'Town Office' as opposed to the research section and sawmill in the industrial quarter. Although it was in town, like many colonial offices it was basic: my father had a desk, a telephone and an enamel bowl of water balanced on a tripod for washing his hands. Today, Abdueli's come here in response to a call that Bwana Bryce's daughter is looking for people who worked with her father. More than that, I'm carrying a photograph of my mother and father standing in line with four of his foresters. It was taken at their farewell party, days before my parents were deported by the Government for being British, colonial, undesirable and backward. Beneath the photo, in my father's writing, are the names of the four men; Abdueli is one of them.

Abdueli is seventy years old, and long retired. Now he's gone back to the way of life that his people, the waChagga, have followed since they arrived in these parts, farming bananas on the mountain slope. When he came, at the age of twenty-two, looking for a job at the Utilisation Section, it was my father who interviewed him. The waChagga value education more than anything except their cherished bananas, and have found their way into professions the length and breadth of the country. So keen was Abdueli to work in a field requiring skills and mental agility he thought nothing of walking two hours to work to arrive at 7am. If it was raining, he'd warm up by the boiler when he arrived. Ten o'clock, tea, twelve-thirty till two, lunch-break, work till four and walk two hours home again. At work, Abdueli did timber grading and drying, made calculations as to density, weights and shrinkage. He was promoted to technical assistant, and did research on the right timber for telegraph poles. By the time he retired, in 1992, he was Principal Laboratory Technician, Grade 2.

But Abdueli never, unlike some colleagues, got chosen to go overseas for further training, or even to Olmotonyi, the forestry school in Arusha, despite his brightness and aptitude. He says he never had a mentor, someone to speak for him. He's smiling, eyes alert and shining. His clothes are clean but old and worn, and he walks upright, in old and much-trodden shoes. Abdueli strikes me as the most dignified person I have met. He is extremely articulate, speaking the careful correct

English of the era before kiSwahili became the medium of education.

A question has been pressing on me, and now I hear myself ask it.

'What did you think of my father?'

'Mr Bryce was a very clever man. He trained us. He was our father and we were very sorry when he left.'

He was our father.

Abdueli's sincere and simple words disable my adult understanding of colonial relationships, mixed up with childhood memories of a fierce

disciplinarian. Jock wasn't an easy father to have, and I had imagined he wouldn't have been an easy boss. Implicit in Abdueli's statement is the desire for education and self-betterment that characterised the Chagga people from the moment the missionaries arrived with a new kind of learning; also, appreciation for an effective teacher. Abdueli's 'our father' expresses a collective sense of filial relationship and respect for an elder, unaffected by difference of class or caste. I am deeply humbled and stare at him, speechless.

Luckily, Abdueli has more to say, going on to describe how the Utilisation Section 'deteriorated' after my father left: there was less discipline and people became less hard-working. Abdueli suffered when it was privatised, after which research and commercial interests were separated, and he was made into a storeman. 'I very much liked my previous job,' he says in a pained tone. Thankfully, after a while he was allowed to go back to researching the potential uses of pine from Rongai.

'How is life now compared with when you started work?'

'In those days, if you were ill, you took a sick sheet to the doctor, who signed it and your employer paid. Now I'm retired there is no medical insurance, and it's very hard. My wife has cancer and the doctors say she must go to the specialist hospital in Dar, but we can't afford it. We are managing with herbs.'

When Abdueli tells you something bad, you can see he isn't looking for anything. He's simply telling you how things are. Now he invites me to visit him and meet his wife in Kidia, the village in Old Moshi where he lives. I accept at once.

Although it pains me, I get caught up in other interviews and it's a few days later than we agreed before I'm able to take a *daladala* to Kidia. Old Moshi, the former kingdom of Chief Mandara, is a spread-out area of villages scattered on the lower slope of the mountain. We're all jolted together on the *daladala* as it lurches for what seems like hours up the rough, steep road. When I get off, one of the other passengers, with great courtesy, shows me where to wait while he goes to call Abdueli.

Abdueli arrives, in gumboots, fresh from his fields. 'I don't believe my eyes,' he exclaims.

On the day we'd agreed, he waited all day for me. I have to do a lot of apologising and explaining before I can convince him it was unavoidable. I had no way of contacting him because Abdueli, unlike most Tanzanians, has no cell phone. But I can see I've offended his sense of propriety and hospitality. Finally he relaxes, as if to say, at least you're here now. It becomes clear he had made arrangements, which he now proceeds to follow. We walk to the office of the Executive District Officer, whom he introduces as a relative of his, and together they escort me on a 'tour of the environment'. Like everywhere else on this mountain it's lush with growth, the green of the banana trees brilliant against the red earth, a waterfall in the distance a cascade of white down a vertical slope of black rock, the sky a clear pale blue. As we pass, we exchange the usual elaborate greetings with women in bright *kangas* and men in boots and shabby work clothes. I'm old enough for the respectful '*shikamoo*' addressed to elders, to which the reply is '*marahaba*', a word of Arabic origin. They look curiously at me, a white visitor off the beaten track, but Abdueli can't be diverted from his mission.

After the tour, Abdueli leads me down a steep muddy path to his compound. A small unpainted block house set in the middle of a neatly-swept yard, surrounded by banana and coffee groves. We enter the first of its two rooms, the only light filtering in through two small windows. In the semi-darkness Abdueli softly calls, 'Mama'. I follow him into the second room, where his wife lies in bed by the window. She struggles into a sitting position, arranging the sheet over her head the way women cover their heads with their *kangas*. In the darkness, her eyes glow. Her voice comes low and husky as she tells me, in kiSwahili, about her illness. Abdueli translates:

'She wants you to know she has cervical cancer, stage two. The doctors prescribed radiotherapy, but it's only available in Dar. I go all the way to a medicine man at the coast for herbs, which cost a lot of money and last for six months. She drinks them mixed with tea, which is what she mainly lives on. Tea, and a little sugar.'

Mama's gaze rests on me as I search for an adequate response. She says something to Abdueli, who laughs and stands.

'She says you look like your father.'

'How does she know?' I ask in surprise.

I follow Abdueli back next door, and in the gloom, make out a black and white photograph on the wall. The only picture in the room, it has hung here for nearly forty years. He takes it down and shows it to me. The entire staff of the Forest Department, Utilisation Section, stand behind my father, who sits in the front row, smiling broadly. It was a farewell photo taken after the government gave him his marching orders, and it must  have been printed after he left because I've never seen it. The other picture, the one I used to track him down, was taken at the party at our house Abdueli says.

'I sat in the best chair and your father warned me that if I sat there too long I'd fall asleep.' I look at my father and he smiles back at me. His ghost has found a way to stay in this place where he lived for twenty years, and greets me now on common ground. The ground we couldn't find when he was alive.

We go back to say goodbye to Mama. Her face shines, and I see a young and beautiful woman, haloed in a white sheet. She glows in the semi-darkness of the room like an icon in an old church. She tells me, 'Come back and see me before I die.'

Abdueli and I walk back up the muddy track to the road, and into a bar where we order Tusker beer. We're quiet a while and then I tell him my mother had cancer too, and died a year after we left Moshi. At his quick and heartfelt sympathy I have to duck my head to control a surge of grief. Abdueli comes to my rescue.

'Mama told me to ask you for a little money to buy sugar for her tea,' he says, and we both laugh.

'This is from my father,' I say, as I give him what he's asked for. In response, he shakes my hand, his grip warm, firm, solid, the grip of a man who loves his life but isn't afraid of death.

As I sit in the *daladala* heading back down the mountain, I feel the touch of his fingers, and a new sensation fills me. For Abdueli, the past I thought was dead is alive, and I am part of it, just as, sitting in the *daladala*, I'm part of the present. Abdueli has shown me how we're all—himself, Mama, my father, my mother and I—swimming in the great sea of time that encompasses both Sasa and Zamani, one flowing endlessly into the other.

PART FOUR: LUSHOTO AND THE USAMBARAS

13. 'Almost like England.'
(Anne Bryce)

I wasn't meant to hear them talking, but I did. They were in their room with the door half-open and half-closed, and I was on my way to weewee when I heard Mummy say, 'She's only eight, it's very young for boarding school.' So I stopped and stayed quiet by the door. Mummy was crying, I could hear her sniffing. Then Daddy said, 'I was a boarder when I was four.' He wasn't cross, but he sounded as if he didn't understand why Mummy was crying. She didn't say anything but I could hear her breathing loud, like when you're crying but trying not to. 'It's only a hundred and forty miles,' he said, 'not like Australia to Papua New Guinea or when I was sent to school in England and they were in Nigeria.' I didn't know about Papua New Guinea or Nigeria, but I knew about England. It was Home to Mummy, like Australia was to Daddy. Then she said, softly, 'But you suffered Jock, and so did Kitty. She told me she still regrets leaving you in that place and going to join George. She says it scarred you for life.' No one said anything for a long time, and I was getting pins and needles in my foot. I was tiptoeing away when I heard Daddy say, 'Look old thing, I survived and so will she. It's not a POW camp she's going to, it's the best school in the territory.' The bed creaked and I went quickly down the corridor to the bathroom.

After that, I couldn't sleep. I didn't know school was anything to worry about because I'd been in Kindergarten and then Primary, and they were all right. I didn't like the stupid grey hat in Primary, but I liked reading and all that. There was a stupid hat at Lushoto too, but I hadn't thought about going a hundred and forty miles and not coming back. How far was a hundred and forty miles? Kibongoto was twenty-four and a half, because Daddy said so when we went to see the Billingtons. Arusha was fifty, because that's how far it was to the baby animal zoo. The next day, I was going on a train with all the other Moshi children, and it would go all night. That was a long time, and I was getting scared. If I closed my eyes, I could see a train because we often saw trains when we drove past the station. However hard I tried, I couldn't see what happened after the train, but now I felt it was something bad because it had made Mummy cry.

I stayed close to Mummy all day and she didn't send me away. I sat on the bed and watched her pack my school things. She had a list and she let me tick things after she put them in. First, she put sheets and towels in a trunk, along with soap and shampoo and Clark's shoes for everyday and tackies for playing sport. Then she put the three grey shorts and three skirts into a suitcase, with the six pairs of grey socks and six white pants and four white Aertex t-shirts and two maroon jumpers. That's what the list called them. There was something called 'mufti', which Mummy said meant your own clothes to wear at weekends or if you went out. So I took my blue dress with the sash, and the dress with roses round the bottom and Mummy said what about jeans in case I wanted to do something rough, so I took those as well. When the list said 'tuck box', she said we needed a tin and took me into the store room. There was the big Cadbury's chocolates tin the Norcrosses gave us for Christmas, or the Assorted Biscuits that came in Auntie Pam's parcel. She said, 'Choose,' so I chose Assorted Biscuits because the lid had a beautiful picture of a girl with yellow curls and a big hat with long pink ribbons.

Then we got Mary and Ally in from the garden and went to town to buy tuck for the tuck box. We went into Mulji's and Mummy said we needed jam, biscuits and sweets. We chose custard creams and Robertson's strawberry jam and a jar of peanut butter. I'd never had my own jam and biscuits, not to share with anyone else. We'd just finished when Helen arrived with her mother and we all said 'hello' and our mothers laughed about how much school was costing and how they hoped we would enjoy the tuck at school. Mummy whispered to Helen's mother and we said goodbye and went on to Ramzan's to get the sweets. I had never been allowed to buy so many at once. Mary and Ally helped me pick Rowntree's Fruit Gums, Sherbet Lemons, Liquorice All Sorts and Aniseed Balls. I wanted chocolates but Mummy said they would melt so I got some of those fruit sweets in a funny wrapper bent at the corners and with soft gooey insides. 'Don't let Daddy see the liquorice,' Mary said, 'he'll eat it.' Mary and Ally got sweets too, but Mummy said they should keep them for later as we were going for a treat.

We went to the Coffee Shop next door to Emslie's Travel Agent and Helen and her mother were there too, so we all sat at a round glass table and had Cokes with straws and could choose any cake we wanted so I had an éclair. I wondered if Helen knew that school was bad because she didn't look frightened. I was glad she was going on the train with me and we compared sweets and agreed to do swaps. When we left Mummy said, 'See you at six o'clock,' and Helen's mother said, 'Yes, we'll be there,' and we got in the car and drove back home to pack the tuck tin in the trunk.

In the afternoon we went to the Town Pool and played diving off the side until Mummy said it was time to go home for tea and to get ready. I was cold from the water and couldn't get warm, even after I had a bath and rubbed myself dry. Mummy made drop scones for tea, and I ate the one in the shape of a J but I couldn't eat more so Mary and Ally had them all. I didn't feel well, but I didn't know what was wrong with me. I needed to go to the bathroom so I ran but before I got there, poo burst out all down my leg. It was slithery and wet and I ran inside and scrubbed it off but my pants were dirty and I didn't know what to do with them. I didn't want to tell anyone I'd pooed my pants, so I took them and put them in the back of the cupboard in the bedroom, where no one would see them. Then I found a clean pair and put them on and went back out, and it was time to go.

Ahmed and Hamisi carried the trunk outside and put it in the boot. Martha stood by the door and when I hugged her I was afraid I'd cry so I ran to the car. Usually Mummy sat in front with Daddy, but on the way to the station, she sat in the back with me and Mary and held my hand and let Ally sit in front next to Daddy. The ring on Mummy's finger had a green stone, with a little white stone on either side. The green stone was called an emerald, and Mummy's hand was soft and the nails had little white half-moons. I kept my head down and looked at them all the way to the station, wondering if I should tell her about the dirty knickers in the cupboard. Eight was too old for accidents, so I didn't.

At the station, lots of children were going on the school train with parents who had come to see them off, and at one end the police band was playing.

'Look,' said Mummy, 'you're getting a proper send-off, like V.I.P.'s.'

'What are V.I.P.'s?' said Mary.

'Very Important People, like people going away to school.'

Mary made a face at me behind Mummy's back to

show I wasn't *that* important, and Ally giggled. I saw Helen, pale and clinging to her mother. Had she heard that school was bad now? I felt my tummy turn and squeezed my bottom so there wouldn't be any more accidents. Daddy took the trunk and suitcase to the luggage van and watched them being loaded on. All the chatter and music and children running around, it could have been a party if something bad wasn't about to happen. There was a lady with a list who looked for people's names and told them what carriage to go in. Our mothers and Mary and Ally came with me and Helen to find our carriage, and then they all kissed us goodbye and got off the train and we stayed on. They all stood in a group on the platform, talking and waving, and we stood by the window and waved back. Daddy came up and smiled and made a funny face to make me laugh, but I didn't.

Mummy came up to the window and put her hand up and I put my hand out and held onto her. Just then the engine began to puff, slowly at first, then faster and faster, and there was a big jolt and it moved. We held on, and Mummy ran along beside the train as it moved slowly out of the station till the platform ended and she let go. I hung out of the window as far as I could, looking back, and saw her standing by herself, waving and waving. Then the train hooted and blew out a big cloud of white smoke and I couldn't see her any more.

We had packed suppers. Mine was banana and honey sandwiches, crisps and a bar of Cadbury's. It was a bit exciting, being on a train on our own. Helen had cards so we played snap on the seat between us till a man in a uniform undid some straps behind us to let down the top bunk. Then he made the beds with proper sheets and a pillow each. There was a basin in the cabin so we brushed our teeth and when we went along the corridor to the lavatory, we had to cross between carriages and we could see the railway lines through the crack in the floor. The lavatory was small and the bowl was bottomless, with the ground rushing by underneath. The sign said, 'Do not use the toilet while the train is standing at the station. EAR & H.' Daddy said that meant East African Railways and Harbours. You couldn't walk straight along the corridor, you had to sort of run from side to side, bouncing off the walls. When we got back, Helen said I could have the top bunk so I climbed up the little ladder. It was narrow so my face was close to the ceiling but I had a light of my own I could switch on and off. We talked a bit but then Helen fell asleep, and I lay awake while the train chugged on and on, plunkety plunk whoosh plunkety plunk whoosh, through the darkness.

We were asleep when the train stopped and the lady with the list came and told us to get dressed. It was still dark when we got off and cold, with mosquitoes whining in our ears, and I felt sleepy and stiff. 'Are we in Lushoto?' I whispered to Helen. 'No, we're in Mombo,' she said, pointing to a big sign. 'Daddy said the railway goes on from here to Tanga, but we have to go up the mountain so a bus will take us.' The lady came and told us to line up with the other children getting onto a big bus in the station courtyard. So even though we had travelled all night, we hadn't gone a hundred and forty miles yet. Mummy had said the school was in the mountains. She had said, 'It's a beautiful climate, much cooler than Moshi. Almost like England.'

When everyone was on, the bus left Mombo. The road went up and up, and the noise and smell of the engine filled the bus till there was no air to breathe. It went slowly, roaring and lurching and swaying. Although I was cold, I was sweating and wanted to be sick but I pushed the sick feeling down into my stomach. I could see Helen had gone even paler and looked sick too. Outside the window, the side of the road dropped away so every time we went round a bend it looked as if we would go over the edge. The bigger children were at the back and ome boys started singing, 'She'll be coming round the mountain when she comes.' It was a funny song, and when they sang, 'She'll be wearing silk pyjamas when she comes,' and 'She'll be eating squashed bananas when she comes,' we laughed and felt better.

Then we reached the top of the mountain and on the left was a valley with a grass field and goalposts and on the other side of the valley, a long low building. We passed a sign saying Lushoto School and soon we were in front of this building, and two ladies, one fat, one thin, were talking to the list lady. Behind

them was an archway and underneath a flight of polished red steps led upwards. We got off the bus. The fat lady spoke in a loud bossy voice. 'All junior girls go with Mrs von Kaufmann. All seniors come with me.' Helen and I were juniors so we followed the thin lady up the steps and down a long corridor, into a hall with long wooden tables and benches where we sat. Each place had a plastic mug filled with a black liquid and a bowl of something like porridge. The thin lady stood at one end of the hall and said, 'Velcome children. I am Mrs von Kaufmann, your matron. You vill now have breakfast.' Helen and I looked at each other and tried not to giggle. The bigger children arrived with the fat lady and sat at the other end. We noticed that the boys from the train and the bus had disappeared and we were all girls. There were so many of them, and I only knew Helen. We had come a hundred and forty miles, and this was school.

It's pouring the day I leave Moshi for Lushoto. It isn't far but the state of the roads makes travel in Tanzania slow and hazardous. Only recently a bus-load of children coming back to school from holidaying in Dar crashed headlong into a lorry. The two drivers got out and ran away. Of the seventy passengers, forty were killed. They used shovels to scrape up the remains. Today, about forty-five of us are crowded in the battered long-distance bus, with rain coming in around the ill-fitting window-glass so it's impossible to keep dry. To shut out the weather we doze fitfully, jolted awake every time the bus stops to allow more people to get on, until the aisle is crammed with standing passengers. At my elbow stands a very tall young man, his stick thin body draped in blankets, his features unmistakably Masai. In memory I see a herdsman standing on one leg, leaning on his spear, at the margin of a herd of humped cattle. Now my Masai neighbour leans down and touches the ring on my finger. 'Amethyst,' he says in English, 'good colour.' In a mixture of Swahili and English he asks me where I'm going, and where I'm going after that. When I ask him where he's going, he makes a wide sweeping gesture. '*Iko hapa*. Roundi-abouti.' Everyone in earshot, including the conductor, laughs, and so do I. What other reply would you expect from a nomad? At the next stop, he swings himself off the bus and he's gone, roundi-abouti.

Once we get to Mombo, at the foot of the Usambara hills, we've been on the bus, hunched and damp, for nearly four hours. We get out, tentatively stretch our legs and visit the toilets at the back of a bar before we climb back aboard. As we leave Mombo and start the climb from 600 feet above sea-level to 4,000 feet, the whole bus wakes and we rock our way up the escarpment to *bongo flava* and Swahili hiphop. I wonder why I remember this journey as depressing and sad. The bus flies around the hairpin bends and in no time we're at Soni, a village a few miles short of Lushoto. This is where I get out. It's still drizzling and I ask a group of boys where I can find a taxi. A man comes with a car, but the price he tells me for going the two kilometres to Maweni Farm, where I'm staying, is nearly twice what I've paid to come this far from Moshi. I haggle for a while but when I see the price isn't coming down, I get in the car.

It takes several attempts to get the door to close, and a few minutes of fancy footwork between clutch and accelerator to get going. We've gone less than a mile when the road dissolves into a great slush of wet mud with no purchase for the tyres. (The boys' name for a dark chocolate pudding once served at Soni School was Tanganyika Mud.) As if to demonstrate his willingness the driver pushes on, but with wheels spinning and steering out of control I concede defeat and get out of the car. He calls a passer-by to help, and this young man, whose name is Ibi, hoists my bag onto his head and sloshes off uphill through the mud. I follow, slipping and sliding and expecting at every moment to find myself face down in the thick sludge that passes for road. When Ibi delivers me and my bag to the door of Maweni Farm I'm more than happy to hand over the equivalent of half the long distance bus-fare for his services. These two kilometres have now cost me one and a half times the hundred and forty-odd miles from Moshi.

What on earth am I doing here? Lushoto, where I went to school, is a few miles further up the mountain. It was Seamus and Desmond who came to Soni School, and Seamus has such bad memories he refuses even to come to the Usambaras, so it's not as if he recommended a visit. We all hated boarding school so I haven't questioned this, and now I think maybe he was right. The truth is I've come on a whim. Maweni Farm used to belong to the Karimjees, a prominent Dar es Salaam Indian family. Rehma Karimjee was at Lushoto and we were good friends, which seemed enough of a reason for this fool's errand. I met Rehma again, years later, in her flat in London and then we lost touch, but I have a vivid memory of her as a child. She had long, thick, glossy black hair I envied because my hair was straight and thin, and her brown neck and cheeks were coated with a soft down.

Once the rain lets up and I can look around, it's not so bad. There's a lovely fish-pond with reeds and birds, and a path to the football pitch of Soni Seminary Secondary School—which was St Michael's School when Seamus and Desmond were there. By the time I've had a hot shower, an early supper with a bottle of Usambara wine and a chat by the fire with an NGO worker and her parents, I feel human again. As I sip the wine, I notice the name on the label is Sakkarani, and my mind goes back to the Rondo. It was the name given by his troops to Tom von Prince, who, after quelling the Hehe revolt, came to Soni to farm. The filament connecting Soni to the south was strengthened further when, in 1946, the Sakkarani farm was taken over by the Ndanda Abbey Benedictines—our neighbours on the Rondo.

The next day I walk in a wide arc, taking in the Soni Falls and Soni Mountain Lodge. Seeing me scrambling up a steep path to the road, a man commends me for taking the 'shorti-cutti' and I'm proud at how I'm finding my way around. But it's cold at this altitude and I haven't brought enough clothes. I'm huddled by the fire at Maweni Farm in the early evening when Bill and Jackie, a missionary couple, take pity on me and Jackie, one of the world's problem-solvers, borrows a fleece from somewhere and promises to bring me extra clothes for tomorrow. Cheered by my fleece, I'm having dinner by myself when a priest from the school turns up and introduces himself as Father Maximilian. Bill, who teaches at the school, has passed on the news that there's an African literature scholar staying at Maweni. Father Maxi is excited and has come to invite me to talk to the students the next day. We have a brief discussion and he tells me they're reading *Things Fall Apart* by Chinua Achebe. As this is a bit like a theology scholar being asked to talk about Genesis, I'm happy to accept.

In the morning Bill brings a bag of clothes from Jackie, a bit on the small side but I manage to layer up, and when I walk to the school after breakfast I'm warm for the first time since I arrived. Mentally, I bless Jackie. I bump into Father Maxi who leads me into a classroom with thirty young Tanzanian men, aged between fifteen and twenty. Bill and Father Maxi settle at the back of the room and everyone looks at me expectantly. Aware of certain difficulties: not everyone has read the book because there aren't enough copies, they aren't accustomed to being taught by a woman, and English isn't their first language, I decide to keep it general. I start by painting the context in which Achebe wrote the book in pre-Independence 1950s Nigeria, and describe the electrifying effect of its publication, the way suddenly people saw that a village in precolonial Nigeria was as valid a subject for the novel in English as Dickens's London or Charlotte Bronte's Yorkshire moors. As I've done so many times, I summarise Achebe's famous declaration that Africans did not hear of culture for the first time from Europeans: they had both philosophy and highly-evolved artistic forms and he saw it as his responsibility as a writer to remind them. Achebe used the Igbo proverb, 'a man who can't tell where the rain began to beat him cannot know where he dried his body', to tell people that the rain started with colonialism, and the African past should be a source of inspiration, not shame.

At this, it seems, Bill can contain himself no longer. Without a by-your-leave he interrupts, wrenching the topic in an unexpected direction.

'Two thousand years ago,' he tells the young men, who listen respectfully, just as they had to me, 'we in Britain were tribal, and the only difference between us and you is that we came through it sooner and moved on faster. Two hundred years ago you were where we were two thousand years ago.'

To my horror, I realise Bill has just contradicted everything I've been telling the students. Between the man of God and me, who will they believe? In fact, I've been hoodwinked into colluding in a discourse my whole career has been devoted to dismantling. Mortified, I sit and bow my head so low I can see nothing but the floor. I hear Martha's gentle voice, 'God made white and black and he made us the same.' I don't remember how it continued: I remember only the terrible shame of that moment and how I wanted to strip off poor Jackie's t-shirt and too-small jumper and run as fast as I could back to Maweni Farm. I wanted to escape.

Most children who went to boarding schools in the decades after the War fantasised about escape. It was a point of honour for my friends and me that we hated our boarding school. We hated being dumped there by our parents for twelve long weeks, with food so disgusting we would hold it in our mouths and spit it out in the lavatory rather than swallow, with constant surveillance and beatings—the cane for boys, a slipper for girls—and shared baths in scummy water and all the stupid meaningless rules we couldn't help breaking. But we were children, and in us was the drive to joy. Playing together we found ways to escape into fantasy, wrapping ourselves in a blanket of make-believe. Though the teachers were old-fashioned they were human, and their humanity showed itself in readings of *The Hobbit*, walks in the neighbourhood, attendance at plays we devised and put on ourselves. Beatings were never so severe as to deter us from risk-taking. The humiliation they inflicted was shared and understood by everyone. The worst thing you could be was a 'goody-goody', because then you were outside the collective resistance to authority that sustained our spirit.

Though many of us had brothers or friends at Soni, we took it for granted that they hated Soni the way we hated Lushoto. No one then had the faintest idea what was going on there, or how much worse it was. Even when I went back as an adult the full extent of what happened there hadn't been revealed. Two years later, former pupils of St Michael's, the colonial school that occupied the seminary school premises from the 1950s until it closed in 1974, started a Yahoo group to share memories of 'Soni prison and torture camp.' Eventually a documentary film would be made, titled *Abused: Breaking the Silence*. Was there some lingering malignancy that had survived the passage of half a century and did I enter its force-field when I stepped into that classroom? Was the humiliation and shame I suffered a distant echo of what had been perpetrated there?

14. Maria Morphopolous's Slipper

To us who came to school from the coast or the plains it seemed Lushoto was always grey and wet, and we shivered in our skimpy grey shorts and Aertex blouses. But for the Germans, Lushoto was one of their favourite places in Tanganyika. At a height of 1,500 metres, it had a climate so cool and temperate they called it Wilhelmstal after the Kaiser and wanted to make it their capital. They built a school for German children that continued, under the British, as a boarding school for children of Europeans, and, until 1973, for anyone who wanted a British education and could pay the fees. When I arrived in 1959, aged eight, I found myself in a barrack-like place, with doorless dormitories opening into each other and onto a corridor at either end, so there was no privacy and the matrons could listen and spy with ease. There was a Girls' End and a Boys' End, and we were not encouraged to fraternise. Girls and boys ate separately in large dining rooms, sitting on benches, mostly in silence, supervised by the Junior and Senior matrons. The Junior matron, Mrs von Kaufmann, was the widow of a German sisal farmer. She was as thin as a stick and we called her Koffee and laughed at her accent behind her back. The Senior matron, Miss Buckle, was enormously fat and rolled along on slippered feet, trailed by her spoilt pug dog on which she lavished a tenderness reserved only for him. We called her Ma Buckle and hated her. Both matrons made liberal use of the slipper to punish us, but compared to Koffee's puny frame, Ma Buckle was big and strong and sadistic and everyone feared her. She was merciless when it came to beating. She would almost quiver with delight as she surveyed her cowering victim, deliberately prolonging the moment to extort maximum pleasure from the whistle as the slipper descended, the thwack onto bare flesh, the searing pain, the burning weals afterwards.

Behind the classroom block was the break-place, a gently rising slope that flattened at the top and led into a grove of eucalyptus trees known as the *Bhundu*. Here too, an invisible line divided the boys' side from the girls', and the *Bhundu* was out of bounds to both. The teacher on duty sat on a bench just below the brow of the hill facing the classrooms and the flat bit where most children played. If you could get behind her without her noticing, you could get above the brow of the hill where you couldn't be seen. If you were daring, you could make a break for the *Bhundu* and disappear. Then you had to listen out for the bell marking the end of break and run like mad back down the break-place to where everyone was lining up, trying to look as if you'd been there all along.

Gillian, Rehma and I loved being in the *Bhundu*. It was quiet and lonely, and the sun filtered through the branches and played on the silvery trunks of the young trees, releasing the sharp medicinal tang of eucalyptus. It tickled our noses and reached into our lungs, like inhaling Vicks. If you were lucky, you found wild golden gooseberries close to the ground, warm and sweet on the tongue. We came so often we'd built a den by sticking sticks close together in the ground and heaving up clumps of the long grass that grew at the *Bhundu*'s edge to wind in and out. We sat in the den and read our precious comics, *Bunty* and *Girl* and *School Friend*. We especially loved 'The Silent Three', a comic strip in *School Friend* where three schoolgirls had a secret pact to go around doing good and daring deeds and not telling anyone it was them. Crouched in our den, we listened to Gillian reading:

'In that pleasant woodland glade, Betty, Peggy and Joan were thinking back over their adventures as The Silent Three. On several occasions at school they had donned their robes to fight against tyranny and injustice. No one had ever appealed in vain to The Silent Three for help.'

We looked at each other: we were in a 'woodland glade' and tyranny and injustice were things we understood. So we made a pact and swore an oath of secrecy. We would be The Silent Three. We could never tell on the others and we had to stay loyal forever.

Everywhere else, we were surrounded by other people and watched over, day and night. Even whispering after lights out was dangerous because you never knew when Ma Buckle was on her rounds, padding past on her soft rubber shoes that made no sound on the concrete floor. She loved to catch you talking so she could send you for a slipper and whack you on your bare backside before sending you back to bed. Inside the den there was only the three of us, the grass wall tickling our backs, breathing the close fragrant smell of dried grass, trampled earth, warm skin, matted hair, crumpled cotton. We were in a capsule where time stood still. We sat hunched over our drawn-up knees, facing each other. You could hear the scuffle of ants in the eucalyptus bark, the chirruping of birds, and faintly, high pitched cries from the break-place. Between us, we had a scrap of paper where Rehma had written: 'We, The Silent Three, do solemnly swear never to reveal each other's names and always to be faithful, loyal and true.' When we had all signed, we looked at each other, wondering what came next.

'We should bury it so no one can find it.'

'But it'll rot in the ground.'

'Put it in a plastic bag?'

'Or in a secret place in the dorm.'

'What secret place? You know Buckle sticks her nose in everything.'

'We can put it in the torn lining of my overnight bag under the bed.'

'Ok, but there's one more thing. We have to Seal the Pact.'

'How do you mean?'

'We have to do a dare and not tell anyone about it.'

'Quick, that's the bell. Run!'

We scrambled out, dazzled by the brightness of sun on leaves after the gloom inside the den. We ran pell-mell through trees and up the open slope of the hillside. The bell was still clanging as we tumbled down the other side, to arrive sweaty and panting at the end of the queue disappearing towards the classrooms.

Seal the Pact. The words chased each other through the afternoon, a challenge and a provocation. The night after we signed the Pact, Gillian stuck her head out of her mosquito net and leaned across the gap between our beds to whisper:

'Let's go down to the river. Tell Rehma.'

I leaned over the other side and whispered to Rehma, who lay still and didn't answer. I saw Gillian slip out of the door and without waiting, I crept out of bed and followed. There was a light at the far end of the corridor, enough to see our way to the head of the stairs leading down to the washrooms. I saw a pyjamaed ghost ahead of me as I flitted along the wall, till my bare feet found the first step. Below me the stairs were a dark well, leading away from safety. I plunged in, toes curling around the edge of each step, fingers trailing the wall, all my senses alert. At the bottom, my heart beat like a drum in the darkness. *I could smell the rubber of flip-flops and tackies*, a faint whiff of soap. Gradually, shapes came into view: sports clothes hanging on pegs, basins under the window, shoe lockers. I moved forward cautiously till I bumped into Gillian and almost screamed.

'Sssh, Buckle'll hear us! Where's Rehma?'

'She's too scared, she hasn't come.'

'Ok, we'll give her a dare later. Let's go.'

We unlatched the door and then we were outside. A yellow square fell onto the dirt driveway from an upstairs window, a fragment of moon showing through the torn clouds. Opposite us was the bank that fell away to the river, another place out of bounds. In the day time, it was a laundry where women washed our sheets on the rocks. As we ran across the road and flung ourselves down the bank, we felt a surge of joy so intense it lifted us off the ground. Held aloft by darkness we floated to the bottom, coming to rest at the river's edge. The moon was fully out, striking the white trumpets of the lilies that grew there so they almost rang aloud, filling our eyes with moonlight like nocturnal creatures. Holding hands we stepped out onto the wide flat rock where the sheets were scrubbed, feeling the day's warmth rising through the soles of our bare feet. Like a cat at a saucer, the water lapped at the rock. Without a word, we slipped out of our pyjamas and stepped in. The water was cool around our ankles, but as we stood, it got warmer, and we went further, further, feeling it rise up our legs, surround our tummies, tickle our arm-pits. Our feet lifted and we were floating, two dark heads breaking the surface, bodies pale and luminous beneath the water. From the reeds, a frog croaked, but otherwise it was silent. Above us loomed the massive outline of the school, with all the sleeping children, guarded by the sleeping matrons. We lay on our backs, eyes filled with moonlight, holding hands.

'Rehma, what'll you do to seal the Pact?'

We were back in the den, discussing the next step. Rehma hung her head, her long black hair making a veil around her face. She wanted to be in the threesome, but she was used to being good. She could no more get out of bed after lights out and creep downstairs than she could fly. So Gillian came up with another idea.

The dormitories were on the first floor, giving onto alcoves with large windows about thirty feet above the school driveway. At night, if we needed to wee, there was a portable toilet in one alcove, its two windows standing open to let out the chemical smell. Ma Buckle was safely in her room, door closed, the radio playing. If she came out, all she would see was three little girls using the portable toilet, and the worst she could do was pack us off back to bed. Gillian and I had done the dare before. It was safe, the safest dare we could think of to seal the Pact, but Rehma looked as if she would cry.

She turned blindly, facing the window. Watching her clamber awkwardly onto the sill, I felt a rush of anxiety. Rehma wasn't good at games, she always dropped catches, she couldn't run fast, and mostly she preferred to sit on the side-line at hockey. Maybe she couldn't do it, maybe we were wrong to ask. But she was already lifting her leg over the sill, as delicate as a cat. Gillian stepped into the cubicle and leaned out through the second window, facing her. There was about six feet of narrow ledge between them.

'Come on Rehma! Just walk!'

Rehma clung to the window frame, trembling. I whispered, 'Go on, it isn't hard, honestly.' The long black hair fell across her face, and she turned her head towards Gillian and the other window. Her narrow feet gripped the ledge as she took one tentative step sideways.

'Do it fast!' I hissed. You had to do it fast, it was the only way. If you stopped and looked down, if you stopped moving, you'd be stuck. Rehma was doing it wrong, taking tiny little steps with long pauses between when she seemed to freeze like a lizard against the wall. It took agonising moments for her to shuffle out into the middle, to the point where her arm was fully extended behind her and she would have to let go. Then she stopped.

'Let go!' I urged, 'You have to let go! Keep moving!'

At the other window, Gillian was up on the sill and leaning towards her, arm outstretched. In a second, Rehma could have touched her, gripped her hand, regained the safety of the second window frame. I saw her small, clenched fingers loosen as she lurched forward another step. Then, at the dead centre, she froze.

The face turned towards Gillian was pale and drenched with tears, the eyes wide with accusation. Below them, the ground beckoned and Gillian knew she had to do something. Without thinking, she lifted her leg and climbed out onto the sill, extending her arm so her fingers touched Rehma's, like figures in a frieze. At that moment, I heard a door open and the rolling tread of a large body in soft shoes advancing towards the alcove. Ma Buckle on her rounds! In a panic I turned and ran in the direction of the dormitory. Too late. I saw the dead white hands gripping the large, heavy flash-light Miss Buckle always carried like a weapon, the shadowy bulk behind it, and then it flicked on, and I was caught there in pyjamas and bare feet, mesmerised like a rabbit in its beam. The cold, clipped voice shot its questions at me: What was I doing out of bed? Why was I running? Who else was with me? What were they up to? I could only squirm, small, stupid, wrongful, rule-breaking, guilty and doomed.

'I thought I heard a noise, Miss Buckle.'

'A noise? Who was making it? Who else was fooling around after lights out? What have I told you girls? Come on now, own up.'

I hung my head, trapped between fear for my friends and fear of Ma Buckle's fat arms wobbling as they raised the slipper above her head. She was getting impatient.

'You don't know who you were with? Maybe I can jog your memory.'

I knew what it meant, and held my breath.

'Go and get Maria Morphopolous's slipper.'

The forty or so of us who used the senior cloakroom all stored our slippers in the foot lockers: rubber flip-flops for the most part, bought in the Indian *dukas* at home, cheap and light and bearable to the skin. But Maria Morphopolous had a different kind of slipper, made of moulded plastic, hard, with ridges in the sole that left a pattern of cuts on the culprit's flesh that lasted days. Maria Morphopolous's slipper was Buckle's most dreaded punishment, reserved for special occasions. This, apparently, was one. I found the slipper easily—everyone knew where it was kept—and crept back upstairs to surrender the instrument of my torture into Buckle's sausage-skin fingers. Silently, I followed her back to the door of the dormitory.

It was only after I had stumbled blindly into the dormitory and crawled under the net, after I had sobbed loudly several minutes, then quietly for several more, after I had shifted and turned to find a place to lie on that didn't hurt, that I remembered the others. Just as I was about to sit up and look around, a hand slipped under the net, followed by a body, then another body. The three of us sat on the bed, faces inches apart, breath mingling.

'Well done. You saved us from Buckle,' breathed Gillian. Rehma was shining with triumph.

'I did it! I did the dare, and you didn't tell. We've sealed the Pact.'

Pain, outrage, humiliation melted. We were The Silent Three, and together we had beaten Miss Buckle, tyranny and injustice—and Maria Morphopolous's slipper.

15. Encounters in the Usambaras

I find myself back in Lushoto in May, the wettest time of year: for the first few days it rains all the time and during trips to town I'm squelching through a sea of mud. In the early 60s, parents coming up for half term would stay at the elegant Lawns Hotel, named for its manicured lawns, and compete for the room with a sunken bath. It felt like the height of sophistication to be served tea in its comfortable lounge or dinner in the dining room. After the food at school, everything set before us struck me as delicious, even bland colonial staples like oxtail soup or mashed potato. It was an oasis of comfort and civilisation in the deprivation of our days.

I suppose I should be pleased to find that, when I visit, it hasn't been modernised at all. In fact, the fabric of the hotel is so old that in places it has rotted into gaping holes now colonised by hornets' nests. The rough wooden floor of the dark and gloomy dining room creaks noisily as you walk. It isn't the hotel's fault that a seasonal plague of locusts has descended, covering the cream-yellow gloss-painted walls with their bright green bodies, flying into your face at every turn, settling on the table as you're eating. My room has panelled walls, a disused fireplace and a wooden floor so soft I fear plunging through to the foundations. I run the taps of the cast iron tub in the bathroom and great black gobbets gush forth with the water. When I pull the plug out, the water splashes straight through the plug-hole onto the floor, soaking my feet. A black moth the size of my hand is nestling in my towel. I dislodge another as I attempt to draw the curtains, and in both cases I utter a piercing scream. Locusts cling to the door and infiltrate the room; corpses litter the floor and I scrunch them underfoot leaving a shiny stain.

The residents take refuge in the bar, where Tony, the friendly and eccentric owner, radiates warmth and good cheer in the surrounding gloom. Tony, a Greek Cypriot remnant of a once-thriving Greek community, is perfectly at home in the strange world he's created for himself, even though his wife couldn't take it and fled to Dar. He tells me he couldn't live anywhere else.

'Because of the political correctness—you can't open your mouth for fear of offending someone.'

He seems to find it natural to be directing a locust-catching operation with his staff, and is oblivious to discomfort. He's a survivor, one of those locals whose family came from elsewhere to settle, and nothing, not failing businesses, political ipheavals nor community ostracism, has kept him away. Before becoming a hotelier, he'd done everything from driving a bulldozer to farming to smuggling, while spiritually, he seems to survive on cable TV news, *Time* magazine and the internet.

'My father's uncle,' he tells me, 'emigrated from Cyprus to Arusha in 1890. My father was the eldest of ten brothers and sisters, so in 1930 he was sent to work with his uncle and send back money to get his sisters married. He worked in coffee estates around Arusha, and by 1939, was working on a German farm inside Ngorongoro Crater. When the War started the owner was interned. My father was a British citizen so he was made custodian of the farm.'

We're walking where the famous lawns used to be, still green but no longer manicured. I remember riding horses with my sisters across these lawns when we stayed here at half-term, or playing tennis on the well-maintained courts. Tony tells me these were taken out when they became a sign of western decadence after Uhuru. He shows me the trees he's planted, which partially screen the dilapidation.

'During the War,' Tony continues, 'the British put the Polish Jewish refugees in camps at Tengeru and Morogoro. My mother was one. My parents got married in Lushoto and afterwards lived in Mombo, where there were fifty Greek families because of the sisal. There was a social club, a coffee shop, gambling. I was born in 1950, and I was sent to the Greek school in Arusha. Two hundred boys and girls went to boarding school by train from Tanga. In '64, after the Zanzibar massacres, at least half the community deserted Tanganyika. At school half the children disappeared overnight.'

The massacres in Zanzibar, taking place just off the coast of Tanganyika three years after Uhuru, deeply unsettled those foreigners who had remained. Though directed at the so-called Arab element of the creolised Zanzibari cultural mix, the violence was carried out in the name of black liberation and who knew if it would spread to the mainland. As one of the few Greeks who remained, Tony lived a precarious existence for years. His father bought the Lawns Hotel in 1985 and when the old man died ten years later, he decided to turn his hand to the hospitality industry and came to Lushoto to run it. Now he says resignedly, 'There's no community here, I'm the only European. Local people are too churchish.'

The Usambaras, like Kilimanjaro and the Rondo Plateau, were heavily Christianised by both German Protestants and British and Irish Catholics. Up the road, a three-way speaker has screamed an anti-Christian, Muslim fundamentalist diatribe for two whole days. It is incongruous in this sleepy, one-street town. Pancras, a fellow guest who went to school in the area and comes back to escape the stress of Dar where he works for the Jane Goodall Trust, tells me such hate-talk is usually shut down because it goes against the idea of Tanzanian togetherness. He says the speaker claims Jesus Christ visited a mosque and so was really a Muslim. The credulous, with no historical background, believe what they hear. In deference to the Muslim population, Nyerere declared at Independence that 'TANU *haina dini*': TANU (then the sole political party) has no religion. Nyerere himself was a Catholic, and he often came on retreat to a government lodge above Lushoto, from where he attended Mass at Gare Mission. Founded by Trappists in 1898, in 1945 this mission was given to the Irish Rosminians, and presided over from 1950 for the next forty-five years by Father Frank Kennedy. Father Frank and Nyerere—known as JKN—became firm friends, and used to have breakfast together after Mass. Seamus told me the story of one of these breakfasts, involving Father Peter—another Rosminian priest and Peggy Brice-Bennett's friend.

When in residence JKN sent a polite handwritten note to Father Frank asking if he could join him for Mass on Sunday. Father Frank would invite him to breakfast, and JKN would always accept. He felt relaxed with Father Frank and could express himself openly. One Sunday, after the usual exchange of notes, Father Frank was called away on urgent business and passed on the responsibility of hosting breakfast to Father Peter.

'But,' he told him sternly, 'the President is on holiday and you're not to bend his ear on any of the subjects—like education—that I know are dear to your heart. Stick to crops and the weather.'

Father Peter celebrated Mass and escorted JKN to breakfast. Over boiled eggs and tea, Father Peter was dutifully addressing the topic of crops and the weather when JKN rounded on him, asking, 'But Father, don't you have any other conversation?'

Father Peter, given to deliberation, thought for a long moment before admitting that, yes, he did. 'But,' he delicately enquired, 'what would the President like to talk *about?*'

'Oh,' said JKN, 'all right then. How about education? What do you think of my educational policies?'

A light came into Father Peter's eyes but he responded cautiously, 'Well, I'm afraid what I have to say might corrupt those two young men who are standing inside the door.'

When JKN turned to his two bodyguards and told them they should go outside, there was great consternation.

'But sir,' one ventured, 'we're supposed to stay with you at all times.'

'Yes, I know,' said the President soothingly, 'but what is the Father going to do to me? Kill me? And if I'm killed by a holy father, I imagine I'll go straight to heaven, so won't he be doing me a favour?'

As soon as the guards had reluctantly stepped outside, JKN turned to Father Peter.

'Now Father, say what you want to say,' he admonished.

What was Father Peter to do? This was the President, after all. So he laid out all his misgivings about the future of Universal Primary Education, JKN's prized policy, in the face of teacher shortages and lack of other resources, which he listed in detail. The President, known as *Mwalimu*, Teacher, defended his policy; more tea was required to fuel the heated debate that ensued. It was brought to an abrupt end at midday by the arrival of Father Frank, who burst into the room, incandescent with rage. He confronted Father Peter.

'I told you this was not to happen! I told you to leave the President alone!' He seemed almost ready to hit Father Peter when JKN took him gently by the arm.

'But Father,' he assured him, 'it was entirely my fault. We've been having a very interesting discussion, so why don't you join us?'

The three sat and more tea was brought. JKN didn't take his leave until he was satisfied Father Frank wasn't going to wait until his back was turned to berate his fellow priest again.

Father Peter is now retired and living in the Rosminian House in Lushoto. I'm curious to meet this survivor from the old Tanzania, who, like the Reverend Richard Norgate at Masasi in the south, has chosen to stay in old age. After Seamus and Desmond's stories, I feel I already know him. The man I meet is long-faced and ponderous, his Irish accent still unmistakable. We sit and talk in a dimly-lit reception room with unadorned walls, furnished only with a couple of wooden armchairs with worn cushions and a plain wooden table. If I'd been wondering what sustained this elderly man in this remote and muddy corner of the world, his energy and sharpness of recall soon put me straight. It's many years since the legendary breakfast with JKN, but Father Peter hasn't lost the gift of the gab. He loves two things, I discover: visual beauty and philosophy, which he's still exploring now in his late 70s.

'What are you reading?' I ask.

'Oh, existentialism, logical positivism, Karl Popper... But in my early life I had no intention of being a priest. I wanted to be a painter and designer. Since I was a child I'd been fascinated with the beauty and colours of nature.'

'How did you become a priest?'

The answer is typical of many poor Irish boys of his generation: faced with few opportunities, they were taken up by the Church, educated and offered what seemed like the supreme privilege of an intellectual life and a role in educating others. It came in the form of a religious vocation that was often less felt than imposed. Father Peter grew up in a small village halfway between Dublin and Limerick where 'everybody was poor'. At primary school his teacher recognised his potential and enabled him to go on to secondary school and thence to an Irish Rosminian house in County Londonderry at sixteen.

When he emerged in 1950, at the age of nineteen, Father Peter was still uncertain of his next step. The only careers guidance was the priests asking, 'Do you want to go on to the novitiate?' but he was hesitating.

'I was painting the stations of the cross when an old priest came to me and asked if I didn't want to go. I said I didn't want to give up my love for beauty. The old priest told me the ancient Greeks held that three things in life were of value: Truth, Goodness and Beauty. He said that Truth and Goodness culminated in Beauty, and Beauty was part of religion. It was the beginning of my love of philosophy.'

So seduced, Father Peter went to Rome to study philosophy and theology. Among its basilicas and museums he felt he had found what he craved. 'I was in my element in the Sistine Chapel. There I could see what beauty was.'

In 1960, Father Peter was ordained and returned to Ireland to await deployment to a suitable post. He fully expected to be sent to the Rosminian house in Tanganyika and was looking forward to it. 'I understood the desire for Independence and the aggression of nationalism,' he told me. 'In my childhood Ireland had just got freedom and was burning everything British except its coal. I was born into a very nationalistic family—they would say patriotic—supporters of de Valera and Fianna Fail. Both my parents had lost a sibling, killed by the Black and Tans.' Instead, he taught philosophy at a study house in Ireland for three years. When at last, 'I was told out of the blue that I was going to Africa, it was a shock because I'd made a huge effort to find my feet as a teacher.'

How did he come to terms with such an abrupt change of direction?

'You'd vowed obedience and that you'd go anywhere at any time to do any job whatsoever. I had no choice because I'd vowed freely, by myself.'

As I listen, I struggle to understand how having no choice because of a vow you'd taken as the inevitable culmination of a long process beginning in childhood, could constitute freedom. Then I recall where he comes from, and how Peggy Brice-Bennett found Cork in Marangu. In 1963, the same year Father Peter arrived in Tanganyika, the Africanist historian, Terence Ranger, became professor of history at University College, Dar es Salaam and started teaching about Ireland. In a short memoir *From Ireland to Africa*, he describes how, when the TANU Youth League protested about the 'alien irrelevance' of Irish history, 'President Julius Nyerere told them that it was, alas, all too relevant.' Ranger also details how during the Zimbabwe war of independence, Irish missionaries, though conservative and disapproving of communism, eventually identified with the freedom fighters against the Rhodesian army. He said of his long career writing and teaching in and about Africa, that, 'For me Ireland and Africa had always been part of the same project... it was the militant and nationalist tradition of Ireland that sustained me over more than forty years.'

In October 1963, two years after Tanganyika's Independence, Father Peter left Ireland alone to begin his new life. Over the next forty or so years, he would be a pastor in various parishes in the Tanga diocese, chaplain to the nuns at the mother-house in the Usambaras, philosophy lecturer at the diocesan senior seminary in Kibosho, Kilimanjaro, and a teacher in Nairobi, before retiring to the Rosminian house in Lushoto, where we now sit.

Remembering the story of the Sunday breakfast, I've been waiting for the moment to ask Father Peter his opinion of Nyerere. Even though I'm accustomed to the veneration he inspires in certain older people, I'm unprepared for his passionate response.

'I adore him. He was one of the best people I ever met. I'd love to see him canonised because he'd be a model to show that to be a leader you don't have to be a tyrant. Nyerere is to Africa what Gandhi is to the world. You can only admire Gandhi and it's the same with Nyerere.'

I'm aware that this is far from being a universally-held opinion. Political opponents and some of his own party who experienced preventative detention, for instance, and Zanzibaris involved in the 1964 uprising—barely three months after Father Peter's arrival—and its consequences, feel very differently about Nyerere, who didn't hesitate to use repressive measures to maintain control. I push him further. What was it about Nyerere, I ask, that makes him feel this way? In reply, Father Peter tells me the story of how Nyerere visited Ireland in 1979 to thank its premier, Prime Minister Garrett Fitzgerald, for the Irish government's long-term support of Tanzania.

'Well,' says Father Peter, 'the PM had all the MPs lined up in O'Connell St to meet Nyerere but before that he asked him what he wanted to do. Nyerere replied that he'd like to pray at the grave in Drogheda of the father who baptised him, so off they went. Nyerere knelt in the mud and prayed for half an hour. Then he stood and said to Fitzgerald, "Now, take me wherever you want."'

Humble, devout, compassionate, faithful—this is the Nyerere Father Peter reveres. For him, after 1964, 'Zanzibar was hell' and thousands of people's lives were in danger when Nyerere stepped in to save them by uniting the island and the mainland as one country, Tanzania. For others, he was complicit in the tyranny of Zanzibar's post-revolutionary leader, Sheikh Abeid Karume. Victims have testified that detentions, torture and disappearances were commonplace both in Zanzibar and in mainland Tanzania. Yet for Father Peter, 'Nyerere's intentions were sincere; how they were implemented wasn't always in his control.' Thinking again of Terence Ranger's words—'For me Ireland and Africa had always been part of the same project'—I wonder whether Father Peter's blindness to the Truth he so much cherishes could be traced to his Irish origins and his desire for the realisation of a new order in his adopted country. Certainly he's in accord with Terence Ranger in seeing the anticolonial struggle in Ireland as a forerunner of similar struggles in Africa.

'But,' Father Peter concedes, 'perhaps Nyerere was idealistic in his aim to return the country to the Garden of Eden. He was obsessed by the Acts of the Apostles. His political philosophy was a strange mixture of the Acts and Plato. Was he right? You have to say he was. Why didn't he succeed? The simple answer is human nature: original sin. He was a natural ascetic and should have been an abbot.'

In the end, then, Father Peter claims JKN and his mission for the Church, casting him as a religious leader whose destiny was hijacked by politics. I'm not a Catholic or even, any longer, a Christian, or perhaps I would have seen much earlier that this was where our conversation was tending. Perhaps, too, this wily reader of human nature deliberately chose not to reveal all he knew to a curious outsider who'd been away almost as long as he'd lived in the country. Getting at the Truth isn't a straightforward process.

On the way out I come on a little group of boys at the gates to the Rosminian house, peering with interest into the garden. They ask me, politely, if it's all right for them to go inside and hunt locusts, a seasonal treat, eaten fresh or fried. I say yes. As I walk away, I see white clouds of insects rising as the kids fall on the bushes. All the way back, kids are locust-hunting, some halfway up the walls of houses. It's a locust free-for-all, a feast. As I reach the Lawns and let myself into my room, scrunching their bodies underfoot, I wonder if Tony couldn't enlist a small army of children to rid the Lawns of its locusts.

16. Return to Lushoto School

All the time I'm in Lushoto, I'm conscious my main purpose in coming here is to visit my old school. This is one of many times I long for a companion, a friendly presence to share the burden of memory. However bad things were at school, we always had each other. When I tell Tony where I'm going, he asks, 'Are you going by footsy?' It's a good question, considering the slog through the mud every walk involves. I set out for the school on a wet, grey day along a road lined with eucalyptus trees, their slender leaves like liquefied silver. I arrive at the gate and stand cowering beneath my umbrella. It is no longer a school. In fact, it's been a number of things since it closed as a school in 1969, and now it's a training college for much-needed primary court magistrates. This is an important detail because it's a government institution so you can't just enter the premises. There's a protocol and I have to explain myself to the security guard.

'I used to be at school here *zamani*,' I tell him. He looks at me with suspicion, but he takes my ID card and disappears for some time, leaving me standing under my dripping umbrella. Eventually he returns and escorts me up the long drive to an office on the ground floor, to the right of the main staircase.

At the door, I hesitate. When it was a school, this office was a sacred space, one we were never permitted to enter. It was the living quarters of Miss Zoë Goodwyn, who taught us French and Hockey and Music Appreciation. In the white families, consisting of parents and children, grandparents were scarcely seen and Miss Goodwyn seemed to us ancient. When my grandmother came to visit my parents on the Rondo from Australia in 1951, the year I was born, life expectancy in the country was around forty-three. She impressed everyone who met her with her majestic age of sixty-eight.

Miss Goodwyn couldn't have been as old as that, but even in the 50s she was an anachronism. Her sturdy figure stood four-square on the earth, except when she was running up and down the hockey field with a whistle in her mouth or riding her beloved horse, Sox, who was stabled at the Lawns Hotel. She was always impeccably dressed for the occasion. She wore outfits: loose 1940s-style wide pants for refereeing hockey; immaculate jodhpurs, with black hat, boots and whip for riding; carefully coordinated skirts and blouses for French and Music

Appreciation classes; more wide trousers for casual evening wear in which to stride the corridor after lights out to sit at the dining room piano and play Brahms and Chopin late into the night. It was the soundtrack to homesickness, every plangent note a falling tear. I have never since those days been able to listen to solo piano without a deep melancholy.

Whatever the outfit or time of day Miss Goodwyn's face was fully made up, her wrinkled skin powdered white, eyebrows painted in, lipstick a scarlet slash across her mouth, cheeks so highly rouged my father once described her as Joan of Arc after she'd been burning for a long time. We called her Goody and feared her sharp tongue and strict discipline, her gimlet eye that saw when you hadn't learnt your vocab or tenses. Her pedagogy was an old-fashioned mixture of learning by rote and fear of public humiliation. When I was doing the entrance exam for Cheltenham, she told me I wouldn't get in because I was too lazy, and repeated what other teachers were allegedly saying about me. Latin: 'I wish she was good all the time instead of good one day and bad the next.' English: 'Her grammar is atrocious.' Funny, I thought, I always get As for both. But Goody wasn't finished.

'You think you can sail through just because you're Jane Bryce. Well, I assure you, you can't!'

I hated her. But when we met a few years later—I was home from school in England and had gone to the station to see my sisters off to Lushoto—she hugged me and called me 'my darling Jane.' What was she doing, this accomplished, bilingual, musical, sporty older woman, teaching in a colonial school in such an out-of-the-way place? She was the daughter of a Cheltenham vicar who became canon of Gloucester Cathedral. It was rumoured she had aristocratic European connections. Why was she unmarried? Had she been jilted, or lost a fiancé in the War? It would never have occurred to us to ask. She was Miss Goodwyn, as immutable as a mountain.

Now, I sit at the Registrar's desk in Miss Goodwyn's bedroom and explain myself to a well-spoken, courteous man who introduces himself as the English lecturer. Everyone else is away as the college is in recess. At first, he's cautious: I suppose it is strange for an elite magistrates' college in a forward-looking African country to double as a place of pilgrimage for nostalgic ex-colonials. Not for the first time, this simultaneous forward and backward-looking makes me slightly dizzy, but once I satisfy him that I'm not a spy, he obligingly takes me on a tour. As we walk around, he tells me that after the school closed in 1969 it became a development institute; then an 'ideological institution' until 1992, when it became the official college for the training of cadres of *Chama Cha Mapinduzi* (as TANU was renamed). My father would have enjoyed the irony. After political liberalisation in 1998 it was established as a magistrates' training college and now has four hundred students. The certification is awarded by the University of Dar and the Principal is a judge.

Double vision. As he talks, I'm taking in the staircase leading to the central courtyard, the assembly hall on one side facing the classroom block, the dormitories at either end, all astonishingly unchanged. In that assembly hall we sang sad, plaintive hymns on Sunday evenings, or watched educational documentaries sent by the British Council about the life-cycle of the mosquito, dental hygiene or the economy of Trinidad and Tobago. It was also where my friends and I performed plays, written and directed by me, and rehearsed on the break-place where we played behind the school. This was a time when my mother wrote to my grandmother, 'Jane is full of fanciful ideas.'

From the assembly hall—the stage, the windows I stared out of during sermons, the shabby walls—we move to the classrooms, and the first room we step into is the very classroom where, joining the lowest form, I began my time at school, struggling for the first time with Latin. At the back near the window, I see myself in the desk, aged eight, uncomfortable in my grey drill shorts, homesick and uncertain how to behave in this new, strange environment. On my first day I tore a page out of one of the small notebooks we had been issued with, to make a list of all my books so as to keep them in order. The teacher beating me with a ruler on the hand was my first lesson.

We walk on, out of the building, my escort proudly showing off the new lecture theatres built on the old break-place. I listen politely, but beyond them I can't help noticing that the *Bhundu,* the patch of wild ground where we built dens and hunted wild gooseberries, is still untouched. Finally, I pluck up the courage to ask if I can see inside the old buildings, and my escort reluctantly lets me through a side door into the old Girls' End (now the men's quarters). Now at last, walking down that endless, grim, gloss-painted concrete corridor, the double vision refocuses and I see it entirely as it was. Here we used to queue for inspection of uniform or line up before meals, there was the cupboard that sheltered the twice-weekly ration of sweets doled out by the matron, and there the dismal dining room where we struggled with food we couldn't eat. Beyond a few improvements for the sake of the adult students—some armchairs in front of a television—it's as dark and grim and brutal as ever. I think (but don't say) that the magistrates must be committed to improving justice to exile themselves here. Every corner brings to mind an incident, imprinted in my brain by danger, risk of punishment or sometimes just the will-to-pleasure of children who must have fun or die.

We re-emerge into the courtyard, and I say goodbye to my host, who goes off to attend other visitors. I wander along the front of the building, peering through the ground-floor windows to see if the bathrooms have changed. The only difference I can spot is that the concrete bathtubs have been replaced by showers, otherwise they're the same as when we bathed two to a tub after hockey games, and I would spit the detested coffee pudding into the toilet bowl after lunch. Across the drive, the outline of the old netball court can dimly be made out but the playing fields have gone back to water-logged pasture. The river, where in the old days laundry-women pounded our clothes and sheets on the rocks, has grown bigger, flooding the surrounding area.

I squelch back through the mud to the Lawns Hotel with its locusts and black bath water, and huddle in the bar watching CNN. Tomorrow I'm moving further up the mountain to a hotel run by Germans, who I'm sure can combat locusts, even at the price of political correctness. I need a little holiday from the past.

17. Forest of a thousand memories

Muller's Mountain Lodge is as far as I go into the Usambaras, the mountain spine stretching 200 kilometres. It's hardly any distance from Lushoto but it's another four hundred metres higher and feels much more remote. The two-storey red-brick building dates from the 1930s, so although today it's owned by Germans, it must have been built under the British. It feels weirdly familiar, but I have no memory of having been here before and put it down to its colonial atmosphere. In my warm, comfortable, insect-free upstairs room a friendly brochure offers advice on walks in the neighbourhood, but warns: 'Please consider, the way is long, stiff and stony and the way back becomes longer and longer. We want you to feel well and not to break down completely knocked out. At the other hand side we don't want to hinder you of a sportsmanlike provocation!'

I decide not to be hindered. I know that thousands of trees have been planted since Uhuru but I want to see if there's any old forest left. I set out next day with a guide, Francis Mshami, aged seventy-two. Francis is Catholic and a retired primary school teacher. He tells me his pension is twenty thousand shillings a month, about eight pounds or sixteen US dollars—which is why he offers his services as a guide. He is courtly, in that formal way of older Tanzanians, and knowledgeable about the area. He was born in a nearby village in 1935 and claims he knows the history and lineage of all the Shambaa kings. The one he names, however, isn't Shambaa, but a Chagga chief of the early 19th century from the north-eastern part of Kilimanjaro. Historians have shown that the Shambaa people of the Usambaras competed with the Chagga under Chief Horombo for control of the ivory and slave routes

that ran from the coast to Kilimanjaro, and it's possible this memory still resonates locally. It's also known that the people who became the Chagga came from many points around Kilimanjaro, including the Usambaras. Is Francis calling on oral memory or something he read long ago? I have no way of knowing, but he tells me confidently, 'King Horombo was as tall as a banana tree. He used to stride through the bananas, pushing them aside.' Francis himself is about four foot ten but as we push further and further into the forest, he strides Horombo-like through the thick undergrowth, slashing a path for us with a stick. Meek as an acolyte, I follow.

In precolonial times, the forests of the Usambaras were home to cultivators as well as incoming pastoralists, who maintained a delicate balance between human and ecological interests. Western 'scientific' notions and the resource needs of first Germany, then Britain, gradually redefined the forests as an industrial tool. In 1921, D.K.S. Grant, the first British conservator of Tanganyika's forests, described mature trees as 'idle capital'. When my father and his colleagues worked for the Forest Department in the 1950s and 60s, the Utilisation research section—which tested timber for different uses—was at Moshi, and the Silvicultural unit—which grew different species in nurseries—was here, in the Usambaras. Since Uhuru, huge numbers of trees have been planted around Lushoto to offset erosion and improve rainfall and present-day forestry policy involves joint forest management between government forest officers and villagers.

When I told Francis I wanted to see the old forest, not new tree plantations, he knew where to take me. We are in Mkwizu Forest, 1,800 feet above sea level, walking beneath immensely tall trees, sixty or seventy years old. Francis knows the names of all the trees and whether they're indigenous or exotic.

'My father was a carpenter,' he explains. 'He learnt from Mr Grant, the forester for this area.'

This is my first missed clue to who he is and where I am, and though I work out he's talking about the 1930s or 40s, my memory remains blank.

We keep walking, Francis keeps talking. 'My father made all the furniture in the lodge. He made the doors and windows too—from Usambara cedar. Mr Grant lived there before. He sold the house to Muller after his wife died. He went back to England when he was ninety-five years old.'

Something is stirring in me at this tale of a grand old man living with his wife in the forest, but still I don't make the connection. I'm too busy working out that if Francis was born in 1935, his father was probably born at the turn of the century and could have told him stories of Horombo, born less than a hundred years earlier. As we go further and further into the otherwise silent forest we're hearing loud chopping. I ask Francis about the village committees that are supposed to prevent illegal tree-felling.

He shakes his head. 'They do nothing. Women chop for firewood, men to sell, and nobody stops them.'

I remember that the Usambara forest estate is 33,000 hectares with only a handful of foresters to oversee it, and meanwhile, food has to be cooked in villages with no electricity. As always, the gap between government policy and local practice is profound.

Now it's hard to talk because we've descended into a valley where even the faintest track has disappeared. For a couple of hours I follow Francis as he slashes through thick creepers and tall, tough grasses with his stick. So intent is he on what he's doing that when a chameleon runs across his back he doesn't notice, though it occurs to me it's the only sign of animal life we've seen. Not even a snake in all this thick underbrush; the only sound the whirr of insects. Meanwhile, I worry he must be getting tired but no, Francis is a woodsman: he reads the track, warning me of nasty spikes and treacherous holes, slashing prickles and thorns out of my way. I stumble behind him until at last the track clears and we come out into a flat, open space with a tinkling stream. I throw myself gratefully on the bank and lay out the hard-boiled eggs, bread and oranges given us for a picnic by the lodge. Francis's eyes widen at the sight of the eggs and he eats three. No doubt his pension doesn't permit much protein.

'You really know the forest,' I tell Francis.

'I was here from a boy,' he replies. 'There used to be leopard, buck and many wild animals. We came with spears and bows and arrows to shoot blue monkeys, or slings to get birds. Now, people are too many and all the animals have gone. Only Colobus monkeys live here, but you hardly see them.'

We go on, and the terrain is gentler, we're walking through small farms, past people's houses. It can't be by design, but on the path we meet a farmer and Francis introduces him as Mr Joseph.

Like Francis, he too remembers old Mr Grant. 'I worked for him as cook and driver,' he says. 'He was my father. He gave me away at my wedding.'

Before I can ask more, Francis gestures at me. 'She was here in the 1960s,' he tells Joseph, who immediately starts talking with great enthusiasm.

'Bwana Grant's son Harry became a District Officer and married Rachel and had two children,' he says, 'Herren and Keit.'

Helen and Keith! But of course, I was at school with them, here at Lushoto! Helen was one of my closest friends. For a time, she and her family lived next door to us in Moshi. Joseph looks at me in delight. Beside us on the path Helen materialises, a small, wiry girl with big brown eyes, her dark hair in a page-boy bob. We shared our packed suppers on the train to Mombo, and later, we boarded the plane together that would take us to our English boarding schools. And at last I've worked it out—Mr Grant was *of course* Helen's grandfather, and I came to the house—then called Grant's Lodge—on outings from school. I'm amazed and flummoxed by my failure to see this until now, but it doesn't diminish the excitement the three of us share.

Standing there in the field with these two elderly men and the ghost of Helen I feel again the closeness of the past. Memory—theirs at least—is long, and relationships are important. Genealogy is an art in Africa, and memories go back generations. Horombo lived nearly two hundred years ago, yet he was with us in the forest. In recalling Grant's grandchildren, invoking Zamani, Joseph has found a way to give me a genealogy; to root me in Sasa, the here and now of the locality.

My mind goes back to one night recently in Moshi, when Jeremiah, the gateman at the house where I was staying, told me he used to work at a farm in Kilimanjaro as a boy, owned by a Danish family called Lund. Like Joseph, he recited the children's names: Karsten, Peter and Birgit, and, like a talisman, brought to life a teenage friendship. I saw myself at fifteen, going to a party at the farm and staying the night, going riding the next day. One of the boys—Karsten— kissed me at the party. Jeremiah and I were the same age, and we shared this memory of the Lund children. Together we paid respect to this link to the past.

I reflect that on this day, as on many other days, what I've been shown is a great delicacy of feeling. Everywhere I walk, the greetings, the questions—'Where are you going? Where are you coming from? *Karibu sana*'—the way the kids practise their primary school English: 'Good morning, this is a window, this is a foot'—are ways people use to show you they've noticed your presence and want to make you welcome. The willingness to remember the bad old colonial days without rancour, with enthusiasm and affection, is an act of extraordinary generosity. Isn't it a way of making the stranger feel at home?

On my pilgrimage to reconstruct the past, my memory is often faulty. I forget important things until someone else remembers on my behalf and the great mesh of memory entangles me. So it is that later, looking through my father's book, *The Commercial Timbers of Tanzania*, published in 1968, I come across a reference to an essay, 'Local Timbers' by D.K.S. Grant, Chief Conservator. Keith Grant, Helen's grandfather, was Head of the Forest Department from 1920 until he retired in 1939, becoming a professional cabinet maker and passing on his skills to Francis's father. In his homage to Mr Grant, I realise my father too was practising genealogy. From the Rondo Plateau in the far south to the Usambaras in the north, forests are living memorials to the people who planted and nurtured trees, and monuments for those who still do. A man or woman who plants a tree knows he or she may not see it grow to its full extent in forty or fifty years. Foresters plant for the future, following the Swahili saying, *misitu ni uhai*—the forest is alive.

It's late in the day when Francis leaves me at the old red-brick farmhouse. I'm exhausted after miles of rough walking, he's as spry as ever. I hobble gratefully into the house that now, to my eyes, looks not weirdly but ordinarily familiar. I see old

Mr Grant in the polished wooden floor, and Francis's father in the skilfully turned wooden chairs and tables. It's my last night in the Usambaras, and though I came a long way not knowing what I was looking for, in the end, I found it.

PART FIVE: MOSHI AND THE MOUNTAIN, 2

18. Music, Coffee, Clans

The way you listened to music at home in the 1950s and 60s was by playing records on a gramophone. The music my parents liked was strictly middle-brow—mostly popular classics like Mozart's 'Eine Kleine Nachtmusik', Handel's 'Water Music', Bizet's opera, 'Carmen' and Tchaikovsky's 'Swan Lake'. Inspired by the album cover with its photograph of ballerinas in feathered tutus, my sisters, Mary and Ally, loved to cavort around the living room doing arabesques. One day, when my mother was entertaining a friend to tea, she heard giggling behind the door and called them into the room. Dressed as usual only in knickers, they said they wanted to show the visitor their dancing. Anne obliged, putting Swan Lake on the gramophone, and the cavorting began.

'Very nice,' said the visitor, applauding. 'What do you call it?'

'We call it,' said Ally, 'the Dance of the Mating Swans.'

My mother had the LP of the musical *South Pacific*, and sang along to 'Some enchanted evening' and 'I'm gonna wash that man right out of my hair.' My father sang raucous renditions of an old Cole Porter number, 'Why was he born so beautiful?' but his high point was when the film of *Zorba the Greek*, based on the novel by Nikos Kazantzakis, came out in 1964. He loved it so much he bought the LP of the music and, to our mingled embarrassment and hilarity, performed Zorba's Dance around the living room, slapping the wall, stumbling into tables and kicking chairs out of the way. In the movie, Zorba's Dance is a ritual of Greek manliness contrasting with the uptight Britishness of the other main character. At moments like these, when his wild side came out, Jock was more Australian than British. When he'd had enough to drink, he'd tie a knot in the four corners of a handkerchief, put it on his head, climb on the dining table and declaim the patriotic 'Song of Australia' at the top of his voice, with gestures to match:

There is a land where summer skies
Are gleaming with a thousand dyes,
Blending in witching harmonies—in har-mon-ies!
And grassy knoll and forest height,
Are flushing in the rosy light,
And all above is azure bright...

Whereupon we'd join in bawling out the chorus: 'Austr-eye-lia, Austr-eye-lia, Austr-eye-lia!' for all we were worth.

When I became a teenager, like everyone else I collected 45 rpm short-playing records by Cliff, Elvis and the Beatles and played them on my precious portable record player. Locally-produced music infiltrated my life only occasionally, like when someone came back from school in South Africa with an album called *Wait a Minim*, recorded in 1961. The song that caught on was 'Ballad of the Southern Suburbs' by Jeremy Taylor, an Englishman poking fun at white South Africans. We knew it as *'Ag, pleez Daddy,'* but were unaware that by mixing English and Afrikaans it was flouting the apartheid ideal of racial purity. There was something deliciously transgressive for me, at eleven, in its ventriloquising of wheedling kids' voices trying to get recalcitrant parents to *pleez* do something interesting, eliciting the explosive *'Voetsak!'* (a very bad word) from the beleaguered father:

> *Ag pleez Daddy*
> *Won't you take us to the drive-in*
> *All six, seven of us, eight, nine, ten*
> *We wanna see a flick about*
> *Tarzan and the Ape Men*
> *And when the show's over*
> *You can bring us back again.*

Between verses—and quite in ignorance of the offensiveness of its language—we would bellow along to the chorus:

> *Popcorn, chewing gum, peanuts and bubble gum*
> *Ice cream, candy floss and Eskimo Pie;*
> *Ag, Daddy how we miss*
> *Nigger Balls and liquorice*
> *Pepsi Cola, Ginger Beer and Canada Dry.*

Years later and long after apartheid, I was travelling in South Africa and stopped in a tiny rural wayside shop to buy a drink from the Afrikaner owner. On the counter was a plastic jar of sweets, and on it a label had been scratched out and Black Balls written over whatever was underneath. That part of the song fell into place.

The other song that infiltrated the diet of western pop was the hauntingly beautiful Swahili love-song, *'Malaika.'* Now everyone knows it thanks to Miriam Makeba's 1974 version, but this was around 1963, so it could only have been the version recorded in Nairobi by Fadhili Williams and the Jambo Boys. I can see myself at twelve or thirteen, next to the radio (usually tuned to the BBC), transported as I listen. The song, addressed by a lover to his sweetheart, is a lament that he's too poor to marry his '*malaika*', his angel, his '*kidege*', little bird. In Williams's version, the swaying slow-dance rhythm alternates with the plangent high notes of the electric guitar—he was one of the first musicians to use the instrument in East Africa. Every note, full of longing and desire, twists my heartstrings now as it did then; the lyric, alternating its mellifluous m's and l's with its hard k's and breathy p's, somehow simultaneously expresses mourning and joy. Swahili is a musical language with a long tradition of poetic composition and performance. 'Malaika' was my unwitting introduction to it in its popular form.

When I went back to Tanzania, I realised music was everywhere—old-style dance bands, *bongo flava* or Swahili hiphop, Zanzibari *taarab* and other religious and traditional musical forms, live or on the radio. The first time I went for a walk in Marangu with a young local guide, he gave me a CD of his own hiphop that he'd recorded with friends. It was the same when I was growing up—live bands making records across East Africa, influences coming in from the Congo, Egypt, India and America—but I was unaware. It was in London in my twenties that I discovered and fell in love with African music.

Decades later, exploring the back-streets in Dar es Salaam, I stumbled on the enticingly named Dar es Salaam Music and Sports Shop. Compared to the self-conscious flashiness of high-end, city-centre, tourist-oriented businesses, the shopfront was old fashioned and down-at-heel. Inside, something of the past still hung in the air, sifting like dust in a beam of light. The original wooden counters were in place, scuffed but kept polished; on the walls, glass fronted record racks were all the emptier for holding a scattering of cassettes. Yellowed LP covers—*The Sound of Music*, Al Stewart, John Denver—rubbed shoulders on the walls with a drum, a couple of guitars, a few badminton and tennis racquets. The acolyte of this neglected shrine, a patient, grey-haired man, stood behind the counter. Ramesh Kothari, the current shop-owner, told me the family's involvement in music started with his uncle.

'He ran the original, Kenyan-owned shop, Assanand and Sons. The shop was already there when I was born in 1944.'

Ramesh was the son of an immigrant from Gujarat, part of the great influx from India that started in the 19th century and built itself into a flourishing merchant class. When his father took over the shop in 1960, he added sports goods to the sale of musical instruments and records.

'I joined my father after leaving school,' Ramesh told me. 'Even after Uhuru most of the customers were foreigners. I became an expert in supplying them with classical music imported from Europe, the USA and India, as well as R&B, blues and jazz. By 1975 most ex-pats had left and we moved into African music from Kenya and Zaire… local bands like Dar es Salaam Jazz, Western Jazz, Morogoro Jazz and Kiko Kids, alongside country music—Jim Reeves, Dolly Parton.'

The Kotharis' business, like so many, was badly hit by socialist policies outlawing private enterprise and ownership. The nationalisation of buildings after 1971 triggered a huge exodus of Indian families. Ramesh's father was one of those who returned to India and later died there. Ramesh stayed, but had to contend with a ban on luxury goods and imports. After liberalisation in 1994 business picked up again, but by then it was competing with the new rage for audio cassettes and pirated recordings.

Standing in his musty shop, Ramesh was a refugee from another era. In colonial days the shop's street address used to be Acacia Avenue, which became Independence and finally Samora Avenue. The ever-grander names traced the town's evolution from colonial port to independent capital to pan-Africanist revolutionary lodestar. Dar had changed around him, and he hardly recognised the placid old city in the high-rise, high-density place it had become. He was, he admitted, ready to retire: glad to relinquish the hassle of handling musical contracts and keeping up with the latest musical trends.

'I am sixty-three,' he said wryly, 'a bit old for hiphop. I knew all about Cliff Richard and Pat Boone, but now my daughters are grown up, for whom am I doing it? There is an end to it.'

One local musician whose records Ramesh must have stocked was Frank Humplick of Moshi. He played with the Jambo Boys of 'Malaika' fame and even composed for them. With his various bands, he made recordings with Gallotone, Troubadour, HMV and East African Records, and was one of the most famous African musicians of the 50s and 60s. There was also a family singing group, Frank Humplick and his Sisters. When I was sixteen, I went with my parents to a dance at the Livingstone Hotel in Moshi, where Frank and his band, the Rhythmites, played every weekend. The Livingstone, a gracious, curved building on the corner of a block in the town centre where all sorts of events were held, was the most glamorous place in Moshi. I wore the 'twist dress' my mother had made me, a straight multicoloured shift to the hips and then a pleated frill, worn with big hooped earrings and shoes with a slight heel. It was 1967, but we were always a few years behind fashion-wise. It was my first grown-up dance, and I was breathless with excitement as boys my age as well as their fathers asked me to dance. When it ended with a cooked buffet breakfast at 2am, I was amazed to discover you could have breakfast in the middle of the night.

It was John Bennett, cousin to the Brice-Bennetts in Marangu, who told me I should look Frank Humplick up in Lushoto. I reached his house down a long muddy track perched precariously on the back of a motorbike taxi. Frank and his wife Betty welcomed me and Betty brought us tea and biscuits. I was sorry when she left us alone as I could see she too had a story, but no one had told me so I wasn't prepared. By the time we met, Frank was eighty and had been retired seventeen years. He and Betty had been married for over half a century.

Frank told me he'd built the house after buying land from departing Europeans post-Uhuru. As we talked, I discovered that, like John himself, he was the mixed-race son of a Chagga mother and a European father, born on his father's coffee estate in Kibosho on the slopes of Kilimanjaro. His mother was one of the very first Chagga Christians, baptised a Catholic in 1898. This would have made her a member of the new elite, born of Christianity and education, that has propelled Chagga people into high positions the length and breadth of Tanzania. Humplick Senior, an Austrian, bought his land in 1911 when the Germans were in control; he died four years after Frank was born in 1927 and Frank and his two sisters—presumably because they were half-white—were left to the trusteeship of the British government. So began a series of mission school experiences under the care of German nuns. 'It was a bit tough,' was his only comment. They recognised his musical ability though, because at school he learned to play trumpet and guitar; afterwards, he studied horticulture, getting a diploma and then a job with the Tanganyika Coffee Board in Moshi.

Frank's story hardly follows a straight course. From running experimental coffee stations he went into business, buying tractors and hiring them out to local farmers. He also drove a taxi in Moshi for three years, when he used to take a young John Bennett to Nairobi to catch the plane to Europe for school. For ten years, from 1970, he managed a coffee estate in Kenya, and in 1984 moved to Lushoto. There he ran a truck business transporting produce to other parts of the country.

Meeting Frank brought home the way children of mixed race resulted from the German occupation, which wasn't so much the case with the British—perhaps because they were there as administrators rather than settlers. Betty, who married Frank in 1954, was the mixed-race daughter of a German farmer and a teacher; Tekla, one of Frank's singing sisters, married a mixed-race person, as did her brother. When I remarked on this Frank reeled off a list of mixed marriages, mostly with Germans, but also Greeks, Italians and Arabs. He said before Uhuru there were places you couldn't go—clubs and hotels that turned you away if you tried to go in—and certain schools, but mixed-race girls (including some fathered by priests) were accepted at Kifungilo Girls' School in Lushoto, founded for orphans in 1935. This was where Betty, Frank's wife, got her primary education. Today, Kifungilo is one of Tanzania's leading girls' schools. Despite the evidence of mixed-race children, according to Frank there was less discrimination under the British.

'The Germans,' he said, 'were very strict. An officer could hang his helmet on a stick and you had to salute it.'

John Bennett, who introduced me to Frank Humplick, is the son of Arthur 'Chagga' Bennett and a Chagga mother, and nephew of Frank, father of the Brice-Bennetts.

Tanzania is a many-storied place, but John's story of racial and cultural entanglement is especially intricate. Arthur Bennett came to Tanganyika when, after fighting in World War One, both in the trenches and as a fighter pilot, he couldn't find work in England. He saw an advertisement for opportunities in Tanganyika Territory and came out as a labour officer in 1921. His first job was to get a sisal estate going at Ruvu, some forty miles from Dar, when the sisal industry was in its infancy.

Although it was so ubiquitous as to appear indigenous, sisal arrived in the country by a roundabout route. An agave that originated in Mexico, sisal was a protected plant, but this didn't stop Dr Richard Hindorf, a German scientist, from smuggling a hundred young sisal plants into Tanganyika in 1890. By the 1950s, Tanganyika was the biggest producer in the world and remained so until nationalisation in 1971. Sisal, whether putting out its fleshy dark green spikes in the fields or as a white fibre drying on racks, was integral to our landscape. As the raw material of rope, mats, bags, twine and, strangely enough, dartboards, it was in demand all over the world.

In the end, it wasn't sisal where Arthur made his mark, but coffee. Kilimanjaro had been the centre of coffee growing since the Arabica bean was introduced at Kilema by Catholic missionaries in the 19th century. Its first champion was a district commissioner in the 1920s, an aristocratic Scot, an anthropologist and author of *Kilimanjaro and its People—a History of the Wachagga*. Charles Dundas was that contradictory entity—a colonial administrator on the side of the native. He saw the potential for the little coffee plantings or *vihamba*, to band together and take on the larger producers, and made himself unpopular with the settler plantation owners by enabling the Chagga farmers to compete on the world market. He's credited with starting Tanganyika's most successful cooperative, the Kilimanjaro Native Cooperative Union (KNCU), which has represented coffee farmers in the region since 1930. When Arthur Bennett was posted to Moshi at the end of the 1920s, he took over the running of the KNCU after Dundas was posted elsewhere. Like his predecessor, Arthur became a champion of the Chagga. He lived the rest of his life in Moshi where he married three times—John's mother, daughter of the Mangi Mkuu (foremost chief) of Rombo, was his first wife.

Throughout the 1950s and 60s coffee, along with education, ensured the development of the Kilimanjaro region. After Uhuru, Nyerere attempted to ounteract colonial capitalism with African socialism, known as *Ujamaa*. This involved forcing farmers and urban dwellers into villages where they were to practise collective agriculture, and was fiercely contested by the Chagga who valued their independence and knew how to organise. The KNCU, which predated post-Uhuru socialist policies by decades, became too successful for its own good and was nationalised in 1977. In 1984 the KNCU partially regained its autonomy, but in the early 1990s liberalisation of the coffee industry meant cooperatives had to compete with private companies. Many did not survive, but the KNCU clung on and eventually regained its pre-eminence as the largest buyer of Kilimanjaro small-holder coffee.

From 1930 the KNCU boasted its own headquarters in Moshi, and in 1950 Charles Dundas laid the foundation stone for a new building. This was described by visiting British administrator, Randal Sadleir, as having 'splendidly equipped modern offices (which) also housed a fully residential KNCU commercial college... an excellent multiracial hotel, the KNCU Hostel... and a top-floor scenic restaurant with wonderful views of the mountain.' We used to go up in the lift—itself an adventure in a place of mainly one-storey buildings—to this scenic restaurant for refreshments when we were out shopping with my mother; it was there I had my last glimpse of Martha. An elegant plaque at street level commemorates Dundas by his title, *Wasaoye-o-Wachagga* (Elder of the Chagga), and bears witness to 'the industry and cooperation of the Wachagga farmers on the slopes of Kilimanjaro'.

Titles are testimony to the respect and esteem in which an individual is held by the community, and Arthur Bennett was also given one: *Mbuya-o-Wachagga* (Friend of the Chagga)—'Chagga' Bennett for short. The writer, John Gunther, who met him when he visited Moshi researching his travel book, *Inside Africa*

(1953), described him as 'one of the wisest white men in Africa,' and advised that, 'Old-fashioned people who do not think that Africans are capable of handling their own affairs should visit the smart, efficiently run headquarters of this cooperative in Moshi... This organisation has given vigour and freshness to the whole community, and opens the way towards what Africa needs above all—the creation of a prosperous middle-class.'

'Chagga' Bennett was a law unto himself. In 1939, when he was put in charge of the detention centre for 'enemy' nationals in Moshi—Germans and Italians, many of whom were his drinking buddies—according to his son John, he allowed at least one to escape. When his brother, Frank Brice-Bennett, died suddenly in 1960 the family went to live with Uncle Arthur in Moshi for a couple of years before returning to Marangu, and Desmond remembers him being relatively wealthy.

'When he sent us for cigarettes, he always said, 'Keep the change, my dear.' And so he died penniless.'

It turned out Arthur's pay was, according to a pre-War agreement, pegged to the market price of coffee, so when coffee boomed after the War he became rich. Having no interest in money, he didn't bother paying tax and gave it all away. When he eventually became senile and was made the ward of Peggy Brice-Bennett, she found herself hounded for back-tax and Arthur's house in Mission St under threat of being impounded by the Tax Office. As Seamus tells me, things are in this parlous state when Peggy receives a phone-call from the office of the President requesting he be allowed to visit his old friend—in the run-up to Uhuru Arthur had been the European representative for the Kilimanjaro area on the Legislative Council in Dar (there were three, European, Asian and African). Peggy prepares for the visit by cleaning the house and coaching Arthur on who his visitor is. It seems all is well until JKN arrives, with a single police car escort, and Peggy leads him into Arthur's room, whereupon Arthur can't remember a thing.

'Arthur,' prompts Peggy, 'it's the President.'

'Which president?' asks Arthur crossly.

'I'm Julius,' says the President, 'not president.' It's no good, and JKN takes his leave with tears in his eyes.

'Such a fine man. I should have visited sooner. But is there anything I can do for him?'

'Well,' admits Peggy, 'his tax affairs are a bit of a mess and the Tax Office is threatening to take his house.'

'Oh dear,' responds JKN. 'Let me see what I can do.'

Days later, Peggy receives another phone-call from Dar with a message from the President: 'Mr Bennett's tax affairs are in order.'

If the Bennetts are a tribe, Arthur's son John is sultan of a small empire on the outskirts of Moshi, where he sits enthroned under the eaves of a roof at one side of a yard crammed with vehicles for hire. His cousin Desmond calls it 'lording it among the Land Rovers'. Here John, glasses on nose, cigarette-holder clenched between teeth, holds court at a battered and pock-marked wooden table, surrounded by cooler chests, old engines, disused fans, cardboard boxes, drums, piles of tyres, trailers and an oily workbench. Though he likes to present a gruff and peremptory exterior, he has time for the many visitors who drop in for a beer and cheerful abuse. If you're there at lunch time, he'll feed you with food from the

Golden Shower restaurant run by his third wife, Vicky.

John Bennett was born in 1946, and lived with his grandfather, the Mangi Mkuu of Rombo—the mountain kingdom that gave its name to Rombo Avenue, where we lived in Moshi. Perhaps because of his chiefly status, he was sent to school in Uganda at the age of seven under the aegis of the King of Buganda. John grew up speaking kiChagga and kiSwahili; in Uganda he learnt kiGanda. One language he didn't learn was English, so when he found himself, at the age of nine, at Cranleigh public school in Surrey, he had to learn it in a hurry. After four years he was moved to the *Ecole d'Humanité* in Switzerland and had to learn French and German. As a result, when he came home in 1959, now aged thirteen, he couldn't communicate even with his mother and had to relearn his two first languages. He had just managed to do so when he was sent off again.

'Sometimes,' he said, 'I had the feeling I wasn't wanted in Tanganyika. I was going to spend the rest of my days in Europe.'

If his grandfather, the Mangi Mkuu, hadn't threatened his father, he might have done, but John belonged more to the Chagga than to the European elite among whom he was being educated. He finally returned home in 1961, by which time his uncle Frank had died and he found he was sharing the house—Karanga House at Kiyungi Estate—with his cousins. When I asked what he did, John said, 'I was a *machinga*—a street trader, someone who marches around selling things.' What John meant by this answer was that he could go anywhere and feel at home. Moshi is a pivotal point for tourism on the so-called Northern Circuit, and in 1977 he started a tour business.

'That's how I was given a Masai wife,' he told me, smiling. 'When I took people to Ngorongoro Crater, I met a lot of Masai there and had many friends. I sent one young boy, Shinini, to school all the way to Standard 6 at age sixteen, and got to know his father very well. I used to visit him in his *boma* in the *manyatta*—the Masai compound. A Masai *boma* is incredibly comfortable and clean. You sleep on hides with a fire in the cold season. Anyway, one day he brought a little girl of three or four. I knew exactly what was going on and I tried to refuse. Several years later, the old man arrives at the house in Moshi accompanied by a friend. With them is a little girl of ten or twelve. Well, I invite them to sit, eat, drink, and then he announces that he's brought this daughter who he's kept intact just for me.

No embellishment, no circumcision. It turned out they'd walked for a day and a half from Lilongo to Ngorongoro, then taken a bus to Arusha, then on to Moshi—altogether over two hundred miles. After that, I couldn't refuse. I called my then wife, Heddy, and told her my dilemma. We already had eight children, but we started teaching the girl kiSwahili and sending her to school. Her name is Serema, and eventually she married a Chagga man. I gave away my "wife", can you imagine? I never even touched her.'

Serema's father died a rich man with ten wives, and John went to pay his respects. ('I slept with the eighth wife on that occasion.') Serema's brother came to John and complained that according to custom, they couldn't circumcise her younger sisters because Serema hadn't undergone the ritual.

'I told him Serema belonged to me.'

Although genital cutting is an important initiation rite in Masai culture, it's painful and dangerous and many Masai girls run away from it and many local activists support them. Through John's protection, Serema was able to avoid genital cutting. Since 2014, Safe Houses, presided over by Mama Rhobi Samwelly, one of Africa's anti-FGM activists, have protected many more.

The Masai, denigrated in socialist Tanzania as *washenzi*—unclothed savages—have seen their culture eroded and lands encroached on by farming and tourism. At the same time, the Masai *moran*, the young male warrior, swathed in red and propped on a spear in his characteristic one-legged stance, is an enduring touristic icon. Driven from their traditional areas and practices, Masai have had to negotiate once unimaginable change. Now, they are everywhere, not only as security guards, an occupation that allows them to draw on their traditional skills, but as writers, doctors, lawyers, rappers, handicraft makers and sellers—even a prime minister. Considering they're plains people, one place where they strike an incongruous note is Zanzibar, where they make a brisk trade selling handmade trinkets to tourists on the seafront.

In 2013, serving on the Main Jury at the Zanzibar International Film Festival (ZIFF), I stepped out onto the roof terrace of my hotel one morning to find two young men having breakfast at one of the tables. Wrapped in *shuka*, the predominantly red plaid cloth that resembles tartan, they were instantly identifiable as Masai. Frank Kaipai Ikoyo was a village headman and subject of a documentary film that was in contention at the festival. The other was his friend, Juma. Ikoyo was a sign of the changes that had come to the Masai. He had completed primary school and, though he was only twenty-six at the time, was elected chief of his community because he was educated, and education was seen as a defence against the many 'lions' threatening the Masai way of life. The film, by German filmmaker, Peter Biello, showed how he had to negotiate the benefits of schooling alongside the desire to retain cultural identity. He thus became an advocate for girls' education while ensuring young warriors would still be trained to hunt lions—the rite of passage for Masai men.

The film, *The Chairman and the Lions*, did a good job of conveying how Frank Kaipai Ikoyo could resolve seemingly insurmountable problems through charisma and diplomacy. As judges, we were allowed to make a personal choice for the Special Jury Award—and we unanimously agreed it should go to *The Chairman and the Lions*. The award ceremony takes place in the Old Fort in Stone Town, which encloses an ancient, semi-circular stone amphitheatre. Ikoyo and Juma came on stage, resplendent in red blankets, and with great dignity accepted the award on behalf of the filmmaker. Later that night, we stood together in the old fort watching a *taarab* band, talking as best we could in a pidgin mashup of Swahili and English. As we walked back to the hotel through the deserted streets of Stone Town, I thought how ironic it was that cinema had brought us together in person to share this moment.

19. The waHindi Clan: Himat and Pushpa

Returning to Tanzania as an adult led to many connections with people I could never have got to know as a child, when life was hedged about with cultural and racial preconceptions and colonial decorum. After Uhuru, Indian children were accepted at Lushoto school where my friend Rehma was a daughter of the great Karimjee dynasty that dominated commerce in Dar. Before Uhuru, however, Indians were a class apart, though this apartness was nuanced. As far back as 1958, Anne described to Kitty how, on a family holiday in Tanga, we'd been invited to tea at the home of 'some wealthy Indians'. No name. I imagine the connection was cricket, which Jock played up and down the country. On those carefully watered pitches, European and Indian teams faced each other, while their families mingled on the side-lines.

I delighted the host when I praised his house as being 'just like the palace of a king'. We were given expensive presents and served sweetened Nescafe from a teapot. Anne and Jock tried to prevent the twins, aged four, from biting off pieces of a pink-lit, marble model of the Taj Mahal. They thought it was a cake. This sort of social mixing suggests Indians, at any rate, didn't see the distinction so carefully preserved by the British. And why should they? They had been there far longer and were, overall, much wealthier than the colonial civil servants. With India's history of colonisation, too, there was nothing strange or mysterious about the British—the shared love of tea and cricket being two examples—and this degree of familiarity must have rubbed off to some extent.

My father, for whom Africans were very much a servant class, always spoke respectfully of Mistry, the Indian carpenter with whom he experimented on different types of wood. Though Mistry is the generic name for a master-craftsman, derived from Portuguese by way of *mestre*, Mistry was his actual family name so he must have come from a long line of them. Mistry's work has outlived him: I still eat at a table he carved, a solid shining rectangular slab of *mvule* set on an angular, art deco base.

A mark of the difference between white relations with African and Indian was the fact that, every so often, Mistry would, like the 'wealthy Indians' in Tanga, invite our family to tea. We would drive into town to the apartment block that housed Mistry's family, with its balconies adorned with washing, and walk upstairs to his quarters. Here we sat in his living room, with its carpets, plushly upholstered ofas and its faint sweetish aroma, around a central coffee table that no doubt he had made. We were entertained by gracious sari-clad ladies, one of whom—Mistry's wife, or mother—poured hot sweet tea boiled up in a kettle with condensed milk. The ladies plied us with small delicate cakes, that looked delicious but when we bit them squirted syrup or crumbled into our laps. Brought up on rice pudding and junket, sponge cake and drop scones, we would be overwhelmed by their sweetness and strangeness. My mother would open the empty handbag she'd brought especially for the purpose and slip into it the food we couldn't eat, so as not to offend. Though it was thrilling to taste things so outside our conventional British-colonial repertoire, it's only now I can name those once-unfamiliar flavours—rose-water, cardamom, pistachio, saffron. Even yogurt was exotic. Of course, we ate curry and samosas, who didn't? Beyond that we had no idea what constituted Indian cooking, or that it varied with region and religion. This tea-time courtesy was one-way—we never reciprocated. Perhaps it was an attempt to approximate a British custom, and perhaps it was beyond my mother to recreate an Indian one—although she had been in India during the War.

After my first return to Moshi, I wrote an account published in a Canadian online journal. It reached the eyes of a reader in Toronto, who wrote to me. Shrikant Mehta had grown up in Moshi but left in 1968—the same year we did—and ended up as an international manager for the Canadian tax authorities.

'Having moved from country to country,' he asked, 'do you ever feel you have locked away parts of your life in little boxes? Boxes you put away in storage and have never opened and shared the contents with anyone. Because, even if you open them, no one will ever understand unless they were there at the time.'

As a long-term immigrant in the Caribbean, I knew what he was talking about. Shrikant reached out of his box and introduced me to his uncle, Himat Shah, who had brought him up, and his wife, Pushpa. Shrikant also showed my Moshi story to another of Himat's nephews in Canada, Kumar Malde, who in turn wrote to me. Kumar had joined the Forest Department Utilisation Section two years after my father left, and knew his book, *The Commercial Timbers of Tanzania*. For three years, until he too emigrated to Canada, he said, 'I continued work on some of the remaining important species and added data to the work of your father.' He remembered Jock in person, not from forestry but from the Moshi Cricket Club—'as a young boy I played a few matches against him.' Kumar, I worked out, was about five years older than me. When my sisters and I were hanging about on the boundary at one of those cricket matches, while Jock bowled and Anne helped set out the cakes for tea, young Kumar was strapping on his pads and marching out to bat.

Through this Indian-Tanzanian-Canadian diaspora, I am introduced to Himat and Pushpa. I've already heard stories of how, in the early 70s as his own property was being nationalised, Himat still found time to drive to outlying farms and warn their owners. Now, on my second return to Moshi, he meets me at the airport. Dressed in a spotless, knee-length *kurta*, his greeting is ceremonious. At first, he comes across as grave and dignified, but then sparkles with humour. He drives me home, to the flat above the shop where they live in the town centre

where I meet Pushpa. Sari-clad and gentle, she exudes grace and warmth. Serious at first, after a while she relaxes and grows talkative. They are hospitable and welcoming, in the simple, straightforward East African way that takes sharing as a given. We sit at a table made by Mistry, identical to the one I inherited, and I taste the first of many delicious south Indian vegetarian meals cooked by Pushpa. She grows and grinds her own spices, sitting on the floor to use a heavy, archaic grinding stone. I get a strong sense of the enjoyment of life from Himat, who in the evening blithely opens bottles of wine and watches *Sopranos* with me. Pushpa is quieter and less social, but both are inclusive and open—an advertisement for the beliefs they share.

I can't believe it's taken me forty years to come across this couple, a decade or so older than me, who were right here in Moshi when I was growing up. Born in 1941, Pushpa has lived here longer than most people alive in the town today. As I sit in Pushpa's own little curio shop drinking *chai tangawizi*—ginger tea—it comes home to me again how narrow a world I inhabited, where Indians were shopkeepers and traders and carpenters but not, to me then, people with rich and interesting lives.

Himat's mother, who was married at fifteen, had nine living children. Of the four brothers only Himat and the eldest, known as Babu Bhai, were left in Moshi. Walking home, Pushpa shows me her parents' house, dated 1949, one of the oldest in the part of town near the railway. In 1971, any privately-owned building not being lived in was taken over, so all business premises were nationalised. Those whose losses were heaviest were coffee and sisal farmers, whose land and houses were taken, and Indian business people. Himat's family, which had been in East Africa seventy years, was among them. When I ask how she feels about the loss of their properties, the splintering of their families, she says, 'I decided not to spoil my soul by being angry.'

This philosophical attitude has a lot to do with Jainism, the religion they practise. She and Himat go to the temple every morning at 6 o'clock and meditate for an hour. I learn from Pushpa that the word Jain comes from *jina*, meaning conqueror, in the sense of someone who has transcended the material world and achieved perfection. She invites me to go to the temple with them for prayers one evening, and I accept. Jainism is more of a philosophy than a religion and can be followed by anyone regardless of faith. I'm relieved to hear this since I don't follow a faith and was put off religion by too much praying at school. It's based on four practical principles: non-violence (hence vegetarianism); non-acquisitiveness; the 'theory of relativity', meaning that it can accommodate all viewpoints ; and karma, or fate. The temple is in the building of the Oswal Association, which was started in 1948 to do work in the community.

This evening there are twelve of us in the temple: five women including me, and seven men, all but me related. We sit on plastic chairs facing a decorative altar hung with flowers and lights and featuring different Hindu gods. I'm impressed by what an active part the women play in the ritual, which doesn't require a priest or celebrant. As we chant and sing prayers the electricity fails, and we sit in semi-darkness with just the glow of candles from the altar. From the shadows a man's voice rises in a beautiful, plangent song. Women's voices are raised in reply. Not understanding the Gujarati words, I'm mesmerised by the slow cadence, the repetitive chorus, the counterpoising of deep and high.

So great is the sense of peace surrounding us it's a jolt when it ends. In the ante-room Pushpa introduces me to her brothers-in-law, and the three of us go off to shop at the supermarket before they drop me home. Filling a basket, standing at the till, part of me is still sitting in the dark in the temple. I feel I've caught a glimpse of the stillness that gives Pushpa her serenity.

When I was growing up, the town centre boasted several Indian emporia named for their owners—Mulji's, Moledina's, Khambaita's. These buildings,

proudly inscribed with their dates of construction, were once thriving businesses selling clothing, groceries or household goods. My parents relied on Mulji's for English delicacies like Branston Pickle (strictly 'not for children') and Cooper's Oxford Marmalade. Today Mulji is a ghostly presence, his name still visible but almost obscured behind a new shopfront. Somehow, the Shahs have held onto their family home, Premcolt House, where the Canadian nephews grew up. Though they are now tenants in their own building, the two-storey building is a landmark of continuity on J.K. Nyerere Road, Moshi's central thoroughfare.

Today it's divided into the upstairs apartment where Himat and Pushpa live, and the shop downstairs, Chui Industries. This is where I meet Babu Bhai, Himat's elder brother. The shop's dim interior is packed with curios, cloth, *kangas*, jewellery, 'I have climbed Kilimanjaro' t-shirts and items of furniture from the factory in another part of town. Babu Bhai is more than a shopkeeper however. His name, an honorific combining affection and respect, means something like Elder Brother, and before Uhuru he was on the Town Council and a member of the Chamber of Commerce. Now aged eighty, he stands upright behind the counter as he unravels the family history.

'My father, Devchand Nathu Shah,' he tells me, 'arrived in Mombasa in 1914 as a boy of thirteen, from the Indian province of Gujarat. He was one of many youngsters who came by steamer in response to the British government's invitation to Indians to come and work in East Africa. They were met by members of the Shah clan or caste, and given jobs in Shah firms. Devchand also joined a Shah firm but within a few months he and his younger brother, both still teenagers, had started their own business, Devchand Nathu and Co Ltd. They sold foodstuffs, then started importing tea from India, and finally went into textiles. In 1918, when he was still only seventeen, Devchand went back to India and returned with a wife, Nandkunver, a girl of fifteen. I, Babu, was born in Mombasa in 1927, their second child and the eldest son.'

'How did they get to Moshi?' I ask.

'The Kenya market was saturated with Shahs. In 1928, aged twenty-seven, Devchand decided to expand into Tanganyika. He chose Moshi for its convenient location on the railway to the coast and numerous relatives followed him. He bought this house, which became the family home, from Barclays Bank in 1935.'

Devchand and his family flourished in Moshi, moving into dairy products and flour milling, and in the process building homes, shops, factories. In 1967, the government declared a monopoly on dairy and grain products and the dairy and flour mill were forced out of business. In the early 70s, they lost the rest of their properties. Most dispossessed people of foreign ancestry left the country, and the Oswal community shrank from five hundred and twenty-five at its height to around fifty today. Born in Tanganyika, Himat and Babu had no links to India; the British government was granting passports to East African citizens, but despite all they had been forced to give up, they renounced their British citizenship and became Tanzanian. The rest of the family, children included, dispersed to Kenya, Britain and Canada. Though Babu has visited India, 'The link is broken.'

Of their enterprises, only one remains. In the 1960s, when he was in his thirties, Himat noticed unwanted bits of hides lying outside the local tanning factory and experimented making coasters and key-rings out of scraps of leather.

'What made you think you could be a leather worker?' I asked him.

Himat shrugged. 'As a child I saw people making shoes in the street. I taught myself from an old book someone gave me, *The Leathercraftsman*, published in 1936.'

With no other training or experience, he launched the business that today is among the country's foremost small industries. But there's more to it than that. In the early morning, in the crowd of people trekking through the dust to work in Moshi's industrial quarter, a man with withered legs pushes himself along the ground with his hands. At the gate to Shah Industries, he joins an albino man, and they enter the factory together. Himat had been in the local Lions' Club for nearly ten years, raising money for wheelchairs and working with disabled people, when one day in 1976, a severely disabled polio victim presented himself at the factory asking for work. Himat took him on. In a country with no safety-net, where polio

is still rife and disabled people tend to be relegated to begging on the street, word spread. Soon other disabled or marginalised people approached Himat for jobs, and he took them on and trained them too. In Tanzania, albinos face a special kind of discrimination and danger, since many believe that their body-parts have magical properties. Many albinos have been hacked to death to make money for medicine men. By the 1980s, of three hundred workers at Shah Industries, fifty-five were handicapped. Though the workforce has now dwindled to forty, seventeen of them are disabled. Hardly another business in the country can claim such a record.

Whether because of its philanthropy or the pleasantness of its surroundings, Himat's factory, while it hums with activity, is somehow an oasis of peace and calm. You approach through a small, well-tended garden abutting the main entrance; on the outside wall, luxuriant creepers compete for space with a Tinga Tinga mural, the brightly-coloured Tanzanian naïve art form depicting wild animals. Inside, the quiet bubbling of fish-tanks and the slow swish of fins offer a muted background to the low murmur of conversation. Everyone is getting on with what they have to do. Small groups are drilling, grinding, tooling, machining, painting, cutting and assembling. There is no overseer. Pastory, the albino man, lifts a giant pair of horns onto a scale, while telling me he's just come back from a convention in Dar he attended at Himat's expense. Among a menagerie of half life-size models of African wild animals, a young man lovingly paints the neck of a giraffe. He shows me how, to make a rhino, giraffe or other animal, an outer leather coat is cut to shape, wetted and plastered onto a wooden frame, where it dries into a perfect replica of the real

thing. So mobile and lifelike is the leather that, once painted, you have trouble distinguishing fake from real, and so you find them decorating safari lodges and hotels up and down the country.

It's complicated being an industrialist in Tanzania. In his office, Himat shows me a newspaper report on World Albino Day, which Pastory attended as a member of the executive of the national Albino Society that fights for albino rights. The report quotes the Prime Minister challenging 'wealthy persons' to support disabled people, unaware of Himat's record. In his upcountry outpost, not only is he somewhat overlooked by those at the coast, he also struggles in an economy with a history of exporting raw materials, not geared to the manufacture or export of locally-made products. Even so, in 1995 Himat was awarded the country's highest honour: the Order of the Arusha Declaration, First Class. It's given to 'Faithful citizens who at considerable personal sacrifices have diligently earned great distinction for the national economy, politically, socially, and in defence of the nation.'

Tanzania today contains this contradiction: the historical residue of Nyerere's great nationalisation experiment even after years of liberalisation. Despite all the personal sacrifices a good citizen may make for the sake of the nation. *Maendeleo*—development—one of the cornerstones of Nyerere's socialism, today means being able to buy the things that signify modernity, to become a consumer. The Shahs, in their modest consumption and almost ascetic way of life, hark back to an earlier period. But a house signifies more than having arrived financially: roots, family, continuity, shelter, hospitality. Belonging. The government still owns Himat's family's properties. He doesn't mind so much about the mill and the dairy. What he finds painful is paying rent to live in his mother's house. He has taken a lawyer and made representations, but this faithful citizen still can't get his house back.

Himat, like Pushpa, has decided not to spoil his soul by being angry. Every day, at the Jain temple, they renew their pact with karma—to do only good, whatever the world does to them.

20. Putting down roots

In February 1967, I wrote to my parents from 'Roderic', my English school boarding house:

> 'I wish I could think of more to tell you but nothing seems important to me any more except thinking about Moshi, which I do constantly, and certainly nothing interesting ever happens here. Please forgive the uninteresting, unenthusiastic letter but I can't seem to summon up enthusiasm for anything much while I'm mouldering in Roderic!'

The mouldering was temporarily alleviated by the visit to me and my sisters of a graceful, elegant woman and her perfect little blonde daughter. Sylvia Emmanuel and her husband Nick, friends of our parents, ran a farm some miles outside Moshi. Sylvia, we were impressed to learn, had been a pupil at our school fifteen or so years before—more evidence we too could survive and have 'normal' adult lives. Her little boy, Greg, was the same age as our youngest sister, Sally, and would later come to her seventh birthday party, in the garden of our last house in Moshi.

Back in Moshi forty years later, I hear that the Emmanuels are still on their farm. Remembering the visit that enlivened our bleak school existence, I contact Sylvia to ask if I can return it. Greg—now in his forties—drives me out to the farm his parents have clung to through thick and thin. Greg went to school in Moshi before studying in the US, becoming an engineer and marrying an American. After thirteen years he returned to manage the farm, with a plan to diversify its output with flowers and vegetables. And the little blonde sister? Well, he has two sisters, one in England and one in Naxos, Greece.

'Why did you come back?' I ask.

'I thought I could do business here,' is the laconic reply. 'The main problems are managing labour and the fact that there's no law.' He thinks for a minute. 'Things change all the time. There's no consistency. Lots of complicated taxes.'

We follow the dirt track through orderly fields of coffee until we arrive at the farmhouse. Sylvia, now in her seventies, meets us on the lawn, erect and slender, her beauty undiminished. She and I amble around her garden with the dogs, admiring the pond and tropical flowerbeds. A cat stalks silently behind us. Sylvia's garden, its shadowy clumps of green and brilliant flashes of colour, brings back

Moshi Garden Club competitions, the women with their exquisite blooms, the children's miniature gardens. I see my mother's shadow on the grass as she waters her precious roses—the bushes brought specially from Nairobi—hear her and her friends as they walk endlessly in each other's gardens, murmuring a mellifluous litany:

Bougainvillea Oleander Portulaca Dahlia
Canna Lantana Zinnia Jacaranda
Poinciana Plumbago Anthurium Antirrhinum
Herald's Trumpet Morning Glory Golden Shower
Bird of Paradise Barbiton Daisy Frangipani
Flame Tree Bottle Brush Tree
Ginger Lily Red-hot Poker
African Violet
Hibiscus
Phlox
Yesterday-today-and-tomorrow

We climb the steps to the verandah of the old German-built one-storey house, long and low and built of bricks, and as I sit I realise it has an unimpeded view of the mountain, shining in the evening sun. It's like having a seat in the stalls. Sylvia pours tea into delicate, flowered, Wedgwood cups, just like the ones that used to appear on the tea trolley alongside the cake and sandwiches every afternoon at four o'clock in Rombo Avenue. Now my sister Ally has them in her London flat. I feel Anne sitting beside us as Sylvia, in her cut-glass English accent, tells her story. (I hear Anne's voice as I write this, saying reprovingly when complimented on her own style of speaking, 'No, I don't have an accent—*you* have the accent.')

Sylvia grew up, it turns out, in Moshi and other places in East Africa, the daughter of an English doctor. In 1950, she was sent, as was I fourteen years later, to school in Cheltenham. Then she read history at Girton College, Cambridge, graduated in 1956, joined the Colonial Service and returned as a teacher, posted to a girls' school in the village of Machame, just up the road from the farm. It was here she met Nick, and they were married in 1961, when she was twenty-seven.

Two things, then, make her remarkable: first, the Cambridge education, at a time—the 1950s—when it was still relatively unusual for women to go to university, and at Cambridge women were a tiny privileged minority—one of them to every ten men. (By 1970, when I found myself at an Oxford women's college, men still outnumbered women by four to one.) Girton, Sylvia's college, founded in 1869, was the first Cambridge women's college, but women weren't accorded full status or proper degrees for nearly another eighty years, until 1947—

nine years before she graduated.

Virginia Woolf never got over being refused entry to a library at one of the men's colleges. She famously gave a lecture at Girton in 1928 that became the basis for her feminist polemic, *A Room of One's Own*. Having been invited to speak on 'Women and Fiction,' she delivered an anti-patriarchal diatribe on how poverty and second-class status inhibited women, concluding: 'A woman must have money and a room of her own if she is to write fiction.' Although things had moved on when I went up to Oxford, the disparity between the women's colleges and those medieval cloisters and combed-grass courtyards where we visited our male colleagues was still glaring. When I read her mischievous description of dining at a women's college, compared to the sumptuous fare served to the men, I recognised it at once.

'One cannot,' she said, 'think well, love well, sleep well, if one has not dined well. The lamp in the spine does not light on beef and prunes.'

Right on, Virginia, pass the port. She wrote about the lecture in her diary, saying she had spoken to an audience of 'starved but valiant young women… intelligent, eager, poor and destined to become schoolmistresses in shoals.' Not quite thirty years later, though not exactly poor, Sylvia was one of those—and women's careers were still limited to teaching and the service professions. My mother, having done a highly technical job as a decoder in the WRNS during the War, afterwards became a secretary, even if a rather elevated one working for a Labour MP.

As a pupil at Cheltenham Ladies College, Sylvia did have the advantage of attending a school that, like Girton, had been founded in the 19th century to advance the cause of women's education. Even though—or maybe because—the school prayer asked God to make us Christian wives and mothers, it had a fast track to university. The school's founder, Dorothea Beale, made sure her girls had somewhere to continue studying by founding St Hilda's College in Oxford in 1893. No doubt Sylvia had teachers who'd been to Girton, just as I ended up at St Anne's because of my English teacher, Ursula ('U.A') Fanthorpe—who later escaped being a schoolmistress and became a celebrated poet. The second way Sylvia was remarkable was that she was one of the few women who independently joined the Colonial Service and came out to Tanganyika alone. Perhaps it was easier for her having, like my mother, lived there before. In both cases, their capacity for self-direction stood them in good stead as colonial wives. In Anne's case, it helped her survive the loneliness and deprivation of the Rondo, separation, distance and the rigours of bringing up four girls in Moshi; in Sylvia's, it was called on in a more extreme way.

Nick and Sylvia had a farm of 2,700 acres, on which they grew coffee and sisal—the crop in which Tanzania was the world leader. The Kilimanjaro area was full of sisal fields, miles of magnificent green spiky plants spaced apart in rows. When I was growing up, the sisal plantation at Kiyungi, just outside Moshi, played an important role in our lives, largely because the estate manager, an Irishman called Bob Wells, had a swimming pool in his garden. 'Going to the Wells' pool' was a treat that sent us children into paroxysms of joy. Bob and his wife May were unfailingly hospitable and welcoming, and we spent hours in the pool, having tea at its edge, diving and racing and splashing, without them ever seeming to wish we'd leave. Their two boys, Mike and Robin, were roughly our age and once I turned thirteen, Mike was considered to be my boyfriend.

Sisal then was the crop Sylvia and Nick husbanded on their farm. Overnight, in October 1973, they found themselves dispossessed. Their bank accounts frozen, cars and machinery impounded, worst of all, they were told to move out of their house. When they pleaded, they were allowed to remain there, where their workers brought them gifts of food to keep them alive. Without a means of making a living, Nick Emmanuel took whatever work he could. For a while he had a consultancy with a Dutch company providing seeds for planting in the Masai traditional grazing area—a problematic farming venture ethically and environmentally. He was away from home for extended periods, during which Sylvia stayed on alone in the farmhouse and looked after their three young children as best she could. Being a Cheltenham Lady had hardly prepared her for such a hand-to-mouth existence.

At this point in the conversation, Nick himself arrives, a spry, brown man with an ironic twinkle in his eye. 'So you have remembered Tanzania?' he says in greeting.

He and Sylvia switch effortlessly between Greek, kiSwahili and English, in all three of which Sylvia retains her cut-glass accent. Their talk is pragmatic, humorous, philosophical by turns. Sylvia, who exudes serenity, erupts occasionally into flashes of anger at 'unfairness' or 'stupidity'.

'You can't just *grow* sisal,' she says, 'it needs capital and know-how.' Her voice is regretful, full of a sense of waste. They lost their sisal plantation and Tanzania lost its sisal—its leading crop. She complains that the way the nationalisation policy was applied was inconsistent—only farms in Kilimanjaro were taken over, not those in nearby Arusha. Then, while British wheat farmers were compensated by the British Government, the Emmanuels waited years before they received any compensation from Tanzania. When they did it was a quarter of the value of the property, paid in ten instalments.

I ask what made them stay. Nick's reply is in the form of another of those familiar stories of migration, assimilation and belonging.

'It's been more than a century since my family arrived. My father came from Greece in 1906 to join a relative who had started the very first commercial coffee farm in Kilimanjaro, and to help him build a coffee factory. I was born only six kilometres away, in the district of Uru, in a house built by my father.'

At nationalisation in 1973, the family company was owned by Nick and his two brothers, both of whom left him to look after their affairs and to make what claims he could. Himat's story, more-or-less. The Greek community, like that of the Asians, was long-established, with its own church and social club. When I was young, the spotless white cupola of the Greek Orthodox church was for me a replica of the snowy peak of Kilimanjaro that floated above it. When most of the Greeks left, it was sold to the Baptist church, and if they want to worship now, the Emmanuels must go to Nairobi.

Though they may be transplants, the Emmanuels are deeply rooted. Nick tells me they have leased back a hundred and twenty acres of their original 2,700 to grow coffee. By staying on despite everything, they've kept their contact with the land unbroken. But much else is broken. Though it was designed to return the land to its rightful owners, the nationalisation of farms and businesses in 1973 led to the collapse of commercial farming and the economy. Yet the story is complicated, with its roots deep in the precolonial and colonial past. Colonialism was founded on the conviction that Africa was up for grabs, and since ownership of the land by peasant farmers and nomads was hereditary and unwritten, it was easily disregarded. In their role as administrators of the Trust Territory of Tanganyika Protectorate after 1919, though the British negotiated land use with local farmers and nomads, large tracts of fertile land on Kilimanjaro came under the ownership of white farmers who regarded it as legally theirs since they had paid for it. This land alienation didn't go uncontested—on nearby Mount Meru, indigenous landowners took their protest against the British to the UN and this could be why Nyerere didn't nationalise the Arusha farms. Generally, though, settler farms had the advantage of being managed by professionals with capital to invest and knowledge of agricultural machinery, so their coffee and sisal estates flourished. The Emmanuels' farm would have been one of those the KNCU was formed to compete with.

As I stand to leave their verandah, it comes to me that the Germans who built the farmhouse in the first wave of colonisation were also subsequently dispossessed. Just as Frank Humplick bought a house in Lushoto previously occupied by Germans, so the Emmanuels' farm must have been vacated by its German owners when the British took over after World War One. So the land has been marked by successive dispossessions—Nick and Sylvia's being the third. As Greg said on the drive over, 'Things change all the time.' Yet the atmosphere, as the sunlight fades on the mountain and shadows grow long across the grass, is one f timeless peace. I wander off among the straight lines of coffee bushes, their glossy leaves sheltering brilliant red berries; the cat follows me.

'I had a farm in Africa.'

The undying opening sentence of Karen Blixen's 1937 memoir, *Out of Africa*, inaugurates a tradition of European women farmers in Africa. For me, the saddest moment in Blixen's story is when she realises she has to leave Kenya and the farm in the Ngong hills: 'I had consented to give away my possessions one by one, as a kind of ransom for my own life, but by the time that I had nothing left, I myself was the lightest thing of all for fate to get rid of.' Sylvia asserted her right to the place she had chosen, declining the tragic narrative of loss. But what about the other side of the story, the one dramatised by Zimbabwean writer, Tsitsi Dangarembga, in the early chapters of her novel, *Nervous Conditions*, or the South African *émigrée* in Botswana, Bessie Head, in *A Question of Power*? What about the experience of the African woman farmer?

Sebastian Chuwa, a botanist and tree conservationist with an NGO in Moshi, told me I had to understand two things. The first is simply the staggering growth in people. When I was born, the population was seven million; at Uhuru ten years later, it was ten million; today, there are fifty-nine million people in Tanzania,

eighty per cent living in rural areas without access to electricity. As it's women who cook and feed families, it's also women who bear responsibility for finding fuel on which to cook. This means foraging for wood in the forests. In the Usambaras, women wending their way home with huge stacks of wood on their heads are a common sight; I heard the chopping of trees as I walked in the forest with Mr Francis. The second thing, as various people pointed out to me, is that for a long, long time women had no title to land, and if they were given any, it was always the worst land and couldn't be inherited. This brought about another problem.

Sebastian told me one simple astounding fact—that because women didn't own land, they weren't allowed to plant trees. He saw this as the single biggest obstacle to women's involvement in conservation, and set out to rectify it. First, he talked to people in local government, then he drafted a bye-law to the effect that everyone, including women, *must* plant trees. This was presented to the local council and passed; then it went on to Parliament where it was passed into law nationally. In Moshi, they heard the news on the radio and rejoiced. When, in 1999, land rights were extended to women, it wasn't only land ownership that changed.

Nothing is ever simply one thing. If you have land rights you can plant trees. If you plant trees, you learn what species serve you best. When you watch trees grow, you want to look after them. You discover there are special, fuel-efficient stoves that mean you don't have to cut so many trees down, or spend so long gathering fuel. When you have more time, you can take an interest in wider issues of conservation and land use, social activism and women's rights. When you form a group with your neighbours you discover the power of collective action. Conservation, education, information, organisation, unite in a virtuous circle of empowerment. Sebastian Chuwa supported and worked with numerous women's groups around Moshi and Kilimanjaro. One, the Green Garden Women's Group, has planted or helped others plant, more than three million trees since 1998.

Sebastian had also started to nurture and plant an endangered indigenous tree species, *mpingo*, or African Blackwood tree. *Mpingo* has traditionally been used by the master carvers of Makonde, a district far to the south beyond Lindi, my birthplace, on either side of the Mozambique border. Makonde carvings, with their marvellously sinuous and interconnected forms, sometimes twisted and grotesque, often more biomorph than human, represent ancestral spirits and supernatural forces affecting human beings. They have become a sign of Tanzanian culture and are much in demand as art and tourist mementos. *Mpingo* trees are the medium through which Makonde carvers channel the spirits, transmuting the material into abstract forms. What animates their carvings is the dynamic process of nature becoming culture. There's a community of Makonde carvers in Moshi, and Sebastian, by organising them into a club, educated them about the wood they use and the need for its conservation. A mature *mpingo* is between seventy and two hundred years old. Now the carvers plant trees, literally putting down roots in the local community and benefitting not only themselves but the entire ecosystem of which they are a part.

As the material of musical instruments like clarinets and saxophones, *mpingo* was also exported to Europe and the Americas. It was in danger of extinction when, in 1992, the BBC made a film about it, *The Tree of Music*. In it, Sebastian talks about what the loss of *mpingo* would mean for the ecology of Tanzania. Whether through the power of cinema to speak to people far away or the guidance of the Makonde spirits, Sebastian and a woodworker from Texas, James Harris, were brought together. The NGO they cofounded in 1996, the African Blackwood Conservation Project (ABCP), has since been responsible for planting more than a million *mpingo* trees.

When I meet Sebastian Chuwa in Moshi, I haven't quite understood how much of a visionary or how influential he is. People have spoken of him to me as someone I ought to talk to, and when I do, he's so humble and down-to-earth it's easy to ask him to take me to his *mpingo* tree nursery. Though he must be in constant demand from all the projects he supports, he doesn't hesitate. In the 4 x 4 bought with money from one of Sebastian's international awards, we drive the few miles out to Mijongweni, a village in the Kiyungi area that donated the two and a half acres for the nursery. Crossing the Karanga river we see, piled on the bank, pyramids of brilliant orange carrots grown in West Kilimanjaro. People stand in the river washing them before they're transported to Dar. We pass a Coca Cola bottling plant and cross a second river, the Weruweru, which Sebastian says flooded a few years ago and the whole area had to be evacuated. Now the river provides water for the tree nursery.

Eventually we arrive and walk around the nursery. Sebastian shows me his bird-scaring devices and irrigation system, how water is pumped from the river through pipes into a reservoir, flowing into a concrete furrow to prevent erosion. As he talks about the types of trees he's nurturing I see the old herbalist, his father, teaching his son the lore of the forest. Always gentle and soft-spoken, his voice takes on the tone of that fatherly presence, explaining how seeds must be allowed to grow for twelve to fifteen months before being transplanted to soil.

He calls their names, like children:

Afzelia, a hardwood tree with beautiful flowers;
Acacia, good for charcoal;
Black Cassia, a shade tree with yellow flowers;
Balanites, whose fruits attract carnivores, whose bark is good for treating amoeba;
Pugnut gives lamp oil;
Gmelina offers shade and firewood;
Camelfoot, a beauty with pretty pink flowers and a bifurcated leaf.

In a further field, Sebastian shows me how they're planting sunflowers in among the *mpingo* saplings to increase the nitrogen level in the soil. He gives me a handful of *mpingo* seeds and I take them with me back to the Caribbean.

At the end of our visit, Sebastian takes me to meet Natalia Sebastian, one of the women involved in his tree nursery. She stands in her immaculately-swept, bare-earth yard surrounded by flowering shrubs in pots and a whole garden of trees, all of which she planted. Her husband and children work elsewhere, so she lives alone with her grandchildren, tending her garden and growing maize. Sebastian teases her that they have the same name.

'So you must be my sister, or my wife.'

Natalia smiles.

Sebastian died in 2014, aged fifty-nine, his memorial a million trees. He was a giant baobab, rooted in the soil of Kilimanjaro while sheltering and nurturing the efforts of hundreds of people and organisations. Today his wife, Elizabeth, and many other local conservationists continue his work.

21. *Misitu ni Uhai*: Forest is Alive

Once, during my series of return visits, I travelled all the way from Moshi by bus to the mouth of the Pangani river, which rises on Kilimanjaro and flows three hundred miles to the coast. Accounts from classical antiquity, including Ptolemy's *Geography*, describe a river called Rhapta, believed to be the same river. The Pangani is the thread linking Moshi and 'the horrid land behind Tanga' to the Indian Ocean.

After a long, arduous, dusty drive on untarred, deeply rutted roads, with a dying shudder the bus ground to a halt where the road ran out, a few yards short of the ocean. It was only thirty-five kilometres from the town of Tanga, but it felt as remote and out of time as if we had arrived in a previous century. Nothing there but palm trees and sandy pathways, the remains of a slave market, an ancient customs house, and other old buildings of crumbling stone. After a day of wandering, I found myself on a boat at sunset, on water like liquid gold beneath a violet sky shot through with the last rays of sunlight. Above us, the first glimmer of a crescent moon, the steady glow of Venus. We glided in perfect silence between the darkling banks of the Pangani river, on the very margin of the Indian Ocean, steering for the jetty lit by a single pale light.

When we were children, we often went with our mother to swim in the Town Pool in Moshi. Now I know this place by other names: prosaically, it's *Idara ya Maji*: Water Department. Moshi is the headquarters of the Pangani River Basin Authority and the spring that fed the pool, called Njoro Juu and once Moshi's main water supply, is a tributary of the Pangani. Melted ice from the glacier finds its way by underground streams down the mountain to bubble up just here, pure and clear and cold, straight from the earth.

The Town Pool wasn't a proper swimming pool like the Wells' pool at Kiyungi, with straight sides and a deep and shallow end. It was a big circular concrete basin with inward-sloping sides you could crack your head on as you dived in. It was the same depth all the way round and you clung to the lip of the pool because there was nowhere to put your foot down, or hauled yourself out on your stomach because there were no nice metal steps. The water was icy cold: Jock said it was melted snow straight from Kilimanjaro. When you came up for air, teeth chattering, you couldn't even sit in the sun to get warm because of the enormous, overhanging trees that shaded the pool and its surrounding grass. We would sit shivering with knees drawn up to our chests, while our mother draped us with towels and gave us tea from a thermos. It was in the middle of town near the railway station but felt utterly remote and cut off from all the town activities. In its mossy, hushed, cool green darkness, it was a magical place.

One day in Moshi I'm walking along a road going somewhere, thinking of something, when a feeling comes over me of walking backwards in time. I falter on the brink of a memory. A certain atmosphere, a stilling of the air, brings it home. The Town Pool. I notice a dirt track leading away from the road. I follow it and come to a wooden gate. It's unlocked and I push it and go in.

It's like entering an enchanted garden, or like a dream where things are familiar and strange in equal measure. As I cross the threshold, external sounds die and a hush descends. I take a few tentative steps, looking for the old pool. I find the buried outline of a circular area now filled with earth and, overhanging it, an immensely tall and ancient tree. I recognise it at once. We swam beneath those branches that filled the sky and blocked the sun. If the pool has gone there's still water somewhere, the sound of it a constant murmur in the quiet air. A little further on I find it, a concrete catchment fed by a little stream, the water as clear and cold as I remember. I kneel and immerse my arms as far as they'll go, splashing my face, letting a trickle run down my throat. When I look up again, a man is standing nearby, calmly watching me.

And so I meet Samweli Mochiwa, keeper of the grove. He walks me slowly around the place, showing me what it has become—a conservation area and tree nursery, with workers, both men and women, busy tending it.

'During the time of *waGerumani* the spring supplied the town of Moshi,' he tells me, 'but now the water is carried by pipe to outlying villages.'

I ask about the ancient tree and he nods.

'Yes, that is a *Newtonia buchananii*, a riverine tree known as *mkufi*. It was planted by *waGerumani* to stabilise the damp soil. Now I have planted strangler fig and sycamore fig-trees because they have long roots and help conserve water. The fig tree has been around on earth between forty and sixty million years, and is sacred in many cultures.'

I tell Samweli that he's very knowledgeable, and he laughs.

'I only went to Standard Four. I do what I do as a service to the earth.'

What Samweli does is protect the spring. Unlike Sebastian Chuwa he has no formal training, but at school a teacher showed them how to raise trees from seedlings and, from then, Samweli was interested in caring for trees. After school

he worked as a mechanic, but he lives near the spring and, noticing the absence of trees where there was water, decided singlehandedly to rehabilitate the area. Every year in March, he says, there's a Water Week to encourage people to conserve water sources and catchments by planting water-friendly trees. In 1999, at the age of thirty-three, he decided, without official funding or support, to plant four hundred seedlings to protect the water reserve from being encroached on. He collected seedlings from the forest. People came to him for trees and he used the proceeds to expand the nursery.

I ask if he knows Sebastian Chuwa and he nods. They are collaborators and both belong to COMPACT (Community Management of Protected Areas Conservation Project), which supports NGOs around Kilimanjaro. He tells me how COMPACT helped him plant trees at Miwaleni spring, a site of twenty acres fifteen kilometres from Moshi. With the cooperation of Moshi Urban Water Authority Sewage and Sanitation he also planted fifteen thousand trees at Nsere, another spring in the Moshi catchment area.

Samweli's project has a name: Kiviwama Indigenous Trees Nursery. In 2004, when developers tried to take control of the land around the spring, Samweli retaliated by planting two thousand tree seedlings. A year later, as though by serendipity, a new Ministry of the Natural Environment came into being, followed by a law aimed at water conservation. Samweli was vindicated, and Moshi Municipality gave the land at Njoro Juu to Kiviwama. Now he wants to extend it into a community botanical garden, but for that different agencies must agree: the District Forestry Office, Pangani River Basin Authority, Moshi Municipality and Moshi District Water Engineering. He's already donated plants to start a botanical garden at his old school, Moreni Primary. Samweli has ambitions for his expanded garden: he wants to raise medicinal trees like baobab, and trees for a paper-making project, producing handmade paper for artists, recyclable bags, lampshades, baskets… He shows me where they've already started on the paper project, with sheets of paper pegged to a line in the process of drying. He wants to see a craft workshop and already has an artist-in-residence.

Nothing is simply one thing. Trees support the spring, which nurtures othe trees, which provide materials for artists and craftsmen to make useful objects tha provide them with a living. At Njoro Juu, it's easy to understand why groves are sacred. Trees are light and life-bringers, embodying vitality, channelling the lifeforce and affecting everything around them. Samweli, keeper of the grove, is also vibrantly alive, channelling his energy into tree-planting and the conservation of sacred spaces. Samweli calls himself a 'zealot', using the Swahili term *kereketwa* as in '*Kikundi cha vijana wakereketwa wa mazingira*', the name for 'groups of youth who zealously care for the environment'. Eco warriors. Just as Sebastian's worldview can encompass science and spirit, tradition and modernity in a world where different fundamentalisms clash, Samweli gently redefines zealotry. Possessiveness, territorial boundaries, fanaticism and intolerance are converted into something inclusive and organic, something we can all share—the need for dirt under our fingernails in the effort to preserve the earth.

When I read *Paradise*, the novel by Zanzibari writer, Abdulrazak Gurnah (who won the Nobel Prize for Literature in 2021), it was the first time I'd seen Moshi represented in fiction. Set in the early years of the twentieth century during the German occupation of Tanganyika, it tells the story of Yusuf, a young boy from the coast, who joins a trading caravan into the interior. The last part of the journey is made by train, on the line that runs from Tanga to Moshi, passing through Mombo—the line that took me to school. Eventually they arrive 'at a small town under a huge snow-capped mountain' where 'the air was cool and pleasant, and the light had the softness of early twilight reflected in boundless water.' In Moshi, he stays with a man from the coast, a Muslim shopkeeper, Hamid, and his wife. One day he accompanies Hamid to trade at a settlement on the mountain. They stop 'under a fig tree, by the bank of a tumbling stream', the air full of the sound of rushing water. When he jumps in the stream, he's surprised to find it's freezing cold and Hamid tells him it's melted ice from the mountain peak. Yusuf walks along the bank to a waterfall and, standing in the spray, thinks he can hear 'the sound of the river God breathing'. They make a camp and as they lie down Hamid says, 'Isn't it pleasant to think that Paradise will be like this?'. Beneath the sound of the water Hamid goes on to describe God's garden, its waterfalls and its four rivers, water everywhere, 'Under the pavilions, by the orchards, running down terraces, alongside the walks by the woods.' The Garden of Eden itself, as promised in *The Qu'ran*:

The righteous will be
Amid gardens
And fountains
Of clear-flowing water.

I know the place on the mountain, the waterfall, the earthly garden resembling the Garden of Eden. This garden takes different forms, but it can be found here and there: in Marangu beneath the waterfall; in the little banana and coffee farms on the mountain slopes; in the hotel garden; in Sylvia's garden on the farm in western Kilimanjaro; and at Njoro Juu.

22. The Prayer Rug

Home was a long way from the Coast. Driving back after the seaside holiday was hot and boring, without the excitement of going away and the sea and all its adventures to look forward to. It was hard when you had to share the back of the car not only with your sisters but Sebastian, who was hot and drooled so his spit was flung about by the breeze from the open window. Everyone's back was burnt and peeling so they couldn't sit still, but they had to try to keep from bumping the seat in front of them. Sometimes Sebastian would climb from the floor onto the seat to stick his snout out of the window, and his claws hurt terribly if you got in the way. This year, though, there was the rug. Rolled on the back seat to keep it out of the dust, its faint, musty fragrance held vague promises of things to come.

Daddy had been so excited when he saw the notice 'Carpet Auction', and Mummy explained it was a sale, and the carpets came from Persia and India. They had gone to the place, in the old part of Mombasa city, with all the carved wooden doors and little windows high up with iron bars. She stayed close to her mother because it wasn't like anywhere she had been before, she wasn't sure of the smell or the narrow streets and the people in their long robes. Inside the auction it was ordinary again, Indian merchants like the ones at home showing you the carpets in a big room, then you sat and they brought you hot sweet tea on a brass tray. The carpets smelt, not bad but different, rich, as if they had come from far away and brought it with them. A man stood at the front, calling out things and people called back, and her father called too and at the end of it, they left with two rolled carpets and a smaller rug that one of the Indian merchant's sons carried to the car. The two carpets had to go on the roof-rack, they were too big for inside, only the small one, the rug, shared the back seat with her. It felt like hers. Her parents were happy and it made her feel grown-up, being there, hearing them talk about the auction.

'That Mori prayer rug,' said Daddy, 'a beautiful piece of work. You don't get a chance like that very often.'

'And the colours, that blue and that red,' said Mummy. 'Like jewels.'

She knew they wouldn't go straight home to the holiday house on the beach. It was an excuse for celebration, bottles of Tusker beer and a Coke for her, spicy

172

samosas, fresh roasted groundnuts, maybe an ice-cream. But she wanted to see the rug unrolled, to look at the colours, like jewels, to feel its softness. Mori prayer rug. The other carpets were patterned all over, the same pattern repeating, with a bright border, one red, one blue. A matching pair. But the rug was different, it had the shape of an arch at one end only. If you held it up it could be a doorway.

'The gateway to Paradise,' Mummy explained. 'Muslims pray on rugs like that, kneeling towards Mecca, their holy place. When you pray, you pass through the gateway.'

She thought of Ahmed, the garden boy at home. He was a Muslim from the Coast. On Friday afternoons, he didn't come to work because he had to go to the mosque in town. She used to watch him leave, in his special clothes like the ones in the old town when they bought the carpets. Once, her mother was driving into town, and they gave him a lift. At the mosque she saw him join a crowd of men taking off their shoes on the steps. Friday afternoon was the only time she saw him in shoes. The rest of the time, he was barefoot and wearing tattered khaki shorts that were too big for him. She craned her neck as they drove away, but she didn't know when he went inside, or what he did there. She knew Allah was inside. More than once, he had let her stay in his room while he prayed, but she had never seen him enter Paradise. Perhaps he needed a rug. Ahmed prayed on a mat facing the wall.

The car spun out the miles in a skein of red dust. Sunburn was easier if you propped yourself on your knees and stared out of the back window, watching the circular swirl of dust, like water going down the plughole in the bath at home. If you were lucky, there might be animals, perhaps a giraffe in the distance, or gazelles in the long savannah grass. Even something dangerous, an elephant, a rhino, but that was rare, and usually only at dusk. So you counted the wooden lightpoles, strung together with a dip in the middle and up at both ends, mile after mile of them, till you got to a hundred and got confused, or sleepy. After hours and hours, they would stop for breakfast at the side of the road, with tea in a thermos that didn't taste like tea, and sandwiches she never felt like eating, because car travel made her sick. Sometimes she *was* sick, and tried to say so in time for the car to stop so she didn't do it all over the back seat. But very, very slowly the sun started to fall down the other side of the sky, and she sat up again, waiting for the first glimpse of the mountain, the first familiar landmarks at the edge of town, the turning off the main road, the driveway. Then they were home, falling gratefully out of the car, stretching aching legs, in a frenzy of barking and patting and romping and things being taken bit by bit into the house.

And now, the rug was home. She watched it being carried inside by Antony, the houseboy. She followed him, saw where he put it, on the floor of the sitting room, watched as her father unrolled it, shook it out and laid it in front of the fireplace. Antony wouldn't know about it, he was a Christian and knelt in church just like they did, not on a rug. Mori. Allah. Paradise. Jewels. She couldn't wait for Ahmed to come to work next day.

She found Ahmed in the garden, where he always was, squatting by a flower-bed, carefully planting seedlings with a trowel. He said nothing when she joined him, squatting silently beside him and watching as he dribbled water into the holes he'd made. She knew if she waited, he would let her help, but she shouldn't ask. She followed him around for half the morning, carrying the watering can, heavy at first, becoming lighter and lighter as they progressed. When she saw him glance at the sky, she knew it was time to stop, and she had earned the right to follow him to his room and watch him eat. She was allowed to taste his food too, but today she was too full of her story.

'Ahmed, we went to an auction. It was in Mombasa. We bought carpets, and a Mori prayer rug. How do you pray with it? Do you enter Paradise?'

He looked at her, smiling at her excitement. 'Mombasa. That's near where I come from.'

He had told her before about his home. It was an island, Pemba, not as big as Zanzibar, but far more beautiful. He had left it when he was very young and grown up in Tanga, on the Coast. Because there were too many children, his father sent him to live with his uncle upcountry, and his uncle had come to her father to ask if he needed a garden boy. She knew Ahmed's uncle too, he worked at her father's office, and he always talked to her when she went there to spend an afternoon. Once a year, he and Ahmed went home to Tanga. It was far, she knew how far, and she was sorry Ahmed only saw his family then. Ahmed said it was the will of Allah. Allah lived at the mosque, but he could hear Ahmed's prayers even from his room at home.

'Ahmed, when you pray, do you enter Paradise? Where is it?'

He was silent, and his face became mysterious, in a way that was familiar to her. He knew wonderful stories, but you couldn't make him tell them. Sometimes when she asked a question, he would just stay quiet, as if he hadn't heard. Other times, he would talk and talk, and she didn't understand half of what he said. He would talk about his family at the Coast, about Pemba and the spirits who lived there, who were very powerful. He knew things no one else knew, even how to read the funny letters in the Koran. It was a big book like the Bible, but the writing was different, and when he read he started at the end and read backwards. Sometimes he read to her, the sounds falling all around like music.

Paradise,' he said. 'Paradise is a garden. It has rivers, and a fountain, and when you go there, you wear silk clothes and drink out of silver and crystal.'

'Where is it, Ahmed?' she asked carefully.

'We cannot find it on earth. But every garden reminds us of it and that we should try to be good, so we can go there one day.'

'Does our garden remind you?'

'Yes, but it is work. *Kazi tu*. In Paradise, young maidens do the work and the faithful rest.'

'Will I go there too?' she asked.

He was silent, then shook his head. 'You are a Christian. Christians have their own place.'

For a moment she was stricken, but then she remembered. 'Ahmed, can I show you the rug? Its colours are like jewels.'

He laughed. 'Ask the *memsahib*,' was all he would say.

She knew it was time for him to rest, and she should go, but she lingered, unsatisfied.

'Go now. I will meet you in Paradise.'

She went.

Antony was cleaning inside, and had put the rug out on the verandah. She had waited days, hoping this would happen. Ahmed had said to ask her mother, but she didn't like to in case she said no. Her world was full of incomprehensible prohibitions: don't cut centipedes in half, don't ride the bicycle outside the garden, don't disturb the servants when they're working. Mostly she did what she wanted when no one was watching. She and Ahmed were digging a watercourse from the furrow to the flowerbed on the top terrace, because he had said Paradise was a garden full of rivers, and theirs had none. In the rains, the furrows circling the garden beyond the hedge were full and rushing with water. Now, they were down to a trickle, but a thunderstorm could come any time. They had dug for days. It had been her idea, but Ahmed welcomed it. He said it would save on the hose water. She ran towards him, stumbling on the terrace, out of breath.

'Ahmed, please come. The rug is on the verandah,' she panted.

He looked up from the hard dry earth he was hacking with a *panga* to loosen it. He glanced towards the house. He knew its rhythm as well as she, knew the parents were both out and they had nothing to fear, but unlike her, he didn't take risks with prohibitions. He was the garden boy, and the house was not his domain. Today, however, the work they had been doing together had pleased him, and he wanted to please her in return. They approached the verandah, stopping just inside the patch of shade cast by the overhanging roof, in the shadow of the house but still outside its confines. They looked at the rug, spread haphazardly on the low concrete balustrade. Eagerly, she looked at his face, but could see nothing against the bright glare of the light behind him. When he spoke, his hushed voice surprised her.

'That's the *mihrab*,' he said reverentially, pointing to the rug. 'The archway that points the way to Mecca. It's on the wall of the mosque too, so we know which way to look when we pray. It's the gateway of the Prophet, who stands in the door of God. When we pray, all together at the same time, we join with Muslims all over the world who are all thinking of Allah. Then we are on the threshold.'

She didn't understand his words. *Mihrab*. Threshold. But he had seen it, that was enough. He had shared it with her. Until he had seen it, it had held its secret from her, but now she knew he would tell her more. She only had to prompt him Shyly, she caught his hand and pulled him backwards, knowing Antony would come soon and catch them. He stepped abruptly back into the brightness, his shorts falling below his belly button. Like him, she was in shorts and barefoot Together, they trudged back up the garden, and squatted on the parched earth under the flame tree. He picked up a fallen seed pod and scratched a line in the dirt.

'Threshold,' he said. 'The door is like this line. One step and you're across it. But to cross, you must know many things, you must be worthy to enter Paradise. If you are not wise enough yourself, you can ask for help. In Pemba, we have a mighty spirit we can call on. He is one of the *djinn* who helped Solomon build the arches in the temple, like the archway on the prayer rug. When Solomon died, they went all over the earth, and a very powerful one came to Pemba.'

She wanted to ask, what are *djinn*? But she didn't dare interrupt his flow. Instead, she stored them in her mind, where she could sip at them slowly. Threshold. Spirit. *Djinn*. *Mihrab*. The words accumulated, pregnant with power. Jewels. She heard his voice resume, still in that hushed tone that was barely above a whisper.

'We are taught that man is made of clay, like this earth.' His fingers scraped the dry ground, his fingernails red with dust. 'It was Allah who breathed the spirit into Adam, and our *djinn* is part of the breath of Allah. In Swahili we say, *p'epo*. It means spirit, breath, Paradise, all three. When we *punga p'epo*, we call the spirit, and it fills us up inside.' Ahmed laid his hands flat, red with dust, over his belly button. 'I have seen it. The women speak with the *djinn's* voice. They are able to cross the threshold. The rest of us can only watch.'

The heat, the smell of the earth, the brilliance of the light, the incantation of words whose meanings eluded her, filled the child with a kind of ecstasy, and her head swam. Ahmed brought his gaze to rest on her flushed face, and smiled.

'You must go inside now, small *memsahib*,' he ordered. 'These things are heavy, and they are only for you. Because of the prayer rug. They are our secret. Even in the mosque, we do not speak of them. There are people who believe *djinn* are evil, that when they open their mouths towards heaven, their breath stinks so bad the angels can't bear it, and so they ask Allah to grant the prayer quickly to stop the smell. They say it's wrong to pray like that, because it molests the angels. But we know that our *djinn* protects us, and breathes the breath of Allah into us.'

Ahmed rose, and in a reversal of the previous gesture, held out his hand to pull her to her feet. She staggered a little, the blood all in her feet, sun and shadow dancing across her vision. Then she went to the house.

She was in disgrace. What she dreaded most, her father's anger, had descended on her, and she still smarted from his hand on her bare legs. Locked in her room at one end of the house, she had wept so much her throat was swollen, and her breath came in hiccups that threatened to choke her. She had tried to explain, to no avail. Her words carried no meaning, no one wanted to hear.

'It was the archway,' she wailed. 'You go through it to reach Paradise. You have to pray and the spirit fills you, then you can pass through. He only has a wall, I wanted him to have the archway...'

They had found the prayer rug in Ahmed's room while he was at the mosque. She had carried it there when she saw him leave, in his *kanzu* and sandals, and less than an hour later, Antony had come to report to her mother that it was missing. Theft was a serious thing, especially by a member of the household. Mummy had waited for Daddy to come home, and he had decreed a search of the servants' quarters. At first, she had stayed quiet, paralysed with fear, as they discussed what to do with Ahmed on his return.

'He'll have to go. We can't have him entering the house like that, let alone taking things. And a carpet...'

'But if it means something in his religion, can't we warn him this time? He probably didn't see it as stealing.'

Daddy always got impatient with Mummy when she made excuses for the servants. 'Don't be silly, they all know what stealing is. You must make an example when this kind of thing happens. You can't afford to be soft.'

Mummy, who shared the house and the garden with Antony and Ahmed, clung to her own version. 'But he's never done anything like this before, and he's such a good *shamba* boy. I don't know where I'll find someone who's so good with plants again.'

It was a while before she realised what it meant. They thought Ahmed had stolen the rug, and they were going to send him away. She knew she had to speak, but it was a while before she could find the words. She waited till Mummy was alone, and whispered it in her ear. She and Mummy had secrets from Daddy, and she begged her not tell, but Mummy looked sad and said it was too serious and she had to tell him or Ahmed would suffer. Daddy was angry. He was cold and hard, and he took her by the wrist and dragged her round the back of the house. She was afraid of him, the way she had to run to keep up, the way he looked straight ahead and his mouth was a thin, straight line. It hurt when he hit her, but what hurt more was that he didn't want to listen. As if she wasn't there, as if there wasn't a reason for what she had done. Ahmed needed the rug; it was the archway. Daddy said she nearly got Ahmed the sack, and what on earth possessed her to be in his room? Then he locked her up, and she heard the car leaving and knew her parents had gone to the club. She listened to the silence and felt the heat in the bedroom lie on her skin, making it hard to breathe. She was still locked up when it began to rain.

She hadn't seen the lightning flash at first, but the thunder broke through her wails. The first crack split the sky, and she screamed. Antony would be in the kitchen, but she was alone. It had never happened before. When there was a thunderstorm, she would be with Mummy, and they would hold each other as they watched the lightning, and she would feel safe. But to be alone, in a locked room, and oh! She screamed again as the thunder boomed and the house shook, and then the rain came. A curtain fell between her and the garden, so heavy was the rain, beating on the roof tiles, flinging itself at the earth. She shivered and trembled, weeping at its ferocity, but her sobs were drowned in the downpour. It grew dark but she was immobilised by misery, too weak to leave the window. To comfort herself, she placed her two hands flat on her belly, as she had seen Ahmed do that day in the garden. She breathed the words she had heard him speak—*djinn, mihrab, threshold*—as if summoning a powerful spirit. Mesmerised by the fall of water, numbed by its drumming on the ground, she was startled back into terror by a voice speaking close to her. It seemed to come from inside the room, and she looked around wildly, but saw nothing. It spoke again, barely a murmur, and now she knew it came from the gloom outside.

'Small *memsahib*, it is me. Ahmed. Don't be afraid. I heard what happened, and that they locked you up. They will be back soon, but I am here now. Don't cry any more. I am here.'

Ahmed. She strained her eyes and could just make him out, pressed against the mosquito netting of the window, sheltering as best he could between the wall of rain pouring from the overhanging roof and the rough exterior wall of the house. He must have come back from the mosque and Antony would have told him the story. Did he know she nearly got him the sack? Did he know Daddy beat her?

It's all right, *memsahib kidogo*. I heard about the rug. It was wrong to take it, but you told the truth and should not have been punished for it. But don't worry, Allah knows. He is everywhere and he will protect you. Did you hear the thunder? That was his voice. He has sent a blessing to the garden. The rain will fill the furrow, and water will flow along our channel, and the garden will have a river, just like we said. Tomorrow, when they go to work, we will visit our Paradise.'

Outside, Ahmed shivered, wet to the skin and frozen. Inside, the girl clung to the window bars, absorbing his voice. Neither knew when the car returned, the crunch of tyres on the gravel obliterated by the rain. She heard the bolt shoot back on the outside of the door, and turned, and saw her mother, her tennis dress streaked with rain, drops of water in her hair. The tennis racquet dropped to the floor as the girl flung herself into her arms.

23. Winds of Change

There are things of which I have no memory. My mother told me that after my sisters were born, I had tantrums and they would lock me in a bedroom and let me scream myself out. I don't find it surprising—I was sent away for two weeks before the twins were born and when I came back, there they were: two of them, where there had just been me. I continued to be a moody and emotional child. I can well imagine how annoying and frustrating this must have been, and certainly my father didn't hide it. I irritated him, and small humiliations—and sometimes physical punishment—were the order of the day. A child, feeling herself powerless, will react in the only way she knows—by lashing out and screaming, or retreating into sulks. I remember as a teenager sobbing to my mother that I hated him. She was the buffer between us, doing her best to keep the peace. When she went to England to have an operation and Jock was left in charge, he wrote to Kitty: 'In the family here, complete accord with Sally, tolerance/resentment/tolerance from the Twins, unending discord with Jane whom I *cannot* like.'

Although things improved as I got older, I puzzle over this dislike. It wasn't all children—Mary and Ally amused him, and as for Sally, when she was two, Anne wrote that, 'Jock is tickled to bits with her and takes far more notice of her than he did any of the others.' In my case, was it because he hadn't bargained for the way I, as the first-born, would get between him and my mother? Was it because he had a terrible relationship with his own father and fought him all his life? Or did it stem from being locked up for two and a half years, living on cabbage stalks, before being forced to march hundreds of miles through the snow by his captors? Was it even, perhaps, because we were too alike—stubborn, opinionated, resistant to authority?

To understand my early relationship with my father I must go back to what Kitty, his mother, told my mother before she married him: 'If you can overlook the rough edges, I venture to promise that you'll have a husband of sterling worth.' This contradiction, I now see, is what made him a tricky father. To his friends, Jock Bryce was the consummate host: the epitome of courtesy, charming to women, jovial with men and playful with children. He could make a roomful of people laugh with his sardonic humour. He would drive miles out of his way to save someone else the trouble. He was dependable, honest, self-deprecating and a good sportsman. He played cricket and tennis, and when he got older, golf, and gave up is time to be president of the Moshi Club where these sports reigned supreme. He played a wicked hand of Bridge, perfected as a prisoner of war who taught other prisoners how to play. He was a *bon viveur* who loved cold Tusker beer with freshly-roasted peanuts, good whisky, often with a cigar, and hot curries, but detested 'foreign *kickshaws*' like garlic—when he met it, which wasn't till we were living in Rome. He was also attractive to women, as Anne reported about one of her friends who apparently fell for him.

'I feel sorry for her,' said Anne, 'when her own perfectly nice husband is so dull, but not enough to lend her Jock!'

But there was another Jock Bryce only his family knew. The man who came home from work in such a mood we dreaded the crunch of his tyres on the gravel. Who came to the table monosyllabic, snarling at servants and children. And yet, he also delighted us by extreme physical clowning, dangling us upside down and scaring us with grotesque noises. At the seaside, he taught me not to be afraid of the water by throwing me into the waves. Teaching us to play Bridge he showed endless patience, warning us (who had never been to London), 'Many a man is walking the Embankment because he didn't draw trumps.' His role as a father was something he wrote himself, having grown up largely without one: when he was young his model of fatherhood was based on holidays spent with his grandfather. 'I had a strict Victorian upbringing,' he boasted, usually in response to some new revelation of the-way-things-are-done-nowadays. He was alternately high-spirited and morose, playful and authoritarian, tolerant and judgmental, a killjoy and the life and soul. He held the world to his own high standards and gave it short shrift when it didn't match up.

If I go back to the old cine films he endlessly made, another Jock emerges. He captured every holiday, every family occasion, with his beloved movie camera, spending hours hunched over his editing machine, painstakingly cutting and splicing the fragile strips of film. Then, in the living room at night, with the collapsible screen, the whirring projector, the darkness, we had our own private movie nights, when we saw ourselves, stars of our own technicolour lives, on screen. Scenes unspool:

The foot-operated ferry at Kilindini on our way to the beach house at Malindi.

All of us belly down on surfboards, rolling in on the waves.

Him climbing a coconut tree barefoot and pretending to get stuck.

Snorkelling expeditions on the reef by *ngalawa*, a narrow wooden Indian Ocean catamaran steered by a fisherman.

Driving hundreds of miles to game parks to see animals in the wild.

Picnics at the side of the road.

Being charged by a bull elephant as he was filming it, having to run for the car and let out the clutch in a hurry.

Finding ourselves in the middle of a herd of rhino, dodging as they charged blindly across the road.

His atavistic delight at hitting an edible bird called a yellowneck at speed on the road, throwing it all bloody in the boot.

Pelting my mother with clods of elephant dung on the rim of Ngurdoto Crater.

Gambling for our pocket money with poker dice.

The times he let me go to work with him and play on the machinery.

The time he spent teaching me to ride his Vespa scooter.

Image and memory coalesce, leaving a residue of excitement at the freedom to take risks, the absence of surveillance—the white man's privilege in Africa. No wonder, once we found ourselves at boarding school, we had such a hard time abiding by the rules.

He could be reckless. There must have been a reason he chose the RAF and got himself trained as a fighter pilot during the War. That impulse to get aloft—to be alone at the controls of a machine moving at speed, to choose the moment to launch your attack—could be seen in his everyday life. He didn't like to be hemmed in. He liked to drive fast for hundreds of miles on dusty roads through an empty landscape with nothing to do but beat his own record. He had many narrow escapes, and sometimes endangered other people. Bob Wells, manager of the sisal estate at Kiyungi, owner of the Wells' Pool, liked to tell the story of how my parents arrived in a lorry and woke him in the middle of the night.

It goes like this. Anne and Jock are invited to an evening at the house of the managing director of the sugar company some fifteen miles from Moshi. They arrive in the afternoon for tennis, after which they have sundowners and dinner, and play Bridge till after 2am. Anne can see Jock's tired but he insists on driving. It's a straight tarmac road, he puts his foot down, falls asleep at the wheel, and drives off the road into a culvert. Waking to find the car has tipped on its side and

Anne is practically lying on him, Jock exclaims, 'Fancy being able to turn over a Ford Zephyr!' He scrambles over Anne, stepping on her face to climb out through the window, pulls her out and they set off on foot towards the lights of Moshi glimmering in the distance. Anne, in tight skirt and high heels, is convinced that the glimmer recedes with every step she takes. After a few miles they are rescued by a passing truck that drops them a mile further on, at the house of their friends, Bob and May Wells, on the sisal estate. The fact they're appalled at the accident only adds to the spice of its telling. Bob drives Jock back to the car in the morning and they pull it out of the ditch with a tow-rope, while May drives Anne home.

Another time, as a teenager, I come home from somewhere late at night to find Jock loitering in the garden in the dark. His disembodied voice comes through the mosquito netting of my bedroom window, asking to be let in.

'Why are you out there?' I ask in confusion.

'Practising walking to work.'

'Why do you need to do that?'

'I've written off the car.'

He's been to pick up my sisters from a party on the mountain and run the car off the road on the way home, ending up vertically over a six-foot drop into a ditch. They're rescued by another driver, but Anne is so angry she won't let him in the house. She sits on Mary's bed and cries. She'll join in the joke when the danger is to herself; when her children are involved, she draws the line. That story isn't funny, but even then, he blunts the edge of it with irony.

'I didn't want that car anyway,' he says. 'Bicycles are better. I might sell the tyres if they haven't been stolen by morning...'

With Anne, things were so much clearer, so much easier to understand. Her love was constant and never in doubt. She was a bulwark and a mediator, softening his harshness, containing his excesses. She was, said Jock, 'like a tiger in defence of her young.' I wouldn't be surprised if, that time he went off the road with my sisters, she hadn't promised to divorce him if he ever did it again. Somehow, she managed to share herself between the three, and later four, of us, so we each felt individually favoured and no one was left out. When we went to school in Lushoto, finding the house deathly quiet and strange, she sat on our beds and cried. To comfort myself at school I had a discarded box of Boots No. 7 face powder. I would take it to bed with me and bury my nose in it under the blankets, inhaling her smell. When she came up for half-term, it was like being readmitted to a special place from which we had been banished. The world made sense again. Until she left.

Throughout his life and until hers ended, Jock's letters to Kitty started 'Dear Mummy'. If I felt abandoned at Lushoto at the age of eight, with my parents a hundred and forty miles away, how did he feel, aged four, in Adelaide, with his parents at a distance of three thousand miles in Malaya? I can see now what Anne saw then—the child inside the man. Perhaps that was why she forgave him so many times.

Like all children, we were spectators of our parents' marriage. When they said, 'Anne' and 'Jock' to each other, we looked at them differently. So, they weren't just our parents, they had a separate existence? Shared jokes and favourite clichés were talismanic utterances:

'Miles and miles of bloody Africa,' as they watched unending brown savannah unfold through the car windows.

'Night fell with tropical swiftness,' as they watched the sunset over a gin and tonic.

'That's the way it goes, professor,' when a philosophical remark was called for.

'Every nerve in my body is screaming for alcohol!' more-or-less every evening.

'Moderation is my middle name,' before pouring the third whisky.

When he said, in response to some routine piece of information, that she amazed him, she retorted that he should be glad she still could. He retaliated by calling her Old Trout. He complained about 'acres and acres of female flesh' and that there were too many women in the house. He said he needed another male to keep him company, so we got Sebastian, the black Labrador, who he called 'the Black Beast' and scandalised us by treading on him. He claimed he didn't know which of us was which, but he assigned us each a nickname, usually based on a colour: Mary was Black Dort, Ally was Purple Dort, Sally, once she arrived, was Pig Dort, or Snort Dort. I was, of all things, Gamboge, the saffron-yellow dye used to colour the robes of Buddhist monks. He would stand outside my bedroom door and wail, 'Gam-booooge,' like the cry of a garbage truck driver, or a ruminant with indigestion. How did he even know the word? He had all sorts of words he liked to use, some real—discombobulate, micturate, condign—some his invention— omstonculate (perturb, amaze), changling (the act of gambling for pocket money), whiskits (the rubbing of a bristled chin along the tender skin of a squealing child). We didn't know the difference. He used the German he'd picked up during the War to tease Anne, telling her, '*Achtung! Auchentoshan!*' (which, it turns out, is the name of a malt whisky), and she would say, 'Stop swearing at me!'

Sometimes, during those movie evenings, the projector would overheat and we'd have to fan it till it cooled. Or two strips of film, so carefully glued together, would part at the splice and the spool would whir uselessly round and round, the film unravelling onto the floor. Life was like that—magical and seamless, until it came apart.

After Uhuru, as the colonial order was dismantled, things changed in ways Jock especially found less and less tolerable. Though he, along with many others, accepted the invitation to stay on in their posts while local people were trained to ake over, he found it an uncomfortable and ambiguous position. From having been secure in his administrative and scientific role, he now had to deal with the sense of racial pride that came with Uhuru.

Taking refuge behind the myth of scientific neutrality he wrote to his mother, 'I am now an expatriate and an increasingly unpopular one, in view of my unbending approach to scientific values.' Looking south, he found himself increasingly making comparisons with apartheid South Africa—where he had never been—and finding it more efficient and, astoundingly, more humane. 'South Africa,' he declared, 'will be vindicated in the end. You can't live in a black republic and still believe in political rights.'

He was far from alone in feeling that self-government, in a country without an educated or administratively experienced cadre, was a contradiction. But, true to form, he made no attempt to hide his disdain for African socialism and the new political class.

Despite her leftist inclinations, Anne was hardly more sophisticated. Commenting on the apartheid ban on interracial relationships in a letter to Kitty, she supposed that, 'Once the gilt starts wearing off the gingerbread it must make a difference if someone has basically the same views as oneself on major subjects. Actually Jock and I don't agree at all on politics, religion, books, films, etc. (Luckily, we do usually like the same people.) However I don't think our different views have worried either of us.'

At that moment Jock was going through a pro-South Africa phase, and when he said that if he were free that was where he'd like to live, Anne retorted that she'd be locked up right away. 'I should feel impelled to go out and ask the first African I met home to tea.' To tea! When we couldn't even reciprocate Mistry's tea parties? The absurdity shows how little they understood, either of them, of the nature of apartheid. What they did know was colonial Tanzania. What they felt was the ground shifting.

This was the era of letter writing, and Anne and Jock both wrote regularly to Kitty—Anne more often than Jock—who kept all their letters. Reading them now, I hear my parents' voices expressing themselves freely and spontaneously without fear of censorship. Their letters were personal, recording family events and feelings; but they are also social documents, providing unguarded access to a time of political upheaval. In all this, Anne and Jock were people of their time—white, colonial, British middle-class. If my politics differ from theirs, that's at least partly a function of where we stand in relation to history—how old we were in the pivotal year of 1968. I was seventeen, they were approaching fifty.

And something else, too—the matter of birth and upbringing. Although I didn't understand what was going on in the country where I lived, I was joined to it by an umbilical cord. Neither Jock nor Anne anticipated the strength of that bond or the way it would shape our lives. Looking back, through the prism of their letters, I see how complicated it was to be in charge one minute, anathema the next. They had fought in the War, suffered, set out again in answer to the same patriotic calling, faced hardship, survived. Like Kitty, I can only salute their courage.

Unsure of the future, for a few years following Uhuru Jock looked around for jobs in different parts of the world: Ceylon, Aberdeen, Oxford, Australia. When the Ceylon government decided he was an undesirable alien and his candidature for a specialist post was unacceptable, he commented ruefully, 'I suppose ex-Colonial Service is enough.' It became apparent he wasn't going to be offered a job if he was still on contract in Tanzania, but with four children to support, he was loath to risk leaving with nothing to go to. Anne felt otherwise. As Jock became more depressed, she said, 'I would give a great deal to be shot of it all and just pray that a firm offer of a job will enable us to leave before too long as I fear Jock will not go without that. I feel things are such in Africa now that one should cut one's losses and go.'

Jock pinned his hopes on the UN agency, the Food and Agriculture Organisation, or FAO, taking over the Utilisation Section, with himself as director. This idea came about as the result of a conference given by FAO in Nairobi in 1962 (the year before Kenya's Independence). The conference was in two legs, the first in Nairobi, the second in Moshi. Jock gave two lectures on the work of the Utilisation Section, and FAO were so impressed they wanted to put money into it. Jock persuaded them the money would be wasted unless they took it over entirely, and wrote a proposal for FAO to that effect, 'so there's a fair chance the institution will be taken out of the hands of the Tanganyikan government and expanded as an East African research institution'—with himself as director. 'Delegates were unanimous in naming their day at my laboratory the outstanding experience of the conference. They simply did not realise that adequate scientific research could be conducted in a British colony.'

Other institutions they had relied on fared less well. Jock reported that the Minister of Health, administering a collapsing health service, had sacked two British doctors because the attitudes of 'colonial medicine' were not in tune with 'a progressive Tanganyika.' Accustomed to segregated facilities, Anne lamented the closure of the European inpatients' hospital in Moshi, forcing them to go to Arusha for operations. Although the general hospital had a Grade A wing it didn't come up to scratch. A European woman, whose baby arrived early, found herself lying there with messengers passing in and out of the delivery room. Outpatients however remained separate for private patients or civil servants, with a 'very nice and efficient Asian surgeon and two young European doctors on contract.' When Anne returned from a week in Malindi with coral poisoning from a cut, she had o queue for hours at the hospital for a penicillin injection. The same thing happened when Alexandra cut her foot on a tin in the waterfall at Marangu and had to go for a tetanus injection. 'How I long,' Anne confessed, 'for a nice old family doctor whom one could telephone! The only European doctor in private practice here is pretty useless and diagnoses everything as malaria.'

As early as 1960, British Prime Minister, Harold Macmillan, had warned, 'The wind of change is blowing through this continent, and whether we like it or not, this growth of national consciousness is a political fact.' Socially things were changing too. People had always moved around the country, or disappeared for several months on home leave, but the community had been stable, with many long-term residents. Now people who had been a part of it for years were leaving for good. A year after Uhuru Anne was complaining, 'I feel bereft of real friends now, so many people have gone and are not being replaced, except by Lutheran missionaries with gaunt-looking wives, or American Peace Corps—worthy do-gooders in octagonal spectacles.' But she was taking French classes, and busy with a women's tennis and Bridge four, library duties and the gardening club. As librarian at the Club, she was disgusted with the level of reading matter and ordered biographies, including one of Rhodes. When she discovered she could get books through The Times Book Club more quickly than ordering through the Twiga Bookshop in town, this annoyed the bookshop owner—who was also Club secretary. A small place, getting smaller. She herself was reading *The Swordbearers: Supreme Command in the First World War* by the military historian, Correlli Barnett, whose close analysis of the role of culture and character in shaping strategy resonated with her own recent war experience.

At work, Jock faced new problems. A clerk came to him to complain that he was a trained typist and was being made to keep the correspondence register and staple papers together.

Jock told him he must do as he was told, whereupon he responded, 'Did you say *must*? That seems a very peculiar word for *you* to use on *me* in these days!'

Another clerk, a Muslim and the Vice President's nephew, told Jock he was 'an imperialist dog' and no free man could work for him. He wrote as much to his friends in the Ministry. 'I'm so *tired*,' said Jock, and Anne had to produce ice packs to soothe his brow when he came home to lunch.

Beyond Moshi and the Forest Department there was the rest of the country, and beyond that, the rest of Africa. They saw and heard about events like the state visit of 'a man called Sekou Toure, president of an obscure African territory called Guinea,' who was entertained by the Vice President, who took him to dinner at the Safari Hotel in Arusha. It was reported that when the guests failed to rise to their feet, the manager was informed he would no longer be allowed to operate his drinks licence, whereupon he turned all the guests out, including a wealthy investor from the US, and closed the restaurant. The slightest hint of discourtesy especially failure to show adequate respect for political figures—such as overtaking a cortege containing the Regional Commissioner—became tantamount to a criminal act.

This was the kind of thing that was discussed over beer and nuts at the Club or at dinner parties, enlivening many an evening. A perennial topic was corruption and Anne regaled Kitty with news of 'a good old government scandal blowing up here—one of the government ministers, now head of maize control, has been arrested, with eight others, for corruption. He took a £1,000 bribe to place the maize contract with an Asian firm. He was supposed to be one of the best— certainly he was charming and westernised. I can't help feeling sorry for people suddenly shot to the top where bribes are concerned—£1,000 must seem like a king's ransom.' Before Uhuru, prison was seen less as a deterrent than a tool of colonial repression, and this attitude, the new government felt, meant some other punishment was needed. Corporal punishment, widely used by the Germans and restricted but not abolished by the British, was now mandated by law and given at the beginning and end of a sentence for corruption and embezzlement. Rumour had it that one Asian given twelve strokes for corruption subsequently died.

'Can you imagine Mr Fenner Brockway's reaction if Britain had been in power?' Anne asked rhetorically. I want to ask my left-leaning mother what she really thought of this prominent anticolonial activist and conscientious objector, who had written a book on Mau Mau in the early 50s, and, in 1963, one on African Socialism. Jock's views I can all too well imagine.

By September 1963, Mary and Alexandra were starting their second year at school in Lushoto. Boarding the school train at the station a year earlier, Alexandra had been in floods of tears and Mary—always the tougher one—had said: 'Poor Alexandra, I *am* sorry for you.' This time, as they were woken for the train in the early morning, both their eyes filled with tears. Anne reminded them that they were so keen to go they used to try and get on the train with me. Mary said, 'Yes, but I've seen it now and I'd rather stay with you.' Once back at school, however, Alexandra wrote that there were a lot of new children who 'cry all day and all night and I'm getting NOT enough sleep because of them.' As for me, now eleven, I was keeping a diary and had a poem, 'The Glorious Birthday', published in the church magazine at Christmas, which my poetry-writing mother thought was 'particularly good and well thought out for her age. She is full of romantic and poetic ideas but I think—and hope—she is developing a fair amount of common sense too.'

That year, Moshi residents were treated to the dramatic spectacle of a huge fire on the heathland above 10,000 feet on Kilimanjaro. For two weeks the slopes below the snow-line glowed a brilliant red, intensifying at night till it seemed the mountain itself was burning. Its origin was mysterious but was most likely accidental carelessness, perhaps poachers, or honey gatherers in the rain forest smoking a hive. For over a century, the upper slopes of the mountain have been getting drier and difficulty of water supply meant about a hundred square miles of the forest belt and its adjacent heathland eventually went up.

Jock was publishing 'a mass of stuff so as to leave something worthwhile to read.' He complained that the Forest Department was almost moribund, everyone with any ability and experience having left Headquarters, but at least salaries were still being paid.

'I really believe I could sit here for another three years and read novels and no one would care. One of the most respected European forest officers was arrested and searched last week, suspected of taking a bribe, because an informer had seen him accept a piece of paper from an Indian in a hotel. Turned out the man was a Kenyan press photographer who wanted more news of our fire and was giving him his name and address.'

Even so, it was a relief when, at the end of the year, the Tanganyika Government invited Jock to stay in Moshi till 1969. He knew the reason for the offer was the many resignations of experienced British staff, but he accepted, largely because I had just passed the entrance exam for Cheltenham and there would be fees to pay. Meanwhile, they waited to hear from FAO.

Colonial holidays, like the Queen's Birthday, celebrated for the last time in September 1962, began to be replaced by East African Independence holidays— in December 1963 there were three in one week: Monday for Tanganyika, Wednesday for Kenya and Thursday for Zanzibar. Anne commented that, 'Holidays come so thick and fast that there is scarcely a fortnight without one.' As Kenya gained its Uhuru, she wrote, 'Things seemed to go quietly in Kenya despite Mr Kenyatta's ceremonial review of ex-Mau Mau fighters and a free pardon to all those still holding out in the forests where many of them have been for the last nine years.' Kenya was a country with which we shared a border, and, unlike Tanganyika, a full British colony. From where we stood, its white-owned farms producing proper beef, milk and cheese, its orderly tea and coffee plantations and its cool, gracious capital, were beacons of civilisation. All through the 1950s, terrifying reports of Mau Mau blood rituals and oathing and settlers hacked to death had been monstrous harbingers of what an anticolonial insurgency might look like. The now venerable President Jomo Kenyatta had been imprisoned as a leader; the Mau Mau general, Dedan Kimathi, had been hanged. My own godfather, John Blower, Jock's colleague in Lindi, had led a police unit known as 'Blowforce' against the Mau Mau, inflicting heavy casualties and killing one of their leaders, General Kago.

Today we know Mau Mau guerrillas as the Land and Freedom Army, which fought for the right to land lost to the huge farms of white settlers. When captured, they were terribly treated by the British and later badly served by their own government. But in 1963, only three years after the state of emergency had ended, the settler killings were still recent and the extent of British atrocities—and the numbers of Kenyans killed, tortured, forcibly removed or detained—had yet to be revealed. As a result, fear of violence lurked in the heart of every ex-colonial who chose to stay on after Uhuru.

On May 1 1964, Jock complained, 'This is our third public holiday in eight days: Id el Hadj, Union with Zanzibar and May Day. No one knows whether we have absorbed Zanzibar or vice versa. All the Communist Ministers in both countries are included in the new cabinet, but they may be hanging from lampposts a fortnight hence.'

The revolution in Zanzibar, to which Jock is referring, happened in early January 1964. The presence of Marxists in the newly-formed Zanzibari Revolutionary Council was enough to label it a Communist plot: one of these, Abdulrahman Babu, an anti-colonialist and nationalist, is remembered today as one of Africa's foremost political thinkers. He had already been locked up by the British and, evidently, was too radical for Nyerere, who later locked him up for another six years. He spent years as a member of the African exile community in London as a correspondent for the journal *New African*, for which I too was writing during the 1980s. But in 1964, the Cold War meant that westerners lived in fear of Communist infiltration.

A week or so after the Zanzibar coup, the expatriate community was further unsettled by a series of dramatic events on mainland Tanganyika, and in Kenya and Uganda. For Jock, attempting to reassure his mother—listening to the news in Australia—it was hard to make sense of events happening at a distance and with minimal reporting. In his letter to Kitty on January 26, he resorted to a breathless succession of detail to convey a week of turmoil:

'You will know as much about it as we do (a) because nothing whatever happened in Moshi and (b) because no official news was or is forthcoming in Tanganyika, and we got our information from Kenya and the BBC. In short, last Sunday night the Tanganyika Rifles mutinied in Dar, took control of the city, of Nyerere's person or at least his residence, and to a certain extent of the police. Two ministers, Oscar Kambona (Minister of Defence) and Job Lusinde (Minister of Home Affairs), retreated steadily throughout Monday and Tuesday (on which day the Tabora battalion also mutinied) and granted all the troops' demands. On Wednesday Nyerere reappeared in public with his cabinet, some say from a tug off-shore (but the wildest rumours were of course going about) and on Thursday held a press conference to say everything was under control. On Friday arrangements with the Navy were presumably completed and on Saturday—

yesterday—at 8am, the Royal Marines invaded and disarmed the so-called Tanganyika Army. It took them less than an hour to assume control. Here in Moshi the Scotsman who still heads the police was the only effective civil authority, the all-African administration being quite without resource or initiative. Our local police continued to take orders and were at least visible on the streets in large numbers armed with rifles. All trade union leaders throughout the country were taken into custody by the police late last night.

'There was no mention of the incident at all in the radio news from Dar, though the disarming of the Kenya Rifles and Uganda Rifles was fully reported. The simultaneous outbreaks in all three countries, following hard on the Communist coup in Zanzibar, have a sinister look, but the old-fashioned proceedings now going on give one confidence, as does the order of battle—the Staffords, the Royal Horse Artillery, the Gordon Highlanders, the Scots Guards, the Marines, an aircraft carrier and a frigate, and a fighter squadron of the Royal Air Force.'

Jock, let it be remembered, had been a pilot in the same Royal Air Force. Historians of this period have pointed out the anomaly of the armies of these three East African countries being, essentially, still structured along the lines of the colonial force set up by the British. The soldiery understandably resented the continued presence, post-Uhuru, of British officers, simultaneously with the loss of their pre-Uhuru elite position and privilege. The fact of British troops being invited by a newly-elected African leader to rescue him from his own army was one of the most sensational and ambiguous moments in Tanganyika's post-Independence history.

'Communist coup' notwithstanding, hindsight would show how Nyerere and Karume, the new leader of Zanzibar, went behind Babu's back to bring about the union of the two countries precisely to deflect suspicion of ideological taint from Communism. This was done with the covert support of the CIA, fresh from its collusion in the overthrow and murder of Patrice Lumumba in the Congo. The US State Department cable read: 'The Department gives its blessing and support to the Tanganyika-Zanzibar Federation or incorporation… which would exclude Babu and his clique.'

Not being privy to these manoeuvrings, Jock regarded the union as confirmation of the government's communist leanings. But was he so far wrong, I wonder? Tanzania has done a good job presenting itself as friendly to the West while remaining closely tied, politically and financially, to China—to this day. If he were to go back now, Jock would no doubt find plenty of evidence to support his view of it as an authoritarian state. Under previous President Magufuli there was censorship of the press, heavy-handed intervention in family planning and HIV prevention and treatment, expulsion of pregnant schoolgirls and harassment and repression of journalists, gays and political dissenters. Tanzania in the second decade of the 21stst century became a place where blogging licences were priced so high most bloggers shut up shop. Meanwhile, its precious wildlife reserves are under pressure from developers—a dam is to be built in the Selous, a new road through the Serengeti, land belonging to the Masai cordoned off as a hunting ground for rich foreigners. Like a veil obscuring all this, the safari myth lives on, promising an adventure in the midst of pristine nature, the roar of lions at sunset.

24. Elephant and Allure

f my parents were experiencing change after Uhuru, 1964 marked a radical shift or me at thirteen. Instead of a journey of a hundred and forty miles by train and ɔus, I was now to fly four thousand miles to boarding school in the Mother Country. My friends and I were sixth formers at Lushoto, our sense of where we ɔelonged inscribed with Italic fountain pen in the front of our exercise books: Lushoto School, Usambara Mountains, Tanganyika, East Africa, Africa, The World, The Universe. Now we sat in rows on wooden benches in the Assembly Hall listening in wonder to a roll call of fabulous place-names: Benenden, St Paul's, Cheltenham Ladies' College... We had sat the 13-plus Common Entrance exam and these English boarding schools were where we were going next. We had turned out perfect essays on 'The Seasons' and 'What I did in my summer holidays', in spite of the fact that the only seasons we knew were Rainy and Dry, and our summer holidays fell at the wettest time of year. We knew Latin and French and Geometry and Hockey and Scottish Country Dancing. What we didn't know was England.

The grass in those English fields was so green, it made me nauseous. Mother and I had flown to England in April to prepare for my new school. I was going to Cheltenham Ladies' College, though I had never heard of Cheltenham and had no idea what a Ladies' College—or even a lady—might be. We set off from Auntie Pam's house in Essex to get the train to Liverpool Street Station in London with a long list of uniform to be bought. At first, I looked out of the window at the English fields and fat English cows eating English grass, but soon I had to keep my eyes inside the carriage. We'd left Moshi in the dry season when everything was scorched yellow as far as the eye could see. So much green was unnatural. I was glad when we reached Liverpool Street and took a taxi to Daniel Neal's, the department store on a square behind Oxford St. The lift carried us to the School Outfitting Department on the fourth floor, where we were taken in hand by a middle-aged lady of great hauteur. She scrutinised the typed list of items we had been sent and sniffed. Without speaking, she walked away, and we followed her as meekly as English sheep.

It was 1964, and even though at home we still dressed as if it was the 50s, we had heard of mini-skirts. Mother was wearing a smart, red wool suit with her hair swept in a beehive beneath the leopard skin pillbox hat that meant she was sometimes mistaken for an East African Airways stewardess. ('Mine's real,' she always kindly explained.) She was wearing stilettos and her skirt stopped exactly at the knee. I was wearing clothes passed down from Miranda, my older cousin—a short black and white dog-tooth check skirt, a black turtle-neck sweater—with large black and white plastic geometric earrings. I thought I looked the bee's knees.

Under the withering gaze of the assistant, I stripped to my white knickers and still-not-filled-out bra. Then began a protracted struggle with a succession of unfamiliar garments. First there was a nylon contraption with dangling metal loops. Seeing my panic, Mother stepped in to fix it round my waist, before showing me how to roll a nylon stocking up each leg and attach the top to the suspenders.

'The seams must be straight,' commanded the assistant in the voice of a Brillo Pad scraping across a recalcitrant saucepan, as she wrenched them into line at the backs of my legs. Then there was a welter of buttons, stiff seams that had to be aligned with sharp tugs, a long-sleeved, white cotton shirt with stiff cuffs and a stiff collar, beneath which the assistant, as though fitting a noose, wound a green and grey striped tie into a tight knot at my throat. I looked at myself in the changing room mirror and saw that the skirt of the green tweed suit I was wearing fell three inches below my knees. What was left of my legs, brown from climbing trees and running around in the sun, seemed to have been overtaken by a fungal growth. The regulation stockings had the pallor of cold Heinz mushroom soup, with fat brown worms snaking up the back. Over the white shirt, a green tweed, double-breasted jacket fell to my hips, and over all of it the remorseless Brillo Pad draped a long, clammy, green gabardine macintosh hanging almost to the brown, indoor shoes she called loafers.

I had never seen, never imagined, anything so ugly as myself in this barbarous get-up. It weighed a ton, and the tie was so tight I could hardly breathe. I felt myself drifting into a state of suspended animation. Gladly I floated to somewhere near the ceiling, where I could look down from a great height at the green creature, the leopard skin pillbox, the sharp nose and iron hair of the assistant. The carpet, the same fungal hue as the stockings, muffled all sound so that my mother's voice came to me as a whisper.

'Don't you think,' she was tentatively suggesting, 'the skirt's a little long?'

'Oh no Madam,' reproached Brillo Pad, 'Ladies are required to wear their skirts below the knee. It's such an elegant uniform, don't you agree?'

'Yes,' my mother acquiesced, 'though isn't it perhaps a little too—*green*?'

'...and the Allure stockings are specially made for the ladies by Aristoc. Now, if you'd help your daughter undress, we'll measure her for the hat.'

A hat! If they added one more item to the load I would plummet into the fungus and never get up again.

Later, after I'd been at the Ladies' College for a while, I came across a book in the house library, *In Search of Charm* by Mary Young, Principal of Mary Young Model School and Agency, 'organiser and chief instructress of courses on Poise, Dress and Personality.' I read it, hoping it might help me navigate the complexities of English feminine etiquette. Under 'Are my stockings the right shade for my outfit?' I learnt that, though '"Nude", "Champagne" or "Sherry" shades look right with most outfits... if you like your legs to have a sun-browned look, try shades such as "Elephant" or "Nigger" in a *very sheer* stocking.' I don't know how the elegant and dignified daughter of the Nigerian High Commissioner, a senior at the school and therefore too lofty to ask, got on with those choices, but I was certainly closer to Elephant than Allure.

A week later, we arrived, my mother and I, each as nervous as the other, on the doorstep of the boarding house where I was to live. My mother drew confidence from the fact that she'd dutifully ticked off all the outfitting requirements. The colonial service salary scale inherited by the Tanganyika Government at Independence could barely cope with the cost of private education in the Mother Country, and my uniform and sports equipment—almost as much as a term's fees—had cost my parents dear. We stood gazing at the shiny door-knocker for a while, and then my mother pulled herself together, lifted her hand and knocked. Footsteps clicked along the hall towards us, the door opened, and a sharp, grey woman stood there. Surely she was Brillo Pad's sister? Taking us in at a glance, she pointed to the brown loafers that protruded from beneath the gabardine.

'Those shoes,' she pronounced, 'simply won't do. Those shoes are for seniors only.'

So began my induction into ladyhood. I was thirteen when the door closed behind me, and, apart from brief interludes, would be eighteen before I was finally let out again. Meanwhile, the 60s, decade of fabulous freedom—dropping out, turning on, getting high—simply passed me by. I saw glimpses on television but I was one of eight hundred girls in green locked up, kept in, laid low. What was important, according to Mary Young, was to 'always remove your gloves by releasing each finger a little at the fingertip, take a firm but feminine grip with one hand of the five fingertips of the other glove, draw off the glove smoothly'. Elderly ladies would phone the house-mistress to report if girls had been spotted without their hats or chamois leather gloves or loitering outside a sweet-shop when they should have been marching to the playing fields for hockey. Mary Young cautioned against too much physical development which 'may be spoiling your looks, figure or grooming', though if you really wanted to play sports, 'there is nothing wrong with this as long as you are sure that everything is well balanced by the feminine things of life'. Dressed for games in white knicker-linings with green over-knickers beneath scratchy green knee-length culottes, topped by white Aertex shirts and finished off with green knee-high socks, we were learning that ladyhood was a form of bondage.

Rules—there were so many. Only walk on the right side of the corridor, don't run, don't talk, use the back stairs, only wash your hair on Tuesdays, don't stretch for the salt, offer it to your neighbour, don't bite into your banana, cut it into slices, polish your shoes till they shine, polish the prefects' shoes till they shine. Often the rules were mysterious—why no long-handled hairbrushes? Or the time I got into bed with a friend because we wanted to talk and the rule was silence after lights-out. The house-mistress, on a snooping tour of the dormitories, dragged us off to her study and spoke to each of us individually. When it was my turn, she asked me if I knew why I shouldn't be in bed with another girl. I didn't. I stared at her and she stared at the carpet. There was silence for a long time, then she sent me back to bed.

You might think we were all spoiled rich kids in our expensive private school, but far from it. When my father wrote to his mother that the fees were a hundred and sixty pounds a term and wondered that people still thought it worthwhile, 'at least for females', she wrote in the margin of the letter, 'How on earth can he pay this—what possessed them? The other three girls will have to go to work at fifteen!' It was a huge relief for my parents when—thanks to my address in England being Auntie Pam's house—I sat an IQ test set by the Essex Education Committee, and was awarded a grant that made the fees manageable. Some were authentically 'posh', but many of my schoolmates came to the school from broken homes or problem families, some, like me, had parents thousands of miles away and some were on scholarship. We survived, like prisoners of war, because of each other. We presented a united front of resistance to authority: all of us broke some of the rules and some of us broke all of them. A friend and I took to creeping out of a downstairs window after lights-out and wandering the streets all night, returning at dawn to crawl into bed before the rising bell rang, just to prove to ourselves we could break out and get away with it. The world outside came to us in short colourful bursts with a rock and roll soundtrack—She loves you, yeah, yeah, yeah, Hey, hey we're the Monkees, *Top of the Pops*, a weekly shot of *The Avengers* with the fabulous Diana Rigg, in skin-tight black leather, kicking ass (though that's not an expression we would have known or used). Not only did Diana Rigg not ease off her gloves from the fingertips or wear nude stockings, she was, by reliable account, an ex-student of our very own school, living proof that we would all get out of there one day and really *live*.

Holidays were a luxury parole from penal servitude. Everything came to life again—colours were brighter, food tasted better, and best of all, we abandoned the green uniform for mini-skirts and jeans. Dutifully, we would leave the boarding house in suit, hat, gloves, tie, Allure stockings and polished regulation outdoor shoes. As soon as we were on the train, we would closet ourselves in the stuffy little toilet (Mary Young: 'Remember the old French maxim, "to be beautiful, you have to suffer"'), emerging triumphantly transformed to ordinary teenagers, no longer 'ladies', expected to walk sedately through town in pairs keeping the seams of our Allure stockings straight.

When I started school in England I could only go home once a year, for the summer holidays. Later, there were miraculous charter flights run by Ethiopian Airways, taking long indirect routes with exotic stopovers. In 1966 my sisters and I flew home for Christmas. They were twelve, I was fifteen, but there was no nonsense about being Unaccompanied Minors. Even better were the dates, which were non-negotiable—we had to leave before the end of one term and return a day late for the next. The flight left Heathrow at 1.40pm for Zürich, where we joined forces with a glossy-haired, sweet-faced Irish girl my age called Deidre, from Tanga. We found a small café and sat drinking Swiss beer and eating cheese rolls, discussing who we knew in common. A large, fair Italian girl called Ala came up and admired my elephant hair bracelet. 'Have you been to Nairobi?' she asked, sitting down with us. Of course, we had, and in quarter of an hour we knew all about her school in Zürich and her boyfriend in Rome and the fur coat she got for her birthday. The electricity failed and the waitresses lit candles. We bought cigarettes and more beer and my sisters had milkshakes. The plane kept being delayed, so we went outside for fresh air, stepping into a magical world of fir trees and crisp white snow.

Eventually, around 9pm, we left for Athens, where Deidre and I roamed the airport, giggling at the sight of two boys who looked like twelve-year-olds, puffing solemnly on pipes. On the next leg, to Khartoum, Deidre and Ala and I amused ourselves by teasing two teenagers, one Swiss, one South African, in the seat in front of us. In retaliation, the Swiss boy threw his newspaper at us, and Deidre threw her Irish one back at him. We were sorry Ala didn't have an Italian one to throw. At daybreak we reached Khartoum, where at last it was hot and we changed into light, summer clothes before taking off again for Uganda's Entebbe airport. Landing involved skimming low over Lake Victoria to touch down seemingly at the last minute on dry land. It was 9.30 in the morning. In Entebbe we started to see other children bound for Moshi, and with mounting excitement found seats together as we took off on the short flight to Nairobi. There, we disembarked and watched as Ala greeted her parents and a noisy crowd of friends with shrieks of joy. At the last minute, she ran back to say goodbye, pressing on each of us a velvet comb case decorated with gold braid. 'I made them as Christmas presents,' she said breathlessly, and ran back to her welcome committee. Deidre rushed off to catch her onward flight to Tanga, and my sisters and I went through Customs. Spotting the precious bottle of duty-free whisky I had bought on my father's instructions, the Customs Officer told me sternly I wasn't old enough to import alcohol; seeing my stricken face, he smiled and waved me through.

Around 1pm, the three of us and a handful of other Moshi children got on a twin-engine Dakota for the final flight. Sleepless, over-stimulated, disorientated, grubby and some of us smelling of cigarettes, we arrived to a grand reception, a mêlée of parents and friends and younger children crowded onto the little semi-circular concrete apron, waiting to receive us. The fire-engine drove out on the tarmac as we taxied to a stop, ready for action if the plane caught fire. Then we were tumbling down the steps, clutching discarded coats and bags and duty-free whisky, the heat rising off the tarmac in a sticky embrace. We had been flying for near enough twenty-four hours.

Today, commercial flights no longer land at Moshi's little airport. The much bigger, modern Kilimanjaro Airport, built to service mountain climbers as well as the game-parks on the Northern Circuit—Serengeti, Ngorongoro, Manyara, Tarangire—is around fifty miles from Kilimanjaro and quite a drive from Moshi. The Moshi airport of my childhood was part of the town. Whenever anyone was going on leave or back to school in another country, family and friends would make the short drive to see them off. On the apron outside the small customs hall, with the plane that would take you to Nairobi parked on the runway a hundred yards away, up to thirty people might gather, chatting, cracking jokes and exchanging last minute hugs. The excitement was enough to keep at bay the homesickness that was waiting to overwhelm you. When it was time to leave you walked across the tarmac to the plane and boarded, turning every few seconds to wave. With a roar you were off, the airport dwindling through the small circular porthole as you craned for a last look. Then a great swoop towards the mountain, and over the border to Kenya.

Leaving for school when I was fourteen, I cried all the way to Nairobi where I found myself in a group of young people waiting for the plane to England. A boy and I started talking. He'd been with his family in Dar, where his dad worked for the British Council. He was tall and slim with an intelligent, humorous expression. Easy to talk to. I had friends in Dar, and we were discussing who we knew in ommon and where we each went to school, when the announcement came that he flight had been delayed several hours. We looked at each other in delight at the eprieve—neither of us wanted to hurry back to boarding school. Then came the uphoric news that the airline was issuing vouchers for a hotel where passengers ould spend the time in comfort, have a meal and relax until called. We joined the queue to collect the vouchers but when it was my turn, the desk clerk asked for my passport.

'You're fourteen,' he said, 'you're an Unaccompanied Minor. That means you have to stay with the stewardess.' My face flushed and I was struggling not to cry when Tony materialised. I was tall, but he towered above me, addressing the clerk with perfectly pitched public school charm.

'I'm over sixteen,' he said, his voice deep, mellow and confident. 'That means I'm an adult, doesn't it? And that means, if you'll allow me, I can save the stewardess the trouble. I'd be delighted to take over responsibility for "accompanying" this young lady.'

Escaping the stewardess, I was driven with Tony to a Nairobi hotel where we spent most of the day. There was an outdoor pool surrounded by red hibiscus and I changed into the holiday bikini I thought I'd packed away for the last time. Tony's eyes told me it made the hoped-for impression. Reclining on a lounger with a long, cool drink, I let the lurking homesickness slink off into the shrubbery. When we got tired of swimming we found our way to the restaurant and ordered our free meal. When we'd had enough to eat, we headed to the bar. I fell for him—he had rescued me from shame. Those blissful stolen hours infused our letters, sent from one boarding school to another, with an enduring aura of romance. He wrote a poem about our first encounter that was published in his school magazine: 'The jets roared as we walked out together,' illustrated with a drawing of him and me walking to the plane. When I complained he'd made my legs look fat, my mother disagreed. 'I think he's got you absolutely.'

25. The Reel Unspools

After the school door closed behind me in April 1964, Anne stayed on in England. My parents were due for leave and Jock, who joined her in August, was selected as one of two representatives from Tanganyika (and almost certainly the only white delegate) to attend a seminar in Berlin around the same time. Though the camp, *Stalag Luft* III, where he had been confined the longest, was just across the border from Berlin, in Poland, his reaction stemmed less from his POW experience and his dislike of 'Huns' than his contempt for the kind of 'togetherness caper' represented by a seminar. This one, he said, appeared to be entirely for the benefit of Germany—representatives from all the English-speaking African countries were to spend five weeks talking about forestry and forest products, and the idea naturally appalled him.

'I haven't the slightest desire to see Berlin, I hate togetherness and the technical problems of forestry in Africa as administered by Africans do not merit five days discussion let alone five weeks at the height of the Test match season.'

So he begged to be excused. Instead, they visited friends all over England and watched a lot of tennis and cricket. After the school holidays, they also went to Aberdeen in Scotland, where Jock was exploring the possibility of a job at the university. It was where George, his father, lived, and they visited him. This was a concession on Jock's part, since he bore a grudge against his father almost as deep as his love for his mother. Early signs were inauspicious: Aberdeen was hosting a Gaelic Festival, and George, an ardent Scottish Nationalist, was reluctant to be distracted from it. Jock, who regarded Scottish Nationalism as a form of tribalism, was most put out when they couldn't get into a hotel and had to put up with 'extreme manifestations of Scotchness along with their constipating food in an unlicensed boarding house.' His father, who seemed unwilling to spare them any time, expected them to attend the festival and enjoy the tribal dancing. They called on him at his boarding house where George's hospitality extended to tea in a freezing front room. When the landlady, trying to make them a little more comfortable, asked if they'd like a radiator, George firmly said no.

Describing the visit to his mother, for whose sake he no doubt made it, Jock said, 'He made it plain he was missing some performances at the festival. Apart from waxing very bitter on the subject of grouse shooting, he enquired after nobody, showed no interest in anyone we could talk about, and claimed not to have seen for years anyone we enquired about… his mind is perfectly sound but is now so fixed on its single track that conversation is impossible. We suggested we might take him to lunch next day but he "usually had macaroni cheese at a snack bar", and said we'd no doubt see him if we attended the festival.'

They did so, in relays because they had Sally with them, aged three, but failed to find him. 'I left a note at his lodgings with a totally false description of our pleasure at Gaelic singing, but even that gesture was fairly generous in the circumstances.' Though this wasn't the last time Jock saw his father, it was emblematic of their relationship— indifference on one side, hostility on the other, grudging compromise brokered by Anne, disillusion inevitable and confirmed.

When they flew back from leave, they were allowed a hundred and thirty pounds of luggage. It sounds a lot, but things were getting harder to find or afford in Tanganyika (which had become Tanzania in their absence), and they had accumulated a mountain of essentials. With a coffee percolator, toaster, typewriter, six pairs of shoes and enough children's books for a year, they struggled to and fro across the road to the weighing machine outside the village chemist's shop trying to make it all stay inside the weight limit.

Back in Moshi early in 1965, Anne found it not greatly changed except for the cost of things in the shops due to import charges imposed by the Government. They were glad they had bought the coffee percolator when they could. And the dark stories resumed: in Lushoto, where all the members of the Forest Department had now resigned, one white forester who tried to pick up an African woman in a bar had been arrested and sentenced to six months in jail. Worse than this puritanical censorship of people's private lives was the double standard now openly operating: an African sentenced for a similar offence was said to have been fined thirty shillings.

In January 1965, Winston Churchill died. It's hard to conjure now the significance of this event to the War generation he had led. At school in England, we were given the day off to watch the state funeral on television, attended by the Queen and members of the royal family, five other monarchs and more than twenty heads of state. In Moshi, Jock and Anne listened to the commentary on the BBC Overseas Service. They agreed the best speech was the eulogy by fellow war-leader Sir Robert Menzies, the Australian Prime Minister, from the crypt of St Paul's Cathedral. Menzies had been holidaying on the P&O liner Arcadia in the Pacific when he heard the news—the very ship we as a family sailed back on from leave in Australia, after Sally was born in Adelaide in 1961. Despite Churchill's unashamed contempt for Australia's insubordinate attitude to the Mother Country, Menzies left the ship at once and flew to London to be a pallbearer. It meant a great to deal to Jock, as to other Australian ex-servicemen and women, for their part in the War to be recognised. No wonder Menzies' words resonated.

'What was at stake was not some theory of government but the whole and personal freedom of men, and women, and children… That battle had to be won not only in the air and on the sea and in the field, but in the hearts and minds of ordinary people with a deep capacity for heroism.'

Surprisingly, Jock reported, even Tanzania recognised the occasion: 'Nyerere, whose colour is now deep red with a streak of yellow, even attended a C of E memorial service, and on the day of the funeral the flag was at half-mast all over the country.'

Affairs of state aside, Jock was facing ever greater difficulties at work, exacerbated by his acrimonious relationship with Chief Conservator Robert Sangster—his nominal boss, who represented everything Jock most despised. Sangster, based at headquarters in Dar, was obliged to negotiate the new political order so as to function, while trying to bring his officers onside. Jock's categorical refusal to conform was the source of unending friction and hearty, mutual dislike.

As a result, said Jock, 'My own existence is as up and down as ever. I had an embittered and all too frank exchange with Chief Conservator Sangster over the telephone, but he is to retire in February. I am chasing jobs all over the world. The Timber Bureau in Canberra hasn't anything. FAO has offered me a really excellent job in charge of the new School of Forestry in Liberia, but only for two years; no news from the library job in Oxford nor from the University of Aberdeen. The trouble is I have set the academic sights fairly high and probably in the end will have refused all these jobs and will finish conducting a bus.'

Caught between pressure to conform to the new dispensation—he refused to hang the President's portrait in his office and insisted on keeping the Queen—and his insecurity about the future, it's no wonder he came home speechless and angry. As with me and all that screaming, he was his own worst enemy.

There were lighter moments. Jock came home one day to relate that his colleague Harry Norcross, a plain-speaking Lancastrian, had been doing a mechanical job with some African employees when he noticed some error in workmanship.

'Crikey! You shouldn't have done it like that!'

A few minutes later the man he had been addressing came up to him and said, 'What was that word you used when you said I had done that job wrong?'

Harry answered, 'I said Crikey.'

'Oh and what does that word mean?' asked the man.

'It means Crikey,' said Harry, 'Go and look it up in the dictionary if you want to know what it means.' The man departed and about half an hour later returned and stood before him again.

'I have looked that word Crikey up in the dictionary and it doesn't give it. But I don't like the sound of that word Crikey and I don't think you should use it to me.'

In February, Anne and Sally went on a working tour with Jock, first to Lushoto, then Morogoro, Anne for the first time since the twins were three months old. She amused herself while Jock was working by a nostalgic visit to the hospital where Mary and Alexandra were born in 1954, but found the old concrete building no longer in use. At the old house, the terraced garden, where my earliest memory is of paddling in the canvas safari bath, was completely gone to seed. They spent a night under canvas at a game park and were impressed by the tent's wire-mesh zip-down windows, which could be firmly closed against marauding animals while still providing fresh air and a view of the night outside. Sally had a special little bed in an annexe at the back of the tent.

From Morogoro they moved on to Dar with its social life, bathing, tennis, Bridge and shops. The night they arrived they went to a big St Valentine's dance on the roof of the Gymkhana Club, where, Anne reported, membership had been opened up and she saw several Japanese, Filipinos and Asians but no Africans. Though Anne was delighted with the shopping and spent time buying dresses for herself and Sally, she told Kitty life in Dar had been impossible because of the official visit of Chou en Lai. The town was stiff with troops with automatic weapons, and they kept closing the one main bridge that led from town to the residential area so no one could get in to work or back home afterwards. He had originally been invited to visit all three East African countries but the visit had been postponed because of the mutinies, and afterwards Kenya and Uganda didn't renew their invitation so he went home again.

Shortly after seeing off Chou en Lai, Nyerere was in Moshi to lay the foundation stone for the new Lutheran Hospital. Anne attended, and remarked he looked very worn and strained, and that the reception at the airport 'did not seem very tumultuous'. At the Police Training School in Moshi, Chou had left fourteen Chinese instructors to teach the art of guerrilla warfare. They could be seen sitting in a circle on the grass at dusk; they were there, said Anne, in case Tanzania invaded Angola or South Africa. That may have been a possibility: Jock commented that, among the impossible burdens imposed by the recent Budget, there was a 5% levy on all income, 'to pay presumably for war with Portugal'. There were also newly-instituted exchange controls, a 50% increase in personal tax, another 15% increase in income tax and a mass of indirect taxation.

'Their politics,' Jock concluded, 'are completely insane (Moshi now well supplied with communist Chinese military) and their financial arrangements completely irresponsible. This is what we meant by not being ready for self-government.'

As far as Jock was concerned, China's influence on Tanzania was insidious Observing the reforms instituted by Nyerere since the mutiny and the subsequent union with Zanzibar, he was characteristically sardonic: 'The capital is an entertaining mixture of privileged capitalists bloated on misappropriated aid funds, and communist slogans. The army is now the People's Defence Force with a Political Commissar; Tshombe (the Congolese puppet leader chosen by the Europeans to neutralise Lumumba) is an imperialist stooge, America a neo-colonialist hyena and Britain a despised milch cow.'

Even in Moshi, he was not to be free of politics. Telephoned by the local commissar and ordered to attend a speech-making ceremony by the Committee of Nine, he asked courteously who these gentlemen were. When the only response was heavy breathing, he agreed to go but naturally 'forgot' when the time came. As he discovered, 'The Committee is apparently a group of ill-disposed, far-left African states who want to dispossess Portugal of Mozambique, so there could hardly have been a less likely attender at their deliberations.' It was the dry season and fiercely hot, and he watched work piling up as the clerical grades, now Africanised, failed to keep pace. Sometimes, overcome by the thought of the paperwork on his desk, he would start at 5am, resulting in complete exhaustion by the time he finished at 6pm. Even so, he was not tempted by another FAO job offer, this time in Pakistan. 'I can't take them very seriously, especially as one needs at least £2,000 a year more in the Far East to earn the same thing as in Africa.'

Anne lamented the withering of her garden and how desperately she was trying 'to get a few flowers to bloom in the wilderness'. She was finding shopping ever more difficult as places catering to European tastes closed. Import restrictions meant many of their favourite brands of food stuffs had disappeared.

'However,' she rejoiced to me in a letter, 'Daddy did manage to find three jars of Cooper's Oxford Marmalade while we were staying in Dar.'

In March, Anne went to Lushoto with Sally to take the twins out for half-term. This too was no longer straightforward. As Jock was busy, she accepted a lift with two other mothers and was shocked by the state of the road—deep corrugations covered in six inches of red dust. They drove the whole way being rattled about at 35 mph, and arrived shaking and covered in dust—'looking like Red Indians'. At the Lawns Hotel, said Anne, 'I was told by the old girl trying to run the hotel that there was trouble about my room as the Area Commissioner's girlfriend was in it and refused to move out. She gave me another room consisting of one single bed and a baby's cot.' Sally was now a well-grown three and half year-old, and Anne kept asking till she got a proper bed.

At the school, Anne found that of the two of them, Mary seemed less settled than Alexandra, was easily distracted and not behaving too well. Once she had earned a bad name among the teachers, she found it hard to shake it off, even though she came fourth in the class rankings—without any apparent effort, according to the class teacher. Is Anne suppressing pride or amusement when she says, 'She will not pretend and refuses to kiss the matron goodnight when she kisses the rest of the dormitory—because she doesn't like her'?

Then in June came the moment Anne revealed to Kitty that she'd discovered a small lump in her right breast. For some time, she hadn't been able to make up her mind whether she was imagining it, though she concealed this from us throughout the Easter holidays and waited till we were all at school to go and see 'the Asian doctor', as he was known. He immediately arranged for her to go and consult the surgeon at the hospital in Dar. She was all ready to go when the plane was unable to land due to bad weather. Jock was driving to Nairobi on a work mission and it was decided she should go with him, even though such a detour caused further delay. From Nairobi she went on to Dar by plane, where she saw the senior surgeon who, she noted approvingly, was a Scottish FRCS. He declared the need for a biopsy and carried it out. He remained reassuring, saying he was sure it was nothing more than a blocked duct.

Anne returned to Moshi to wait for the results. Jock was on a duty trip in Tanga and she was alone in the house when she got the call from Dar. The surgeon himself was on the line.

'I was very surprised,' he said 'and I'm very sorry to tell you that the biopsy shows the lump is malignant.'

Jock wasn't due back till the following evening so she was alone with the news for a day and a half. Her writing desk, a wooden escritoire made by Mistry with a drop-down flap and little pigeon-holes for letters, was in the sitting room. There, she took refuge in writing to Kitty.

'The surgeon advised flying home to England to have it seen to as the proper aftercare isn't available here,' she told her. 'As you can imagine I feel rather shattered and unfortunately Jock is away in Tanga and does not return until this evening.'

Shattered and alone, how did she fill those hours till Jock returned? She had survived the War, stalking leopard, charging elephant and Jock's driving. She had shown she was brave, but she had four daughters, the youngest only three. As well as the letter to Kitty she tried to distil her feelings into a poem:

So—must I leave, so soon?
Hearing an echo of children's tears and I
Unable to turn back?

What she dreaded most was leaving us alone, but, as she sternly reminded herself, she'd had twenty years longer than many friends who'd died in the War. In her folder of poems, written in her twenties, is one titled 'Beauty':

> She goes
> With tears,
> All her flowers are dead.
> She is not dancing
> For the years
> Lie heavily, the melody
> Disappears
> And every song has fled.

Now, at forty-four, she counted her blessings one by one—love, children, animals flowers, friends, cooking smells, and this:

> Twenty years—to walk barefoot on hot sand
> Along a beach in Africa, with casuarinas moving
> In the white hot sun.
> To swim in warm seas with the tropic fish
> All liquid fire, banded with iridescent colour
> In their noiseless world...

... till she simply ran out of words and trailed off, 'Dear wonderful world I cannot...' Ahead of her were four more years of heart-breaking struggle. She never complained and, though she was much afraid, never spoke of fear.

She flew to England the following week, leaving Sally with Jock and Martha, who was still with us in 1965 and now Sally's *ayah*. As she assured Kitty, 'People here are very good and kind at helping at times like these as no one has any relatives to take over and everything devolves on one's friends.' She herself had nursed numerous sick friends, visiting or taking them into the house until they recovered. She was also popular and highly thought-of, and what was left of Moshi society mobilised in support. In her turn, Kitty replied to Anne's letter, spelling out the depth of their bond.

'I love you so much and have always felt deeply about you. The thought of you crowds out everything else.'

In England, Anne went into Addenbrooke's Hospital in Cambridge at its ultra-modern new location. After a mastectomy she came home to her sister, our Auntie Pam's house in Thaxted, with a pad to fill out where the breast was missing. There was no reconstructive surgery and the prosthetics were primitive. There was a consensus that we shouldn't be told what was wrong with her. That's how it was in the 60s. People hadn't got to the point of talking openly about surviving cancer, making a statement about being breastless or bald. Auntie Pam explained to me, in all seriousness, that breastfeeding could cause milk to get stuck in a duct and solidify into a lump. Nowadays, you'd go straight online. There was no way of checking then, and you tended to believe what adults told you.

When she was well enough after the operation, Anne flew back to Moshi, one of six passengers and three stewardesses on a BOAC Comet. Changing planes in Nairobi, she declared two children's dresses at Customs and was told she'd have to pay 50% duty, but when she opened her purse to pay, the Customs officer decided he'd let her off. She missed her onward connection to Moshi where we were anxiously waiting at the airport. It was August and when we'd flown home weeks earlier for the summer holidays the house had seemed empty without her. She managed to get on a flight to Arusha, we got back in the car and Jock drove fifty miles at breakneck speed to meet her there. We were overjoyed she'd come back to us. We had lunch at a hotel, and drove home to a houseful of flowers from well-wishers and a cake baked by Martha.

Since her days in Tanga during the War, Anne had always loved the coast. Some of our happiest times as a family were holidays at Waridi, a house at Malindi on the Kenyan coast, where you ran from the verandah directly into the surf that broke and surged only yards away. Now Jock had organised a restorative week for us all at a Kenyan seaside hotel called Trade Winds twenty miles south of Mombasa. Before mass tourism, such hotels were plain and simple. This one was a series of thatched *bandas* strung along the beach, with wooden tables outside on the sand shaded by casuarinas that sighed in the slightest breeze. Jock and Anne had a *banda* to themselves, the four of us shared another one. Outside, we sat at the tables drinking Coke and cups of tea. Nearby, young local men shinned effortlessly up coconut trees, their feet bound together to help them grip the trunk. Jock made us scream with laughter by trying to climb one himself. He got half way and looked down with comical dismay, before sliding painfully back to the foot.

All along the beach vendors sold plaited baskets, shells and little boats and windmills made of coconut fronds. The twins, aged eleven, were entranced. They had recently started getting pocket money and spent their time in commercial wrangles with one group or another, until it ran out. At fourteen, I was happy playing big sister to three-year-old Sally, building sand castles and taking her paddling. Because of the operation Anne couldn't swim until the wound healed, but she could sit gazing across white, palm-fringed sand at aquamarine water. She could walk barefoot in the hot sand leaving her arched footprints, and cool her toes at the water's edge. In the evening, a bright orange moon swam up out of the sea.

On the two hundred mile drive to Trade Winds, we had to wait over an hour on the road due to the arrival of President Kenyatta at a village. We joined the crowd looking on as he got out of his Rolls Royce to hear schoolboys sing a psalm of welcome. 'He's looking old,' said Anne, alert to signs of humanity behind the façade of power. Jock started his movie camera rolling and an officious, plain-clothes policeman turned on him.

'No photographs! No photographs!' he commanded.

Jock ignored him, continuing to film. With unexpected violence the man grabbed his arm, and Jock responded with a peremptory, 'Take your hands off me!' For a moment Anne was afraid Jock would hit him. Luckily, at that moment the cortège moved off and the policeman dropped Jock's arm and ran for his car. Someone in the car ahead had been less lucky—he'd had his film removed and holiday snapshots spoiled. On the return journey, when we stopped to board the ferry from Mombasa island to the mainland, we met the procession again. This time it seemed the rules had changed as people were photographing freely.

'All part of 'Freedom' I suppose,' said Anne with a shrug. She at least had learnt to be philosophical about the huge deference demanded by political figures, the whimsicality of rules made up on the spot. Jock had not. When both Tanganyika and Kenya had been under British rule, there had been free movement across the border. Now there was a frontier between Tanzania and Kenya where Tanzanian cars were inspected and sometimes searched. Jock had scant respect and no patience for such manifestations of officialdom.

The border crossing at Taveta was only twenty-five miles from Moshi but we got there fractious and late in the day. Even though the family car was now a spacious old Mercedes, four sunburnt children sharing the back seat for six or seven hours was wearisome for everyone. A constable approached the car and peered in the driver's window.

'Papers!' he ordered, holding out a peremptory hand.

Jock complied, but when the man opened the boot and insisted on going through the bags of wet swimsuits and picnic things, Jock got out of the car. Ostentatiously, he took out the notebook he always carried and wrote down the constable's number. It was only two years since Kenya's Independence and the slightest mark of disrespect of an African official by a European was tantamount to a crime. The next thing we knew, Jock was carted off to the police station, leaving the five of us sitting in the car. Sally wailed and we all tried to distract her, ut couldn't disguise our suspense. Would our father be arrested and would we have to go home without him?

He was conducted indoors and paraded before an inspector, who luckily was polite and pleasant, but wanted to know what Bwana could mean by such an odd action.

'In order,' said Jock, 'to report the constable for truculence and foul manners, repeated on so many occasions that your police station is damaging Kenya's reputation among tourists and foreign visitors.' Slightly taken aback, the inspector asked how it was that no one else had complained.

'Because,' said Jock, 'they are mostly private citizens or business people who do not care to take risks or to involve themselves with authority. But *I*,' he said, warming to his subject, 'am a senior civil servant of a neighbouring country, I am not in the least frightened of you and not in the least prepared to put up with over-officious, junior policemen.'

This counter-attack worked because the inspector persuaded him that, rather than reporting to the Commissioner of Police, he could report to him. Jock duly did so before being returned under escort to the car, where we had been waiting for forty-five minutes in the dark. We were scared and fidgety and Anne had spent the time trying to reassure us that everything was going to be all right. She was rigid with tension, but as we drove away Jock was laughing.

'Kenyans are infinitely more arrogant and threatening than Tanzanians,' he said gleefully, 'but they don't know how to deal with counter-attack. Whereas in Tanzania counter-attack doesn't work because the system is more completely authoritarian.'

In the back seat, the twins and I exchanged looks and tried not to giggle. We'd grown up watching our father flouting the rules and didn't care too much for them ourselves. He glanced sideways at Anne.

'Never mind,' he said, 'at least the scenery is just as good both sides of the border.' Anne didn't laugh. It was dark and we were still a long way from home.

26. 'That's the way it goes, professor.'

Jock having escaped arrest for disrespect, the holiday was healing in other ways. I had visited my mother in Addenbrooke's—driven over from Thaxted by Auntie Pam—before flying home, and knew she had had a breast removed. Though even that didn't alert me to the truth of her condition, it was a watershed moment. Like most teenagers I was totally self-absorbed, and it jolted me into being more considerate to spare her stress. Perhaps as a result, Anne told Kitty, 'Jane's nature is easier than it used to be. I don't think she and Jock are really compatible in the way he and Sally are but they get on a lot better than they did when she was smaller. Even so, I can see she annoys him at times, and then, knowing how her mind works so well, I can see how he upsets her without realising it. But I suppose these things always happen in families.'

The key to my release from being regarded as the intractable daughter was the arrival of Sally, an enchanting smiling child, adored by all of us. I was ten when she was born and the age difference allowed me to demonstrate my precarious maturity. That was impossible with Mary and Ally, who had the same disrespect for hierarchy as Jock and I. When they were very young they were a self-sufficient entity with their own language. As they got older, they grudgingly allowed me into their games, embarrassed me at puberty and in time became competitive about boys I was seeing. Sally refocused the equation, so by the time I went back to school in England in September 1965, Anne was able to observe:

'The time with Jane seemed to fly by and I could hardly bear to part with her after only three weeks. She and Jock hit it off better towards the end of the holiday. I don't think she is jealous of the twins nowadays; Sally seems to have redressed the balance and Jane is terribly fond of her and very good with her.'

Then my mother, who never admitted to hating anyone and always spoke about her childhood with nostalgic affection, made an unusual onfession. Her own father, who died when she was very young, was no more than revered memory. After his death, her mother had taken her two young daughters ɔ live in Cardiff, Wales, where her own mother and redoubtable collection of ɯnts lived. I inherited an album of black and white photos showing leggy girls on ᴡelsh beaches, standing outside the Boathouse at Laugharne, wearing the ɴiform of Howell's School, Llandaff.

'However,' my mother confided in her mother-in-law thirty or more years fter these pictures were taken, 'there's no accounting for the play of temperament. still feel guilty because I *loathed* my maternal grandmother although I realise ɯow she was a most praiseworthy character. I hated her for all the three years I ɯved with her in Cardiff and her terrible, old-fashioned, heavily-carved furniture ɯnd bead curtains which used to tinkle in the wind and which she loved. I ɽemember feeling terribly guilty when she died because I could not really feel ɔorry.'

Those bead curtains—I can hear them tinkling.

After I left, the twins, aged eleven and thrilled by what they could do with ɱoney, won a lot of it playing Tombola at the Club. They too must have been ɑffected by Anne's illness and absence because before they went back to school, ᴛhey spent all of it on presents: headscarves or hankies for all Anne's friends, a ɱouth organ and bubble liquid for Sally, Liquorice Allsorts for Jock. For Anne, ᴛhey bought two bars of soap, nail varnish remover and a small bottle of scent.

'At the end of all that,' wrote Anne, 'they had exactly eighty cents left so they gave fifty cents to Harry the Houseboy and thirty cents to Martha. Now they've gone back to school, but I'm afraid Lushoto isn't the right place for them any more as they aren't kept occupied. It's fine educationally, but there aren't enough bigger children or spare time activities.'

In October Anne and Jock went again to Nairobi for the FAO Conference on Timber Statistics—a subject Jock found unutterably dull and the conference chairs unbearably hard. This was compensated for by the fact Nairobi still had attractions for small-town dwellers, from restaurants to theatre to shopping. As part of the FAO proceedings, they were guests at a reception given by the Kenya government and attended by government ministers. Among them was another luminary of the anticolonial and Independence movement—Tom Mboya, a renowned pan-Africanist who had founded the trade union movement in Kenya and was now Minister for Economic Planning. In the 1950s, in partnership with then Senator J.F. Kennedy and Martin Luther King he had established the African Airlifts, taking Kenyans to study in the US. Famously, one of these would become Barack Obama's father.

In this exalted company, Anne was interested to meet delegates from other African countries and surprised by how human and approachable she found them, including 'a charming Abyssinian, aged twenty-nine and ex-Oxford, and an extremely fat and amusing Sudanese who, while drinking his third whisk informed me he was a strict Mohammedan.' This was possibly her first clos encounter with an educated African elite. Did it occur to her to wonder whethe class and education might have shaped her racial attitudes? With a tiny fractio of children in school and only seventy university graduates by 1961, the colonia education system had scarcely prepared Tanganyika for Independence. Througl his education at the hands of the Catholic Church, Nyerere was a rare exception In 1949, as Anne and Jock headed to the Rondo, he was taking up a scholarshi to study history, politics and law at the University of Edinburgh.

Four years after the reception in Nairobi, in July 1969, Tom Mboya was sho dead as he picked up a prescription at Chaani's Pharmacy in Nairobi. According to one account, as he went in he bumped into Obama Sr, who joked that from the way he'd parked he'd get a ticket. A minute later, Mboya was shot by a political assassin. When he heard the news, Jock was outraged. Was the fact that the suave and articulate Mboya was also 'ex-Oxford' a factor in his admiration of him? If so the contradictions proliferate: Babu, the Marxist, studied English Literature and Philosophy in England before returning to Zanzibar. Both Babu and Mboya were intellectuals whose political activism and charismatic popularity were seen as threatening by the presidents of the day. Even being associated with them was suspect, it seems—according to a newspaper report by Henry Indangasi of the University of Nairobi, Obama's testimony at the trial of Mboya's killer was enough to put him beyond the pale as far as the Kenyatta government was concerned. Kenyatta was a Kikuyu while Obama and Mboya were both Luos from the western part of the country. Kenyan politics are notoriously ethnically driven, and Indangasi suggests that this accounts for Obama remaining jobless for some years afterwards. In his memoir, *Dreams From My Father*, his more famous son writes of hearing all this years after the event from his sister. Anne and Jock stood in the outermost eddies of this onrushing political tide.

Work was central to Jock's life, and much of his suffering was caused by politics having taken precedence. It had therefore meant a great deal when in 1964 he'd been awarded Fellowship of the UK Institute of Wood Science for his work in advancing the knowledge of wood technology. He was also working on the book that would eventually be published in 1967, *The Commercial Timbers of Tanzania*. This was an annotated index of every type of wood grown in the country for industrial use, and, apart from years of research, took hours and hours of painstaking compilation and checking for errors. By the end, it was a family production: we spread the proofs on Mistry's dining table and went through them together, reading aloud.

At last, in 1965, FAO came through with the long-promised job as director of the Utilisation Unit in Moshi. The move from civil servant to UN 'international expert' meant an end to government housing, and for a while we camped in the church bungalow down the road while we looked for a house. For Jock, the security of being employed by an international agency and no longer being beholden to the government was a reprieve and a vindication.

For me and my sisters, oblivious to politics, the last years in Moshi were concentrated bursts of freedom in our rule-bound boarding school lives. For me, at fifteen, sixteen and seventeen, life at home was a welter of friends and social activities. Everything happened in groups—playing tennis, snooker, table tennis, watching rugby, hockey, cricket, learning golf, swimming, hanging out in each other's houses, going to tea parties, sundowners, dinner parties and dance parties. We drank and smoked and listened to records, and went to movies at the Plaza and the Everest, running the gauntlet of the Indian youths who sat on the bonnets of cars outside and mocked us from a safe distance. The old social segregation was slowly breaking down as schools became more mixed and even the Club extended

its membership. My friends included Italians, Greeks, Danes, Germans and Americans, as well as Scots, Irish and English, and a few rare local Indians. Still no Africans. Sex ran like an electric current through our encounters, but in practice it hardly went beyond kissing and hand-holding. In town, a favourite haunt was the slightly disreputable Bamboo Bar, where hookers rubbed shoulders with respectable patrons and where we could drink and flirt unobserved by parents or their friends, speeding home afterwards on the backs of motor scooters or all squeezed into the backs of cars.

In the early 60s volunteers from the British organisation, Voluntary Service Overseas, appeared in Moshi. In their early twenties, they were only a few years older than we were and added a veneer of sophistication to the mix. One day in 1967 I came home to find a young man in bed in my sisters' room—their school term obviously hadn't finished. Alan Wallman was a VSO working with Jock in the Utilisation Section. He had a septic ankle and a fever and Anne and Jock had brought him home to look after him. He was twenty-two and I was sixteen and starstruck. With my passion for the Beatles, he was exotic: a Londoner who'd studied at Liverpool University, who talked about jam butties and footie and later, after a few sessions of making out in the back of the government Roho, would refer to me as his bird. He couldn't get up for meals, so Jock and Anne moved Sunday lunch into his room and we sat round his bed balancing plates on our laps and drinking Bloody Marys. I lingered long after my parents left. When he recovered and went back to the bungalow he shared with other volunteers, he sent both Anne and me bouquets of flowers. Mine were red roses: for love, said Anne. It was the most romantic thing that had ever happened to me.

My sisters and I were back in Cheltenham when, early in 1968, Jock received a peremptory phone call summoning him to Dar. He and Anne wavered between the options: good news, bad news? Next day as he was leaving, Anne had the presence of mind to push a small flask of whisky into his overnight bag. For hours she waited anxiously by the phone, unable to concentrate on anything. By the time he rang it was late at night and his voice sounded far away.

'We've got three weeks to leave,' he said.

As with so many political decisions taken in the capital, the fall-out was contrary to ideological expectations. Moshi people, being mostly Chagga, had always had their own ideas about how things should be run and wouldn't go along happily with edicts from the coast. Knowing from experience that deportees' accounts could be frozen, the next day Anne went to the bank to withdraw all the money she could. The clerk who served her had been her student at the College of Commerce and was so flustered he could only stare at her in alarm. Patiently, she talked him through what she needed. Word got out quickly and a stream of visitors called at the house to commiserate. For Jock's office staff the commiseration was personal, and they had to be plied with beer to make them feel better.

'Departure day had better come quickly,' said Jock to Anne, 'for the sake of my liver.'

How, in three weeks, do you sort and pack the accumulation of nineteen years, of a marriage, a family, a career? It was at best a haphazard flinging of things into boxes, random selection and snap decisions—a letting go. The house was full of objects picked up over time and incorporated into our daily lives. Jock was a keen photographer and struggled for years to capture a satisfactory image of a dhow in full sail. At last he did, and the framed colour photograph of that seductive sight had pride of place on the sitting room wall. Would it retain its poetry, torn from its context? What use would there be in future, in an unspecified place, for an ebony rose bowl, a zebra-tail fly-whisk, a beaten copper tray purchased on a beach at dusk from passing traders? That reproduction of Constable's 'The Hay Wain', the carvings of Masai warriors? The prayer rug bought at auction from Arab carpet sellers in Mombasa Old Town, that nearly got Ahmed the sack? Anne's kidney-shaped dressing table with the frilly yellow curtain, made by Jock's works' arpenter from a tree he had helped to grow? In what space would these objects have meaning, uprooted, shorn of their associations?

When they arrived in Rome, and eventually found themselves in an apartment, Anne unpacked the boxes. Among the things she found there were twenty wire coat-hangers, three packets of spaghetti and several well-thumbed issues of *Time* magazine. Something to hang a new life on? Sustenance for the journey? A title to remind us that all things must change?

At this cataclysmic moment, I was seventeen. By now my sisters had joined me at the Ladies' College, where they were having an even harder being ladies than I was. They had always gone their own way, answerable only to each other. Subjecting them to English manners was like caging wild birds. They were constantly in trouble, didn't understand the uniform, had no notion of etiquette. I wasn't much help—I was as homesick as they were. The only telephone belonged to the housemistress, and calls were a rare event, reserved for emergencies. We lived for letters, avidly checking the hall table where the morning post was laid out for collection. If you were lucky, there was just time between breakfast and walking to class to read one. It was March when the flimsy blue airmail letter arrived. A mournful wind whined around the house, rattling the window panes and threatening rain.

In our school house there was a room known as the 'Drawing Room'. Unlike the dormitories and study-rooms it was carpeted and cushioned, with armchairs and a grand piano. It was used for receiving visiting parents, and for evening prayers before we filed into the dining room for supper. Otherwise, you could go there if you wanted peace and quiet. We skipped quickly from the front hall into the Drawing Room and crowded into a window embrasure for privacy. It was a bay window with a sofa that formed a protective barrier if you sat behind it on the floor. Though we always sat on the ground at home it was harder when you were encumbered by shoes and stockings and tweed skirts. Once we were safely hidden, Ally read the letter aloud. She'd hardly begun when we heard the words, 'Daddy has been recalled to Rome and we are leaving Moshi at once.'

Curtains, carpet and cushions faded. We were in the garden in Rombo Avenue, dressed only in knickers, sitting in a triangle on the scratchy grass, brown legs outstretched, bare feet touching, forming a barrier around three fluffy squeaking ducklings. The shrill of cicadas, the rich melodious call of wood pigeons. From inside, clacking of claws on the concrete as the dog looked for a spot to cool his belly. Somewhere nearby, a scuffling in the grass. We sat still, hardly breathing. Leaving Moshi? What did it mean? We looked at each other, eyes enormous and already brimming with tears. Beside us, rain streaked the window pane and somewhere in the depths of the house a bell rang. We were out of time. Desperately, we scanned the letter for an answer.

It seemed it meant we were leaving Tanzania altogether, with hardly a clue as to what was to happen next. Mother had, she said, no idea where we would live or even in what country. She promised to tell us as soon as she knew.

'We have been so lucky with our happy life in dear old Moshi all these years, it has been home to us,' she continued. 'Sorry to have to send you news which I know will distress you so much.'

Distress? The word made no sense. We were never going home again. It was as if the bus on the road to Lushoto had skidded on a hairpin bend and plummeted off the cliff. Or like the time we came back from school expecting to see Sebastian barking and rushing at us, and Mother had to break the news that he had died of tick-fever. Our beloved dog was nothing more than a mound of earth under the lemon tree. Time was suspended and life lost direction, spinning us off-kilter.

In that moment, I was back on the school bench in Lushoto, facing the unknown, but without the comfort of knowing where I stood in relation to The World, The Universe. When my mother said in her letter, 'Perhaps you will manage to visit here again one day,' she didn't know that homelessness would become a permanent state of being. Or that it would take another thirty-six years, several switches of country, and the birth of my own daughter, before I made that journey back.

27. The Dead are Not Dead

By late March 1968, Jock, Anne and Sally were in Rome, where FAO was headquartered. After all his African experience, Jock was appointed officer in charge of FAO's Field Projects in the Mediterranean, Near East and South East Asia. Instead of puttering off in shorts on his Vespa to his downtown office, he drove to work in a multi-storey, blue-glass building opposite the Colosseum he called The Sacred Precinct. With the end of colonialism FAO had become a haven for many old Africa hands. Jock and Anne arrived in Rome to find Dick and Pauline Willan, ex-Lushoto, already there. Before long, Jock would be working on conservation projects in Bhutan and Nepal with his old colleague, my godfather John Blower, who had previously helped the Emperor Haile Selassie establish conservation areas in Ethiopia.

After fourteen years in Moshi Anne was euphoric at being in a European city in spring, visiting art galleries and museums, eating *saltimbocca* and fresh peaches and drinking wine at pavement tables. In Moshi, I'd had my first introduction to European art through Anne's collection of large, hardback books with tissue-paper inter-leaved reproductions of the Old Masters. As though in a dream, Anne now found herself in a world of Baroque facades and Renaissance frescoes, Roman columns and heroic statues, dimly-lit ancient churches and sun-drenched piazzas. She and Pauline spent long days gazing at it all, sipping cappuccino, walking the cobblestone streets of the old city.

As she was discovering Rome, Anne was also coming to terms with being unwell. She attended Italian classes and one day wrote to tell me she'd had to stop and sit on the steps of the Metro because she couldn't breathe. I heard what she said but didn't see the implications. In June, Pauline, a devout Catholic who believed in miracles, took her south to the town of San Giovanni Rotondo, home of a living saint, Padre (now Santo) Pio, who had the power of healing through the laying on of hands. Those hands symbolised his holiness, because in them he had received the stigmata—wounds in his palms as though he had been nailed to a cross. So great was Pauline's faith that Anne was given to hope, but by the time my sisters and I came home to the Rome apartment for the summer holidays, she was in Guy's Hospital in London. We still didn't understand what it meant, hadn't heard of metastasis.

Rome was exotic to us little African girls, a playground full of admiring young men, multiple flavours of ice-cream, Italian pop, discos, cappuccino and cornetti delicious horn-shaped pastries eaten standing at counters. And Anne was far away out of sight. Suddenly Guy's called to say there was an emergency and Jock departed overnight for London, leaving me and my slightly older cousin, Miranda who was visiting, in charge of the apartment. In the week he was away we held open house: a party that went on all day and all night, with the four of us teenage girls and an army of young men who came and went at all hours. We were too innocent for sex, but all the beds were full, and boys slept on the sofas and floors. Music played, ash-trays overflowed, and while the more sophisticated among us smoked joints, the rest of us drank cheap red wine from two-litre bottles. Of course, the money ran out, so when one visitor paid for a couple of overseas calls he made on our phone, we dipped into it for food. When Dick and Pauline came round to check on us, we cleaned up as much as we could and boys hid under the beds or jumped off the first-floor balcony and ran away.

Then Jock came home. There was an indelible stain where a bottle of red wine had spilled across the terrazzo, the sheets all had burn marks from people smoking in bed, and there wasn't enough money to pay the phone bill. I was surprised he wasn't angrier. It was as if his mind was somewhere else and our exploits irrelevant. He told us our mother had nearly died. When, earlier that summer, he had announced in tones of outrage, 'Those poor Czechs, the Russians have invaded them,' we'd looked at him in incomprehension. Now what he said was equally unreal.

The summer holidays ended and we went back to school; when Anne came out of hospital she visited us there. You got a cubicle when you were in the Upper Sixth, it was considered a privilege and gave you privacy. She and I sat in mine, talking about her recent treatment. She said something about further tests and I looked at her hard.

'Do you think it could be cancer?' I blurted. She was only months away from death, and she said no.

I knew anyway. I existed on two planes: on one, I was working for my A-levels, studying hard and thinking about university, on the other, I stood on the brink of a catastrophe. My mind kept turning away from it, as though by not thinking it I could stop it happening. Eventually she could no longer leave the hospital (no hospices then) and we were visiting her whenever we could. The Easter holidays went by, during which my daily trips to Guy's—the tube to London Bridge, the trudge through the grey hospital buildings, the institutional corridors and vestibules and stairwells—almost felt routine.

In May we were back at school when we were told she had reached the end. It was the middle of term and my A-levels were a month away, but the three of us moved back to London. For a week, my sisters stayed with family, Jock and I were given rooms in the hospital so we could spend our time at her bedside. She had a room to herself, a small quiet space off a busy corridor leading to a ward, where she lay propped up on pillows. A cupboard, a window, a door, two chairs. The iron bedstead. Around her the great hospital hummed, and beyond it, the city, with its millions of people on the move. Everything that mattered was concentrated at this still point of the turning world. Anne was weak and had difficulty breathing; the oxygen cylinder beside the bed hissed as she pulled the mask over her nose. On her last day someone brought strawberries but when I tried to feed them to her, she smiled an apology.

'I'll have them for my pud,' she said, as if there were other courses to come.

With that brave disclaimer she summoned the memory of all she loved, a lifetime of feelings shared. But she had already moved on. At two o'clock in the afternoon, Jock and I sat one on each side of her bed, listening to her breathing. At last, she asked him to take her left arm and pull it towards him, and as he did it, she died.

Once, she had written from Moshi: 'I don't think I would ever get over the ache if I were permanently severed from England.' There was a poem by A.E Housman she loved to recite:

'Loveliest of trees, the cherry now
Is hung with blossom on the bough
And stands about the woodland ride
Wearing white for Eastertide.'

It was spring when she died and the streets were covered in a drift of white cherry blossom.

She was forty-eight. I was eighteen, Mary and Ally fifteen, Sally eight: four girls adrift without an anchor.

Anne's ashes were buried in Thaxted churchyard, under a little stone hard up against the eastern wall of its monumental church. But where, I wonder, does her spirit reside? Or does it roam, restless? Over the years I've had a recurring dream, that I meet her again, now. The astonishment of recognition, the bafflement of unexplained absence. She's always the age she was when she died: not young, not old. I'm the age I am. I ask her, but where have you been? And the hard, unsmiling truth is borne in on me: she didn't want me to know where she was. She kept herself away, was somewhere else on purpose. The red hot torrent of feeling is all one way.

I want to release us both from this frozen stasis. I want her to walk with me again along the paths she used to know. I want to set her spirit free.

After Uhuru, there was a choice: give up your foreign citizenship and become Tanzanian, or claim British citizenship by virtue of living in a Trust Territory. For Jock this wasn't even a choice, and we stayed resolutely British. Himat and his brother Babu Bhai became Tanzanian. Seamus inherited British citizenship, which probably stood him in good stead as a London copper. But now, having come back for good, he wants full Tanzanian citizenship. It's not an easy process. Seamus tells me how as part of his application, he must go for an interview with the Regional Commissioner. He dresses in a suit and tie to attend the appointment at the regional council offices. He and two other applicants, a Ugandan woman and an Indian imam who wants to stay in Tanzania 'because it's peaceful', arrive in the morning and wait all day until 4pm. They're the last item on the regional council's agenda. When he's at last called in, Seamus stands before the members, arrayed on three sides of the room. The Regional Commissioner greets him politely and enquires after Marangu. After they've exchanged courtesies, the Commissioner introduces him to the rest of the council, including the Chief Inspector of Police.

Then he turns to Seamus. 'So,' he says, 'why do you want to become a Tanzanian?'

Seamus is ready for this. 'I was born here and though I left for some years to study and work in Britain, I came back thirteen years ago when my mother was becoming ill. I feel Tanzanian, and I hope to die in Tanzania.' One of the members asks him what work he did in Britain.

'I was a policeman. I became a Chief Superintendent.'

'Oh,' says the Chief Inspector approvingly, 'I thought you stood like a policeman.' Someone else asks what he would bring to Tanzania, and Seamus talks about the contribution of Marangu Hotel to the tourism economy. One of the members asks what happened to his mother and he says she died.

'And where is she buried?'

'Here in Moshi.'

Finally, the Regional Commissioner explains that the application must now be sent to Dar, and Seamus is dismissed. The whole interview has been conducted in Swahili.

Which of Seamus's attributes carried more weight? Was it, in an aid-afflicted country, his economic contribution? His ability to communicate in Swahili? Or his policemanlike uprightness? Or was it the fact that his mother is buried in Moshi soil, that he himself hopes to die here? If you die in a country, you become part of its spirit-life. You linger in the trees and rocks; the sighs of the bush are the ancestors breathing. Though he needs no passport to the spirit-world, the council members acknowledge his living presence as a Tanzanian. They recommend him for citizenship.

The dry season had extended and extended, grass yellow, air dust-laden. Even the trees looked exhausted. We were at the Club, Anne playing tennis, the three of us amusing ourselves on the swings with the other children. The Club had the best view of the mountain at sunset. From the golf course, you could have aimed a golf ball at the crater, there was nothing in the way. Normally, we sat on the verandah to drink our Cokes and watch the snow on the summit flush pink before slowly paling to blue, then grey, before it was blotted out by the descent of darkness. Tonight a storm was coming, heralded by a great pink glow in the east caused by red dust blown up from the plain by the rising wind. It made a wall a thousand feet high. Forked lightning illuminated mud-coloured clouds like drapes across the sky. The mountain had disappeared. Little currents of air played over our bare skin, raising unaccustomed goosebumps. The first drops of rain raised a flurry in the red Moshi dust, releasing the fragrance of returning life from the parched earth.

Anne appeared beside the table where we sat, holding her racquet, ready to go. 'We should get home.'

It hadn't rained for three months, and what was coming was an end-of-dry-season electric storm. You could feel the tension in the air, as if the world was holding its breath. Anne drove home as quickly as she could in the deepening dusk. As we turned into the drive the first thunderclap exploded overhead, like a huge gong signalling the start of the drama. We hurried indoors, and as she flicked the light switch, Anne said, 'Oh no, the electricity's gone.' The house was very dark but she knew what to do. Suddenly, lightning lit up the sky directly overhead illuminating three white faces and Anne, already feeling her way towards the fusebox.

The rain started. It was as if someone had opened a sluice in the sky. As the great wave hit, another thunderclap broke directly overhead and all three of us screamed. Terror, excitement—an uncontrollable energy exploded out of us and drove us outside, tearing off our clothes to dance naked in the pounding rain. The ground was already sodden, we splashed each other with mud as we ran up and down the terraces, screaming for joy. Something had released the wild in us and we'd become part of the storm.

Then, as if Anne had captured lightning and channelled it through the fusebox, the house lit up. We saw her outlined against a window and that was where we wanted to be—inside with her, warm and dry, with the storm outside. Shrieking, we ran for the verandah, shivering as the water poured off us puddling the floor. Anne hurried towards us, towels in her arms. She wrapped them around us and over our heads and we dashed inside like cloaked intruders, leaving a muddy trail across the sitting room floor. Domesticated again, no longer whirling dervishes galvanised by the storm. Normal children, ready for a hot bath and supper.

Five decades later, Mary, Ally and I, each with our one daughter apiece, are staying at Marangu Hotel. The Brice-Bennetts, used to hosting colonial returnees, give us a great welcome. One day, Desmond offers to take us to see the Moshi railway station. This station, where we cried as we boarded the train for school, where Anne ran the length of the platform holding my hand through the carriage window, is no longer in use, but our daughters have grown up hearing stories of Moshi and Lushoto and they want to see it. The Tanga to Moshi line, built by the Germans in 1891, no longer gasps with steam from the pulsing engines of its trains. But there are still signs for the ticket office and the offices of *Steshen Foamen* and *Steshen Masta*. There's even a Railway Station Social Club with a bar, and we sit on the old platform by the disused rails and drink Kilimanjaro beer with the mountain as backdrop. Afterwards, as I wander up and down the platform, a man sitting on one of the concrete benches asks me curiously what I'm doing.

'I was born here *zamani*, a long time ago. I used to go

o school from this station.' He looks at me and smiles.

'*Karibu ndugu,*' he says.

There are different kinds of belonging. There's the kind that comes with a passport, and there's a kind of helpless, spiritual attachment. The second is easy to refute, if you care to, if you deny the right of ex-colonials to any stake in your country fifty or more years after Uhuru. But *karibu* means welcome and *ndugu* means kin, and over and over when I tell people I was born here, this is their generous response. It spells recognition and acceptance. It spells *heshima*—the bestowal of respect.

Msuya is a taxi driver in Moshi and has been taking us here and there. On our last day, we ask him if he knows where the old Utilisation Section is. As so often happens in this small, relatively unchanging place, it turns out Msuya used to work here in the 70s and knows exactly where it is. In fact, he says he remembers Bwana Bryce and he's glad to meet his children. So it's a family outing. Six of us cram into his car and we drive across the railway tracks to the industrial part of town, pulling up at a gate with a sign saying Kiliwood. It's a lumber company and looks deserted, but an elderly guard comes out of a hut by the gate and greets us courteously. Msuya explains who we are and what we want, and the guard calls two more courtly, dignified, elderly men. They all look at us.

'We worked with Bwana Bryce,' says the first guard.

He opens the gates and we drive in. It turns out these men worked in the Utilisation Section in the 1960s and stayed on through all the changes.

The yard is poorly maintained but Msuya and the guards conduct us across it to Jock's old office, a free-standing, one-room wooden building with a spectacular

view of the mountain. The office where the president's picture never hung, where Jock came at five in the morning to deal with paperwork. It's locked and we stand around outside, nobody saying anything much. Three daughters, three granddaughters and three old employees, each with their own thoughts.

Msuya drives us back to town and as he lets us out of the car he says, 'I'm happy to meet Mr Bryce's family. He was a good man.'

Of course, it's not true that things don't change. Today, on the mountain peak,

the snow is melting. In time, if climate change continues its present course, it wi
be gone and the mountain with the unrememberable name will no longer dazzl
the eyes of onlookers. The great snowy peak will have joined Zamani.

I've been strolling through the *shambas* around Marangu and I've come onc
again to the river. I step carefully out across the rocks and sit down midstream. Th
past is close; the ghosts of who we were assemble in silence. Three children play i
the water. Anne walks in a garden at twilight, chanting her litany of names. Joc
smiles down from a wall in a two-room house on the mountain. As they pass b
together on foot safari, far in the south, Anne places a stone on a cairn.

They are in the water, they are in the stones.

A young girl appears on the bank and picks her way over the stones. She sits besid
me.

'*Mimi ni Furahi,*' she tells me. 'My name is Happiness.'

'Are you happy?' I ask her.

She smiles. 'I am very happy.'

It's dusk, and as we sit there the air cools and colour slowly drains from the
sky. All that's left is the whimpering of the stream as it winds around the rocks.

ACKNOWLEDGEMENTS

It took a long time to write this book—fourteen years or a lifetime, depending on how you look at it. I couldn't have done it without material support and emotional encouragement from all sorts of people.

In Marangu, Desmond, Fionnuala, Seamus and Jackie Brice-Bennett welcomed me as a long-lost friend. At different times, I stayed at Marangu Hotel at cut prices, Seamus and Jackie lent me their house in Moshi, Fionnuala rented me her cottage and they all offered support in many ways. Though they all shared their stories, the voices of Seamus and Desmond especially resonate, while Desmond never lost patience with my endless requests for information. In Moshi, John Bennett kindly tolerated me hanging out at his garage, eating his food and raiding his library. Himat and Pushpa Shah not only shared their stories, their house and their friends and family, they opened up a previously unseen world and invited me in.

I had supportive and critical early draft readers in Jane Borges, Desmond Brice-Bennett, Stewart Brown, Mary Bryce, Ally Bryce, Eleo Carson, Denise DeCaires Narain, Gabriel Gbadamosi, Abdulrazak Gurnah, Julie Kitchener, Bjorn Sverre Kristensen, Philip Nanton, Kim Robinson, Richard Synge, Mike Wells, Clare Wenner, Dick Willan and Caroline Wintersgill. Your comments and responses have made this a much better book.

Thanks to fellow attendees of the Arvon memoir-writing retreat at the Hurst, Shropshire, led by Hannah Lowe and Horatio Clare in 2017; members of the Writers.com online memoir-writing workshop, led by Anya Achtenberg in 2018; and the Cornerstones Edit Your Novel course, led by Kathryn Price in 2021. Two of my fellow Cornerstones writers, Tamsin Hickson and Felicity Goodall, became true friends, reading and commenting on successive revisions and offering precious advice about publishing. Polly Pattullo of Papillote Press gave practical help and encouragement just when it was most needed. My writing homies in Barbados—Sharma Taylor, Anderson Lowe, Lafleur Cockburn and Brian Franklin—never stopped believing in me. Philip Nanton stayed close to me and the writing. To all of you—*asanteni sana!*

BIBLIOGRAPHY AND SOURCE MATERIAL

Blixen, Karen, *Out of Africa*, Putnam, 1937, now owned by Penguin, Random House.

Carleton, Caroline, 'Song of Australia', 1859.

Coupland, R, *East Africa and its invaders: from the earliest times to the death of Seyyid Said*, Oxford Clarendon Press, 1938.

Diop, Birago, poem: 'Spirits', or 'Sighs' (trans), variously anthologised.

Eggeling, W.J., Chief Conservator. Annual Reports, Forest Department of Tanganyika (58, 59). Rhodes House archives, Oxford.

Johnston, Sir Harry, *The Kilima-Njaro Expedition: A Record of Scientific Exploration in Eastern Equatorial Africa. And a General Description of the Natural History, Languages, and Commerce of the Kilima-Njaro District*, London: Paul Trench, 1886.

Macmillan, Harold, 'Wind of change' speech to the SA Parliament in Cape Town, 3 February, 1960.

Menzies, Robert, Transcripts @ *https://pmtranscripts.pmc.gov.au/*

Mbiti, John, *African Religions and Philosophy*, Heinemann Kenya/East African Educational Publisher, 1969.

Gunther, John, *Inside Africa*, Harper & Brothers, 1955.

Housman, A.E., 'Loveliest of Trees', from *A Shropshire Lad*, 1896.

Qu'ran, Surah 15, verse 45. King Fahd Holy Qu'ran Printing Complex, Saudi Arabia.

Ranger, Terence, 'From Ireland to Africa', *History Ireland*, Issue 4 (Jul/Aug 2006), Volume 14.

Sadleir, Randal, *Tanzania: Journey to Republic*, Radcliffe Press, 1999.

Schneppen, Heinz, *Why Kilimanjaro is in Tanzania*, National Museums of Tanzania Occasional Paper No.9.

School Friend Annual, 'Foiled by The Silent Three', UK Comic Books 1957, now owned by Rebellion Support.

Taylor, Jeremy, 'Ballad of the Southern Suburbs'/'Ag Pleez Deddy' on *Wait a Minim*, 1961 Decca, UK, 1964.

US State Department cable re Zanzibar, 1963

Williamson, J A., *Builders of the Empire*, Oxford Clarendon Press, 1925.

Woolf, Virginia, *A Room of One's Own*, Hogarth Press, London, 1929.

Young, Mary, *In Search of Charm*, Brockhampton Press, 1962.

Printed in the USA
CPSIA information can be obtained
at www.ICGtesting.com
LVHW090104151023
761010LV00003B/248

9 781788 649865